Ravé Mehta's THE INVENTOR

THE STORY OF TESLA

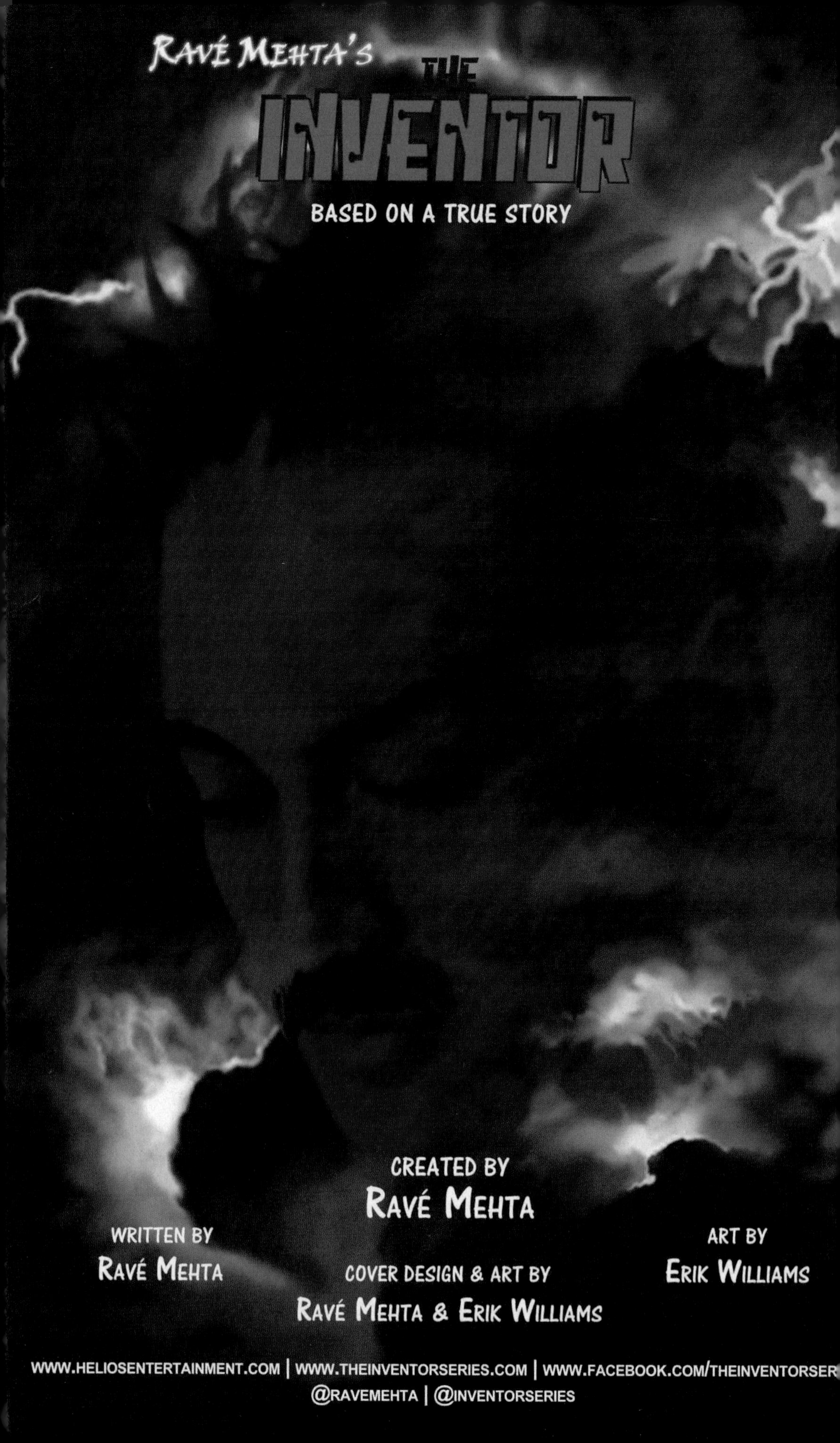

Ravé Mehta's

The Inventor

BASED ON A TRUE STORY

CREATED BY
Ravé Mehta

WRITTEN BY
Ravé Mehta

COVER DESIGN & ART BY
Ravé Mehta & Erik Williams

ART BY
Erik Williams

WWW.HELIOSENTERTAINMENT.COM | WWW.THEINVENTORSERIES.COM | WWW.FACEBOOK.COM/THEINVENTORSER
@RAVEMEHTA | @INVENTORSERIES

AT THE END OF THE 19TH CENTURY DURING A TIME WHEN INVENTORS WERE KNOWN AS WIZARDS AND CORPORATIONS WERE THEIR KINGDOMS, EMERGED AN EXTRAORDINARY LEAGUE OF GENTLEMEN WHO SHAPED THE MODERN WORLD WITH THEIR MINDS, MONEY AND MACHINES. AT THE EYE OF THIS STORM STOOD NIKOLA TESLA, A MYSTIC INVENTOR WHOSE GENIUS BLURRED THE LINES BETWEEN MAGIC AND SCIENCE. HIS IDEAS AND INVENTIONS WERE SO PROGRESSIVE THAT HE CATALYZED THE SECOND INDUSTRIAL REVOLUTION AND FASHIONED THE 20TH CENTURY IN THE COMPANY OF GEORGE WESTINGHOUSE, J.P. MORGAN, GUGLIELMO MARCONI, MARK TWAIN, LORD KELVIN, YOGI VIVEKANANDA AND NOT TO MENTION HIS GREATEST MENTOR YET MOST RESOLUTE ADVERSARY, THOMAS EDISON. YET, DESPITE HIS GENIUS, PASSION AND IMPACT ON HUMANITY, IN THE END IT WAS OTHERS WHO MADE GREAT FORTUNES BASED ON HIS INVENTIONS WHILE HE ENDED UP PENNILESS, ALONE AND FORGOTTEN...UNTIL NOW.

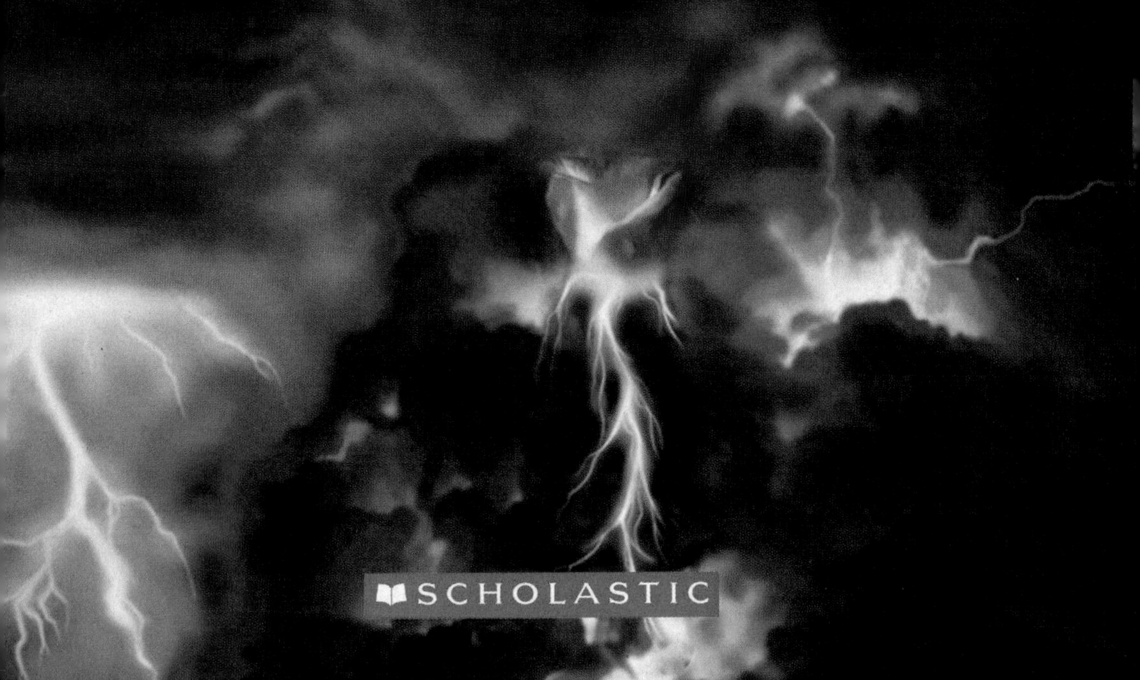

SCHOLASTIC

SCHOLASTIC AND HELIOS ENTERTAINMENT PRESENT THE INVENTOR Digital Print. May 2013.

ISBN: 978-0-9893379-0-8 | Printed in Canada

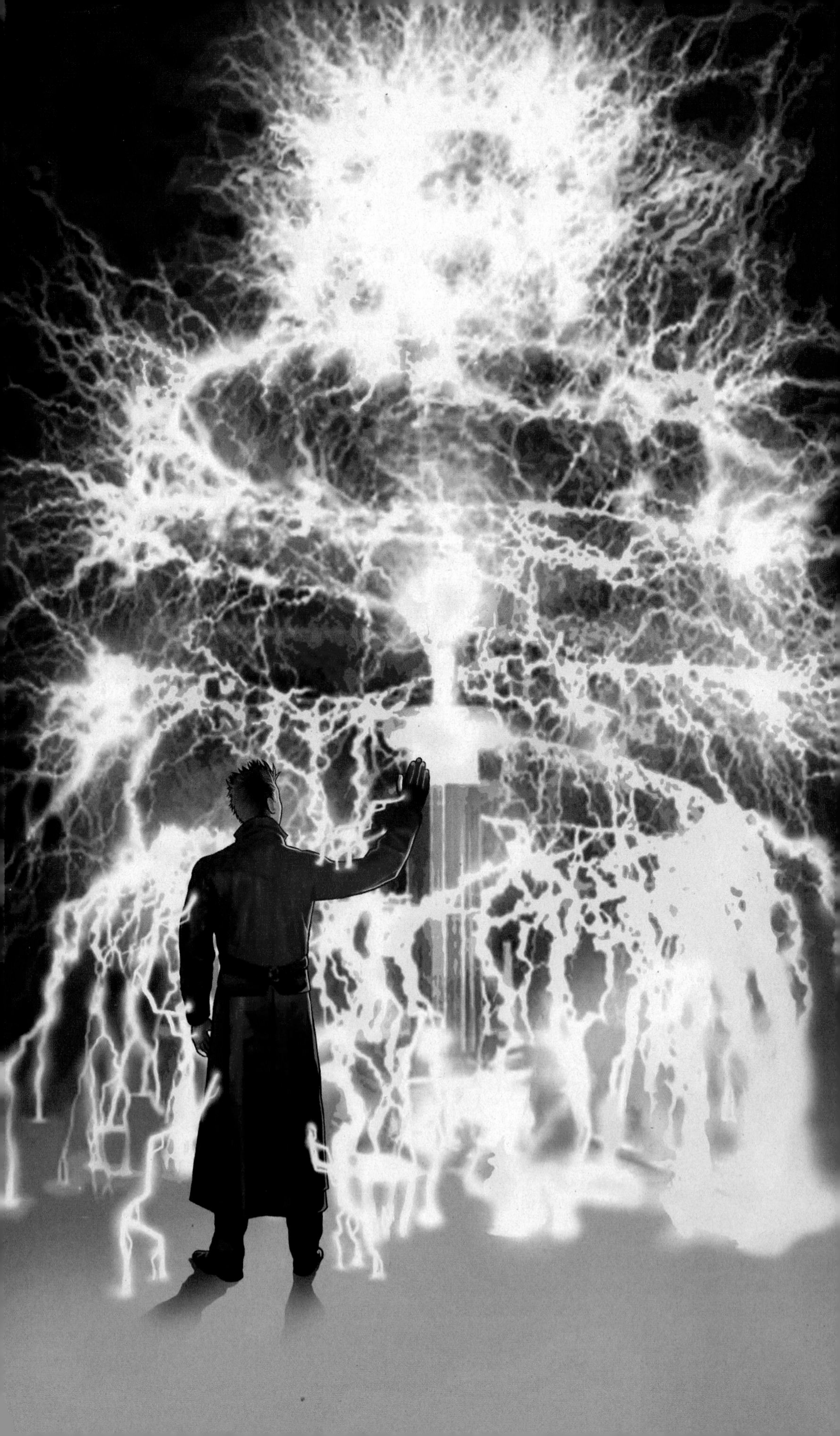

DEDICATED TO NIKOLA TESLA

THE MAN, THE ENGINEER AND THE VISIONARY INVENTOR WHOSE
IMPACT ON HUMANITY IS STILL FLOWING THROUGH THE RIVERS OF
TIME WITH GREAT MERIT AND INCONCEIVABLE POTENTIAL FOR THE
HUMAN RACE...AND WHOSE COMPLETE VISION FOR OUR SPECIES HAS
YET TO BE FULFILLED.

- RAVÉ MEHTA

"UP TO THE AGE OF EIGHT YEARS, MY CHARACTER WAS WEAK AND VACILLATING. I HAD NEITHER COURAGE OR STRENGTH TO FORM A FIRM RESOLVE. MY FEELINGS CAME IN WAVES AND SURGES AND VIBRATED UNCEASINGLY BETWEEN EXTREMES. MY WISHES WERE OF CONSUMING FORCE AND LIKE THE HEADS OF THE HYDRA, THEY MULTIPLIED. I WAS OPPRESSED BY THOUGHTS OF PAIN IN LIFE AND DEATH AND RELIGIOUS FEAR. I WAS SWAYED BY SUPERSTITIOUS BELIEF AND LIVED IN CONSTANT DREAD OF THE SPIRIT OF EVIL, OF GHOSTS, AND OGRES AND OTHER UNHOLY MONSTERS OF THE DARK. THEN, ALL AT ONCE, THERE CAME A TREMENDOUS CHANGE WHICH ALTERED THE COURSE OF MY WHOLE EXISTENCE."

- NIKOLA TESLA (1856-1943)

Chapter I
Undercurrent

IT IS OFTEN SAID THAT TESLA WAS BORN OF LIGHTNING AND PUT ON THIS EARTH TO LEAD MAN INTO OUR NEXT EVOLUTION...INTO OUR NEXT REVOLUTION. HE WAS NOT A GOD, NOR WAS HE YOUR ORDINARY MORTAL, BUT SOMEWHERE IN BETWEEN. HIS PIERCING BLUE EYES WERE THE WINDOWS TO HIS MIND AND HIS IMAGINATION WAS HIS SUPERPOWER THAT ELECTRIFIED THE WORLD. WITH HIS ABILITY TO LOOK AT THE FORCES OF NATURE AND CREATE MACHINES THAT COULD HARNESS ITS POWER TO SERVE MAN, HE STOOD AS HUMANITY'S GREATEST HOPE TO ASCEND US TO OUR NEXT PLATEAU OF EXISTENCE.

YET, HIS PATH WAS NOT AN EASY ONE. EVEN HIS CHILDHOOD WAS RIDDLED WITH HURDLES, AS IF THE GODS THEMSELVES USED THESE FORCES TO SHAPE HIM AND GIVE HIM STRENGTH TO FULFILL HIS DESTINY. ESCAPING THE COILS OF DEATH MULTIPLE TIMES, HE TRAVELED FAR ACROSS LAND AND OCEAN TO MAKE HIS WAY TO THE DOORSTEP OF HIS FINAL TEACHER...SO HE CAN 'BEGIN' HIS WORK.

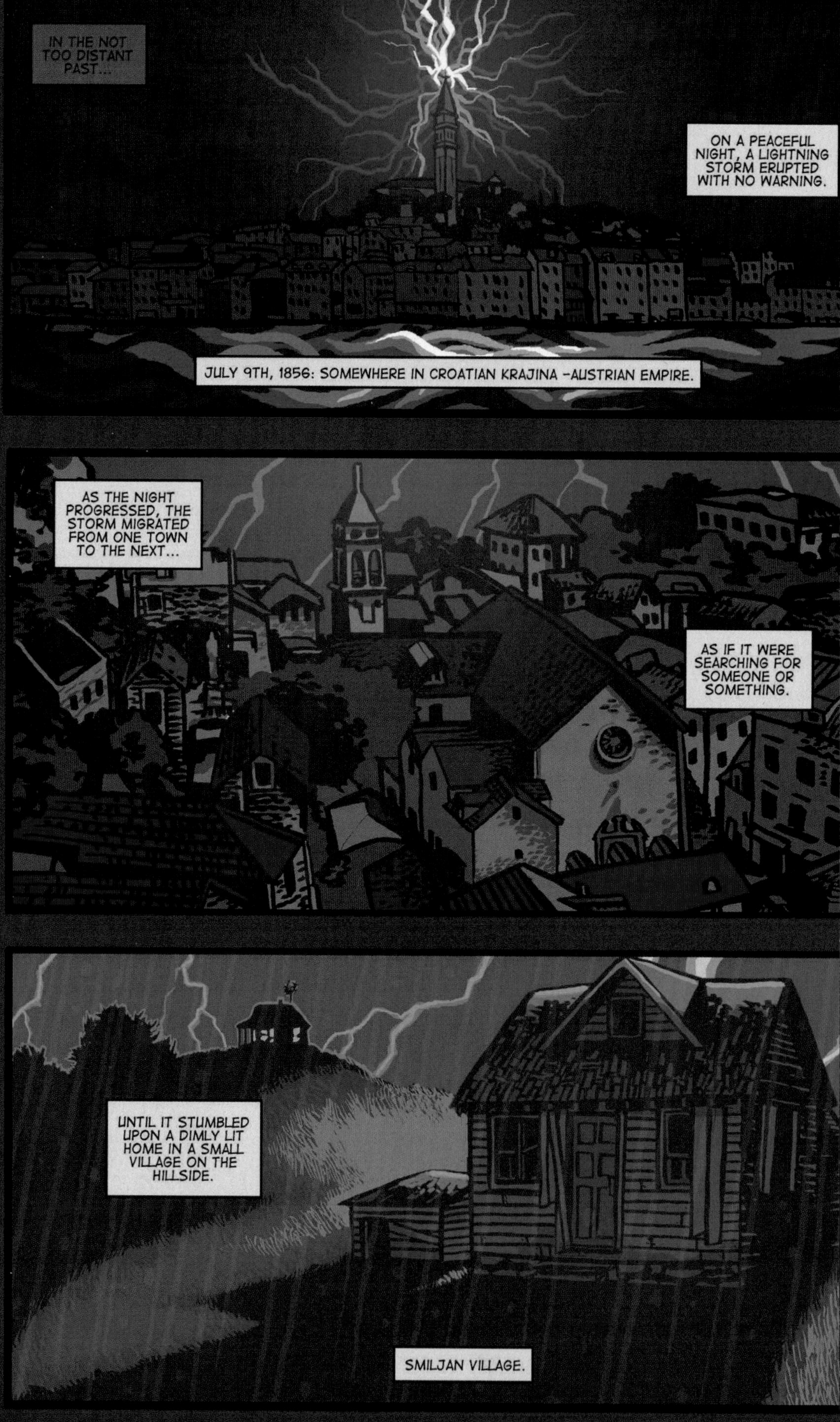
IN THE NOT TOO DISTANT PAST...
ON A PEACEFUL NIGHT, A LIGHTNING STORM ERUPTED WITH NO WARNING.
JULY 9TH, 1856: SOMEWHERE IN CROATIAN KRAJINA -AUSTRIAN EMPIRE.
AS THE NIGHT PROGRESSED, THE STORM MIGRATED FROM ONE TOWN TO THE NEXT...
AS IF IT WERE SEARCHING FOR SOMEONE OR SOMETHING.
UNTIL IT STUMBLED UPON A DIMLY LIT HOME IN A SMALL VILLAGE ON THE HILLSIDE.
SMILJAN VILLAGE.

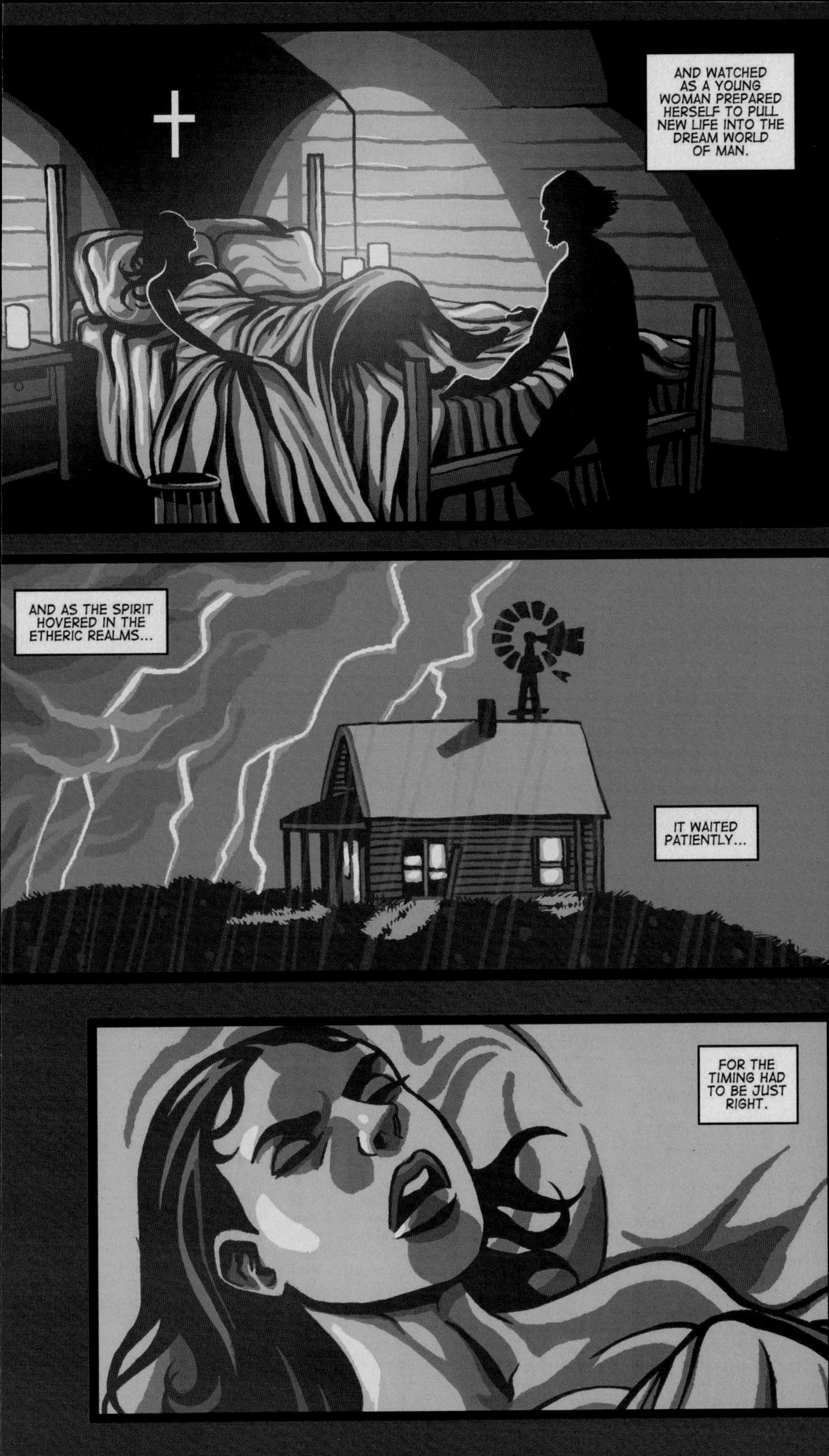
AND WATCHED AS A YOUNG WOMAN PREPARED HERSELF TO PULL NEW LIFE INTO THE DREAM WORLD OF MAN.
AND AS THE SPIRIT HOVERED IN THE ETHERIC REALMS...
IT WAITED PATIENTLY...
FOR THE TIMING HAD TO BE JUST RIGHT.

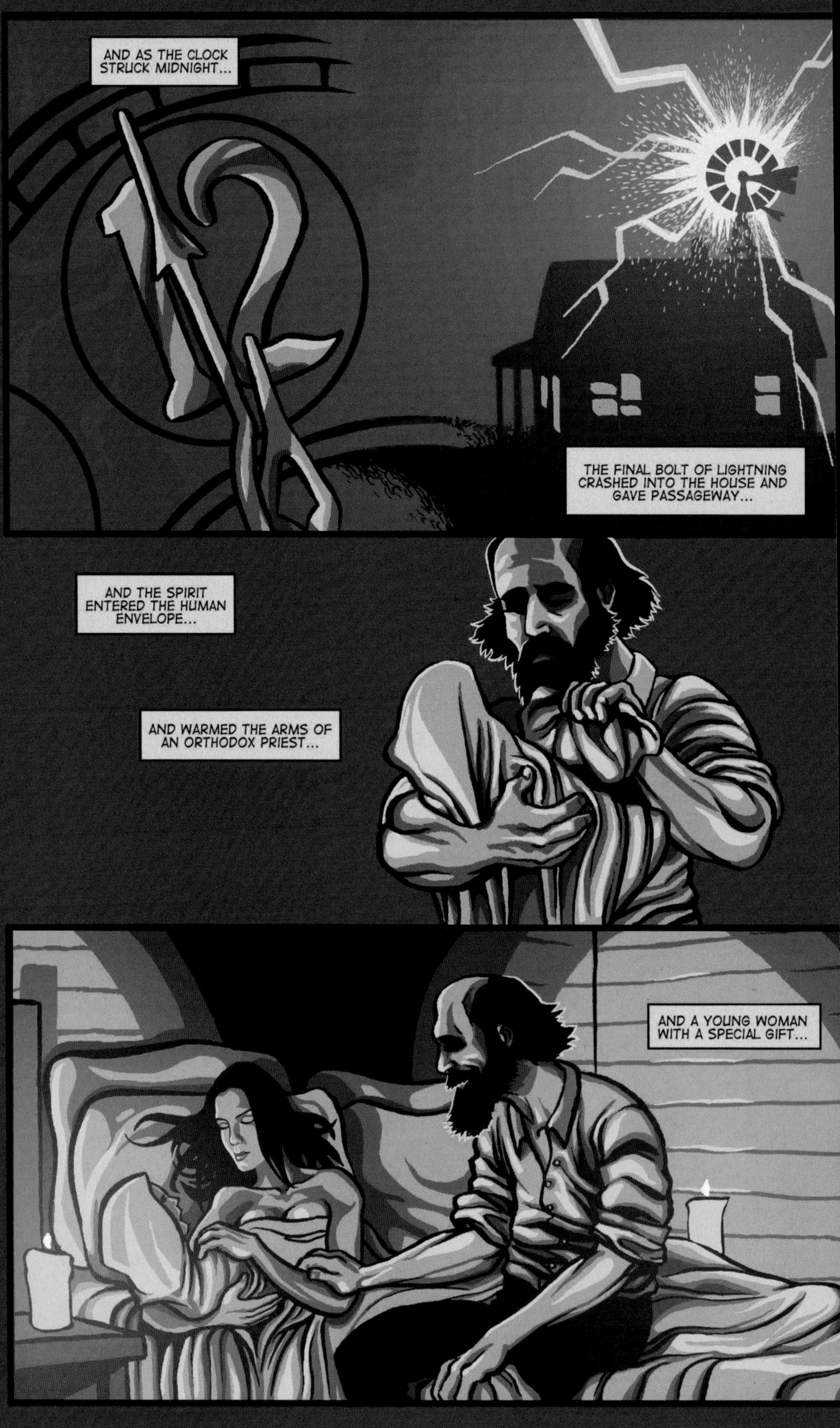
AND AS THE CLOCK STRUCK MIDNIGHT...
THE FINAL BOLT OF LIGHTNING CRASHED INTO THE HOUSE AND GAVE PASSAGEWAY...
AND THE SPIRIT ENTERED THE HUMAN ENVELOPE...
AND WARMED THE ARMS OF AN ORTHODOX PRIEST...
AND A YOUNG WOMAN WITH A SPECIAL GIFT...

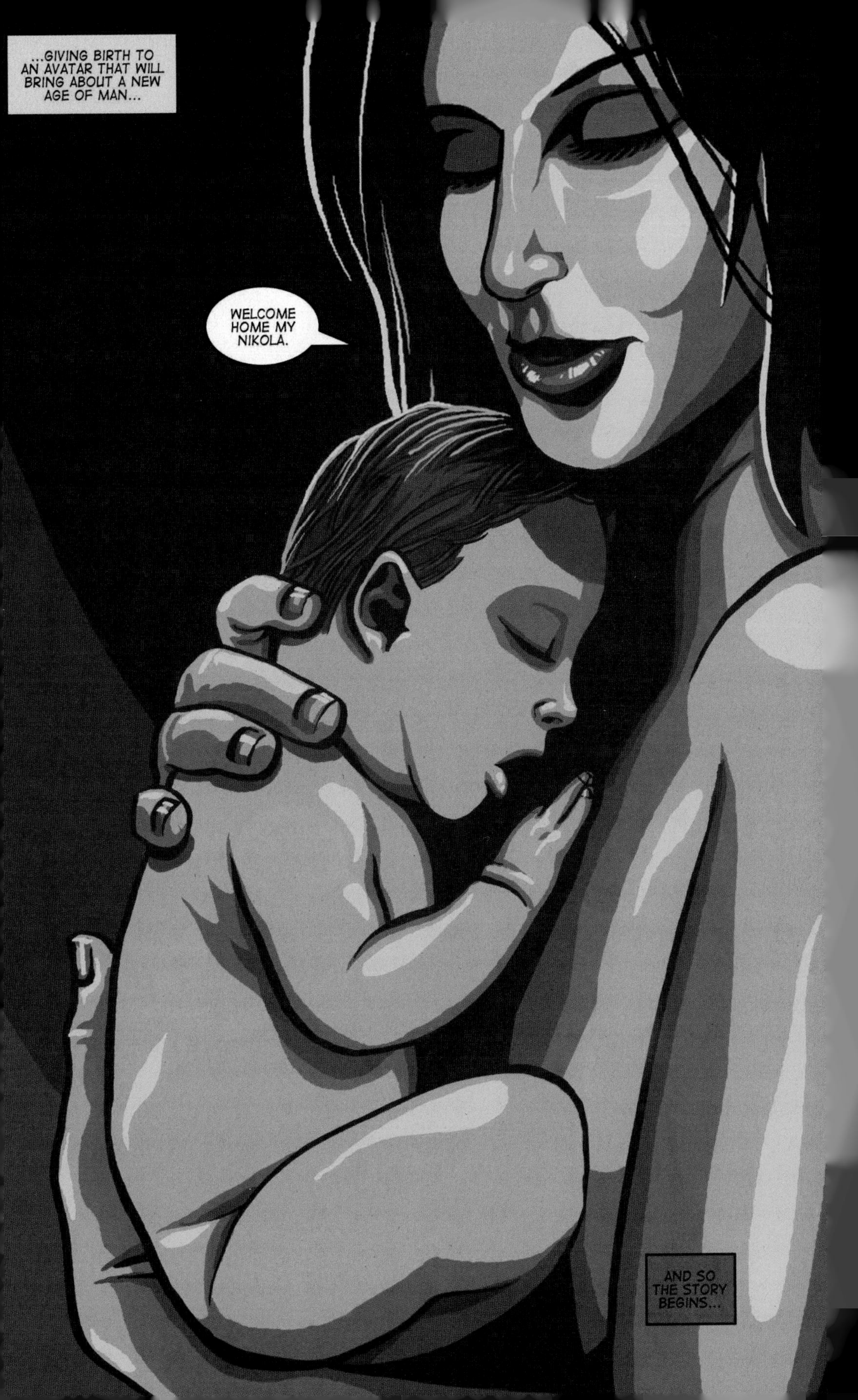
...GIVING BIRTH TO AN AVATAR THAT WILL BRING ABOUT A NEW AGE OF MAN...
WELCOME HOME MY NIKOLA.
AND SO THE STORY BEGINS...

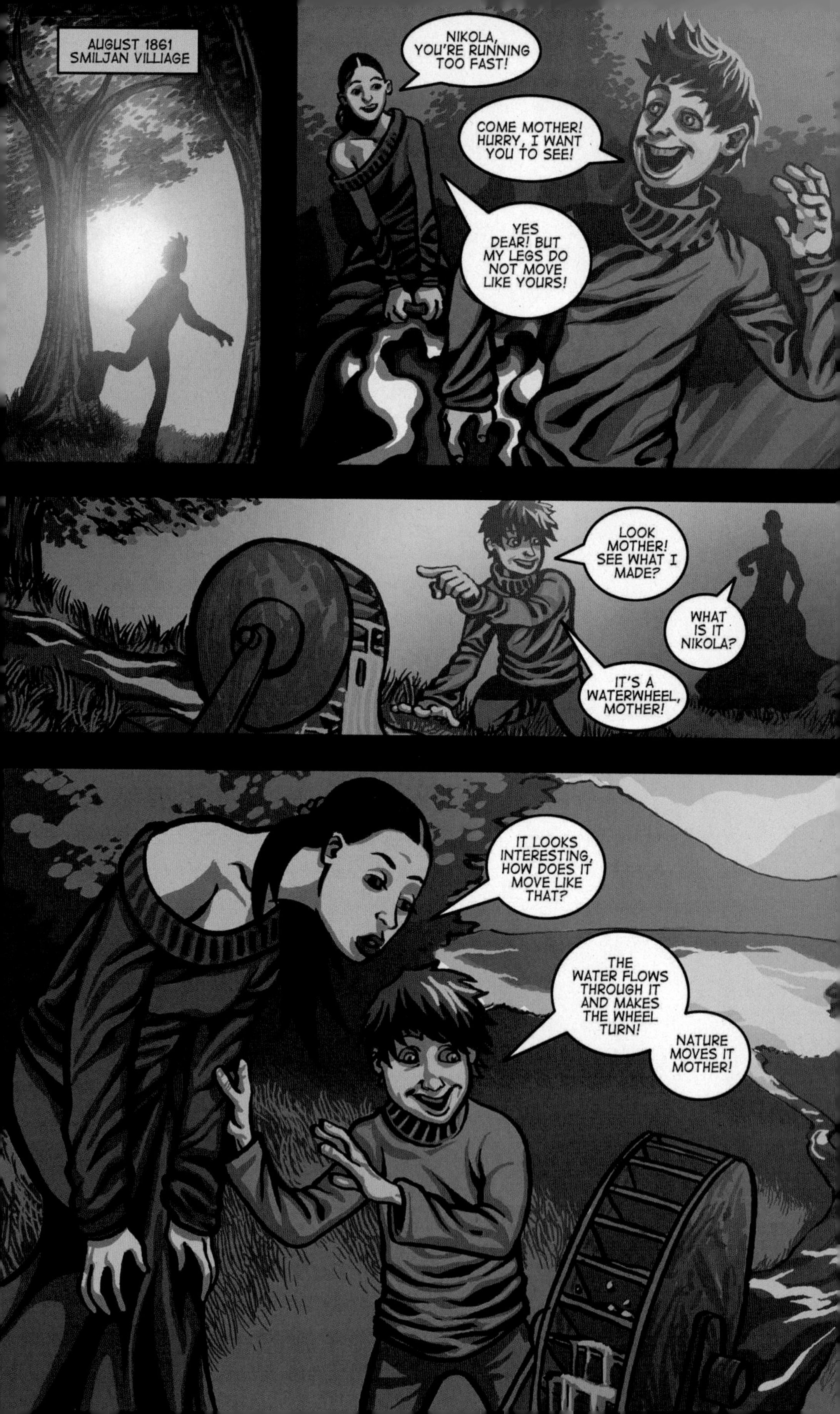
AUGUST 1861
SMILJAN VILLIAGE
NIKOLA, YOU'RE RUNNING TOO FAST!
COME MOTHER! HURRY, I WANT YOU TO SEE!
YES DEAR! BUT MY LEGS DO NOT MOVE LIKE YOURS!
LOOK MOTHER! SEE WHAT I MADE?
WHAT IS IT NIKOLA?
IT'S A WATERWHEEL, MOTHER!
IT LOOKS INTERESTING, HOW DOES IT MOVE LIKE THAT?
THE WATER FLOWS THROUGH IT AND MAKES THE WHEEL TURN!
NATURE MOVES IT MOTHER!

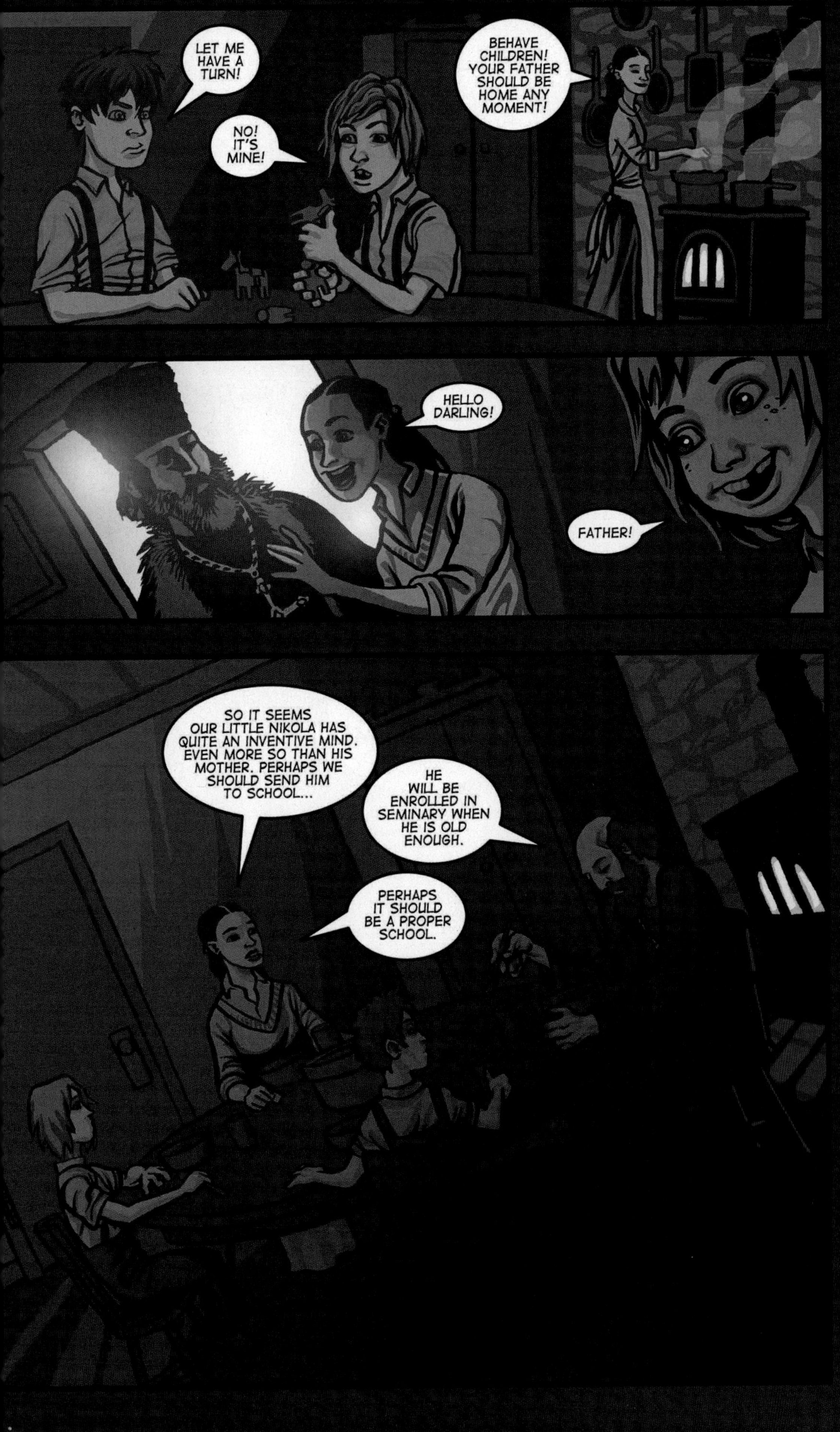
LET ME HAVE A TURN!
NO! IT'S MINE!
BEHAVE CHILDREN! YOUR FATHER SHOULD BE HOME ANY MOMENT!
HELLO DARLING!
FATHER!
SO IT SEEMS OUR LITTLE NIKOLA HAS QUITE AN INVENTIVE MIND. EVEN MORE SO THAN HIS MOTHER. PERHAPS WE SHOULD SEND HIM TO SCHOOL...
HE WILL BE ENROLLED IN SEMINARY WHEN HE IS OLD ENOUGH.
PERHAPS IT SHOULD BE A PROPER SCHOOL.

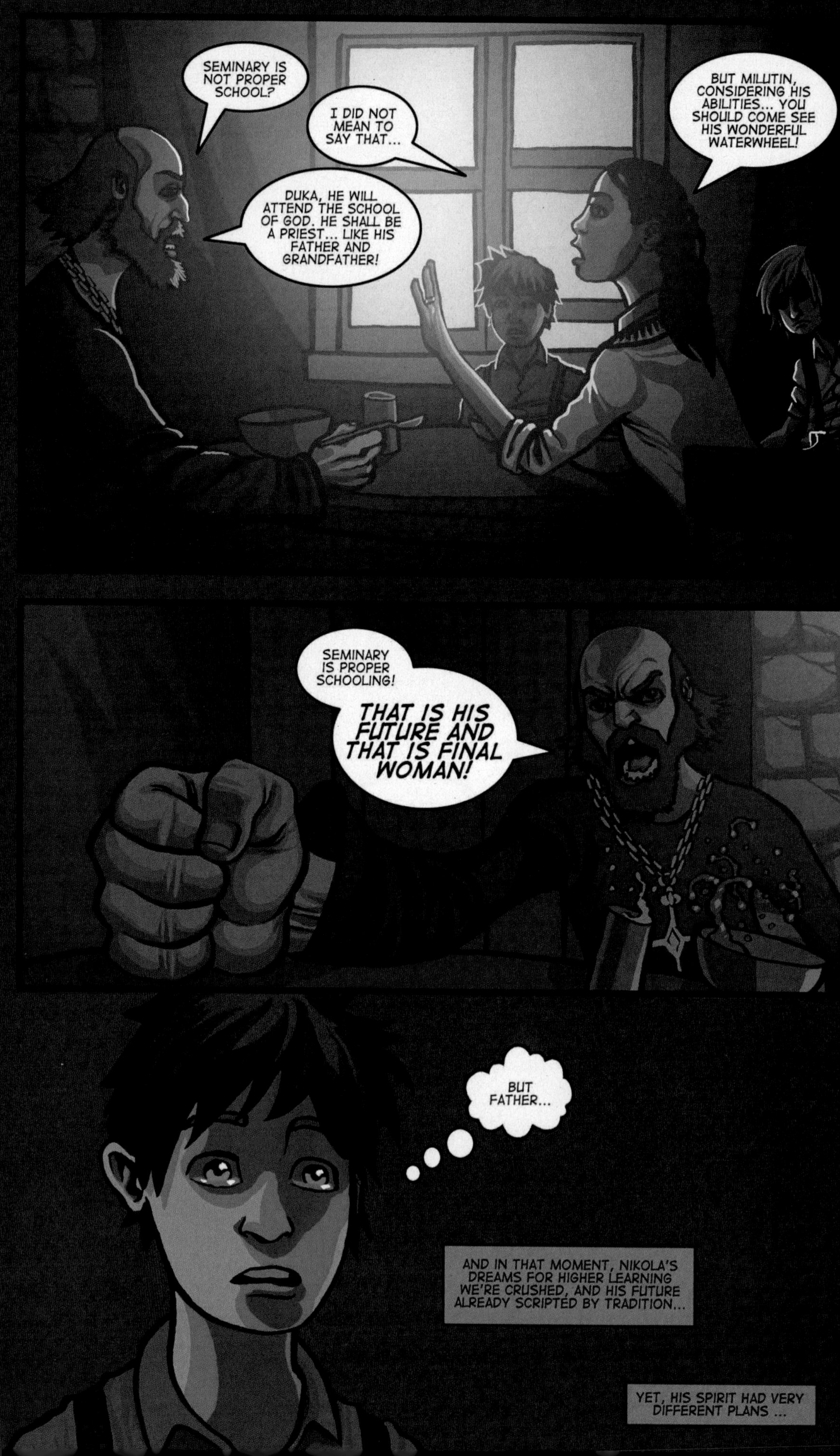

SEMINARY IS NOT PROPER SCHOOL?
I DID NOT MEAN TO SAY THAT...
BUT MILUTIN, CONSIDERING HIS ABILITIES... YOU SHOULD COME SEE HIS WONDERFUL WATERWHEEL!
DUKA, HE WILL ATTEND THE SCHOOL OF GOD. HE SHALL BE A PRIEST... LIKE HIS FATHER AND GRANDFATHER!
SEMINARY IS PROPER SCHOOLING!
THAT IS HIS FUTURE AND THAT IS FINAL WOMAN!
BUT FATHER...
AND IN THAT MOMENT, NIKOLA'S DREAMS FOR HIGHER LEARNING WE'RE CRUSHED, AND HIS FUTURE ALREADY SCRIPTED BY TRADITION...
YET, HIS SPIRIT HAD VERY DIFFERENT PLANS ...

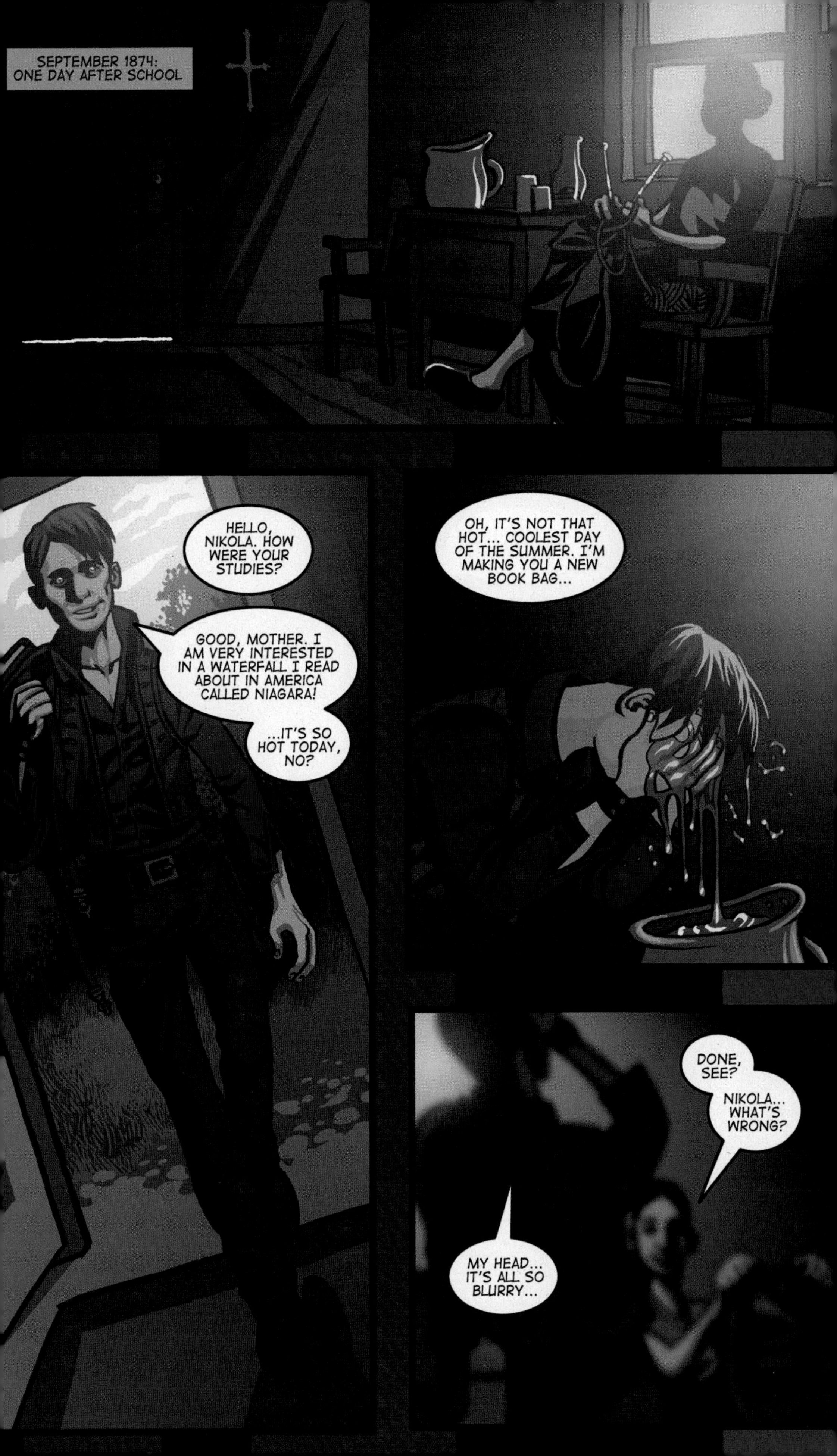
SEPTEMBER 1874: ONE DAY AFTER SCHOOL
HELLO, NIKOLA. HOW WERE YOUR STUDIES?
GOOD, MOTHER. I AM VERY INTERESTED IN A WATERFALL I READ ABOUT IN AMERICA CALLED NIAGARA!
...IT'S SO HOT TODAY, NO?
OH, IT'S NOT THAT HOT... COOLEST DAY OF THE SUMMER. I'M MAKING YOU A NEW BOOK BAG...
DONE, SEE?
NIKOLA... WHAT'S WRONG?
MY HEAD... IT'S ALL SO BLURRY...

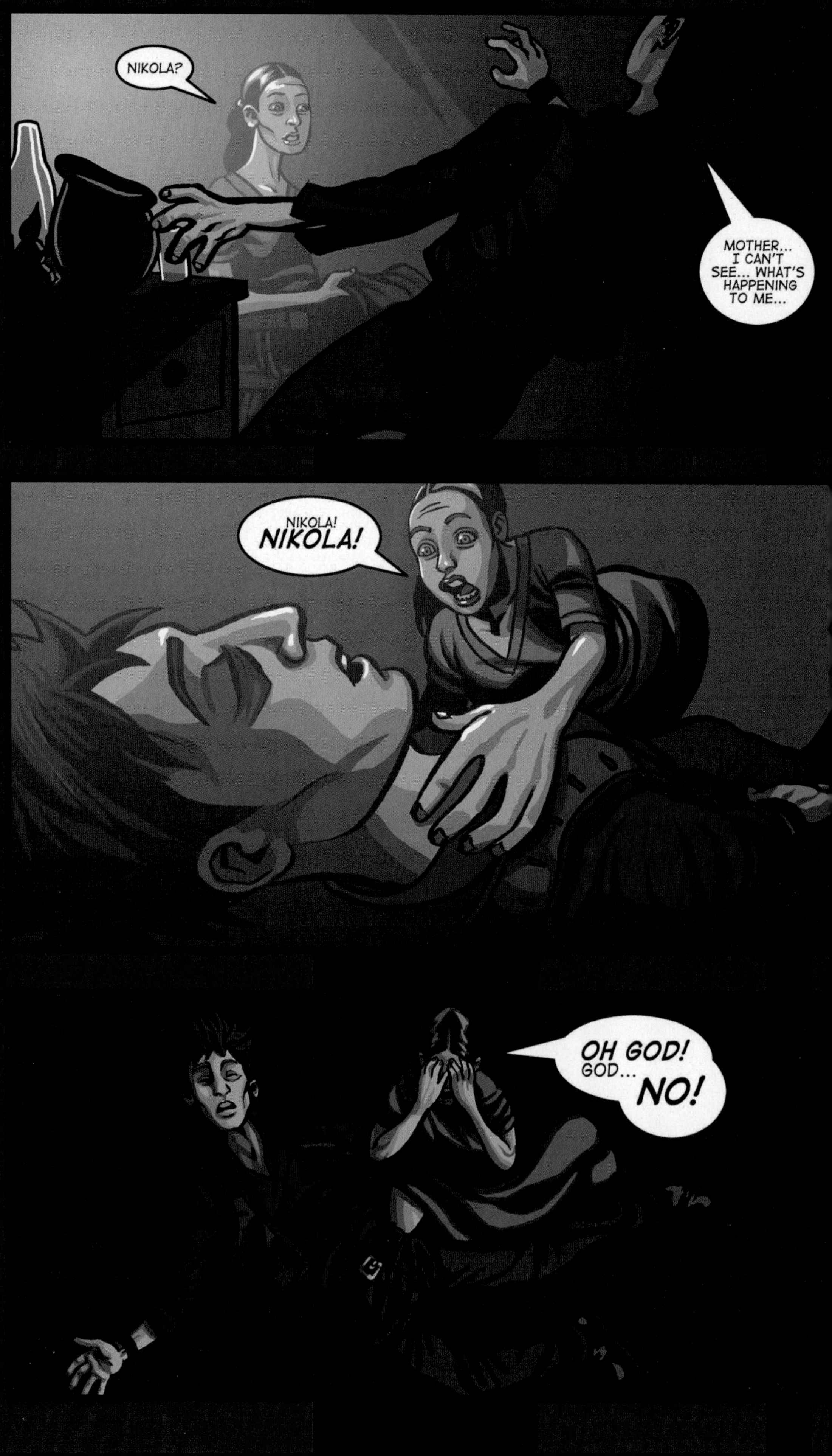
NIKOLA?
MOTHER... I CAN'T SEE... WHAT'S HAPPENING TO ME...
NIKOLA! NIKOLA!
OH GOD! GOD... NO!

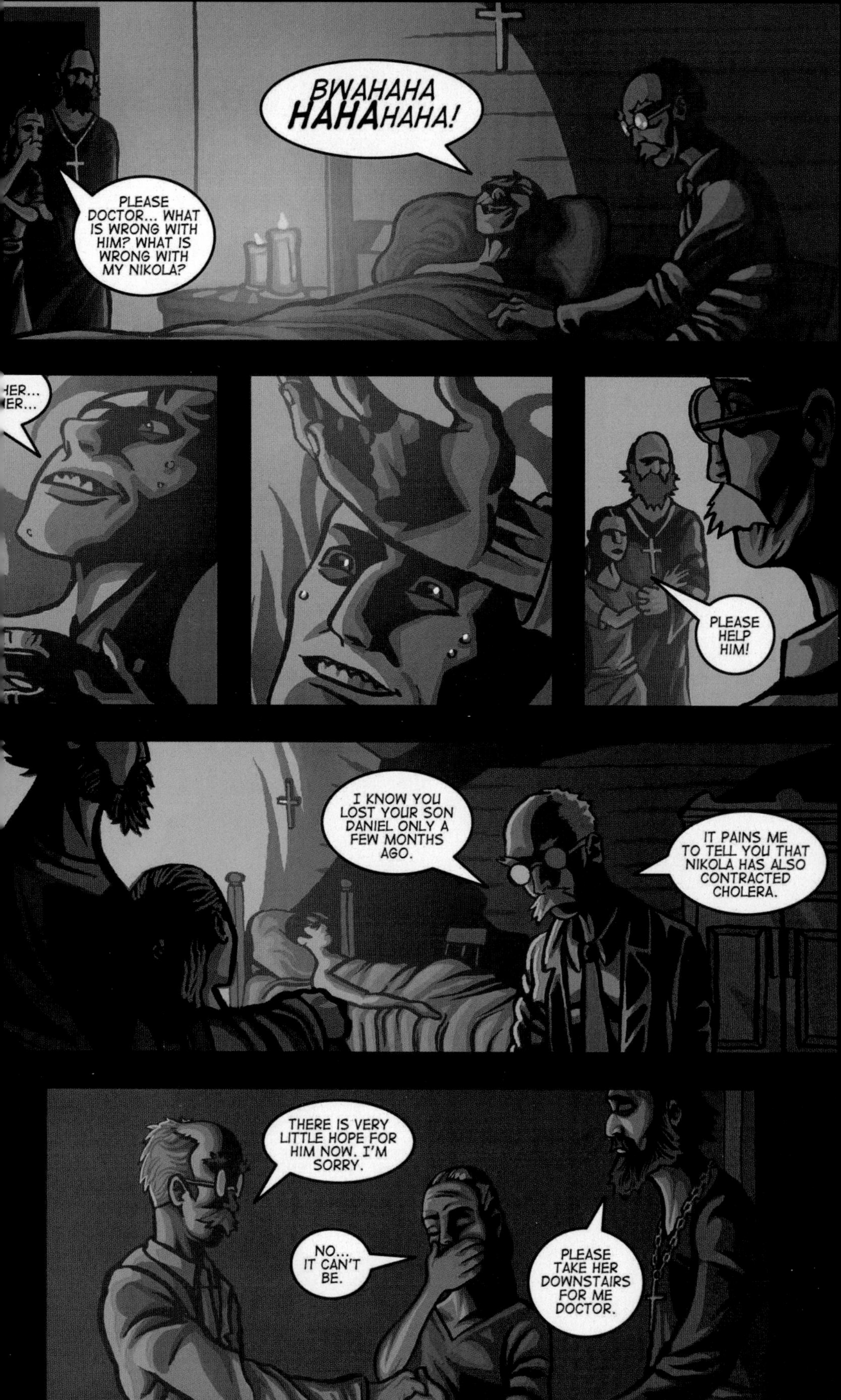
BWAHAHA HAHAHAHA!
PLEASE DOCTOR... WHAT IS WRONG WITH HIM? WHAT IS WRONG WITH MY NIKOLA?
PLEASE HELP HIM!
I KNOW YOU LOST YOUR SON DANIEL ONLY A FEW MONTHS AGO.
IT PAINS ME TO TELL YOU THAT NIKOLA HAS ALSO CONTRACTED CHOLERA.
THERE IS VERY LITTLE HOPE FOR HIM NOW. I'M SORRY.
NO... IT CAN'T BE.
PLEASE TAKE HER DOWNSTAIRS FOR ME DOCTOR.

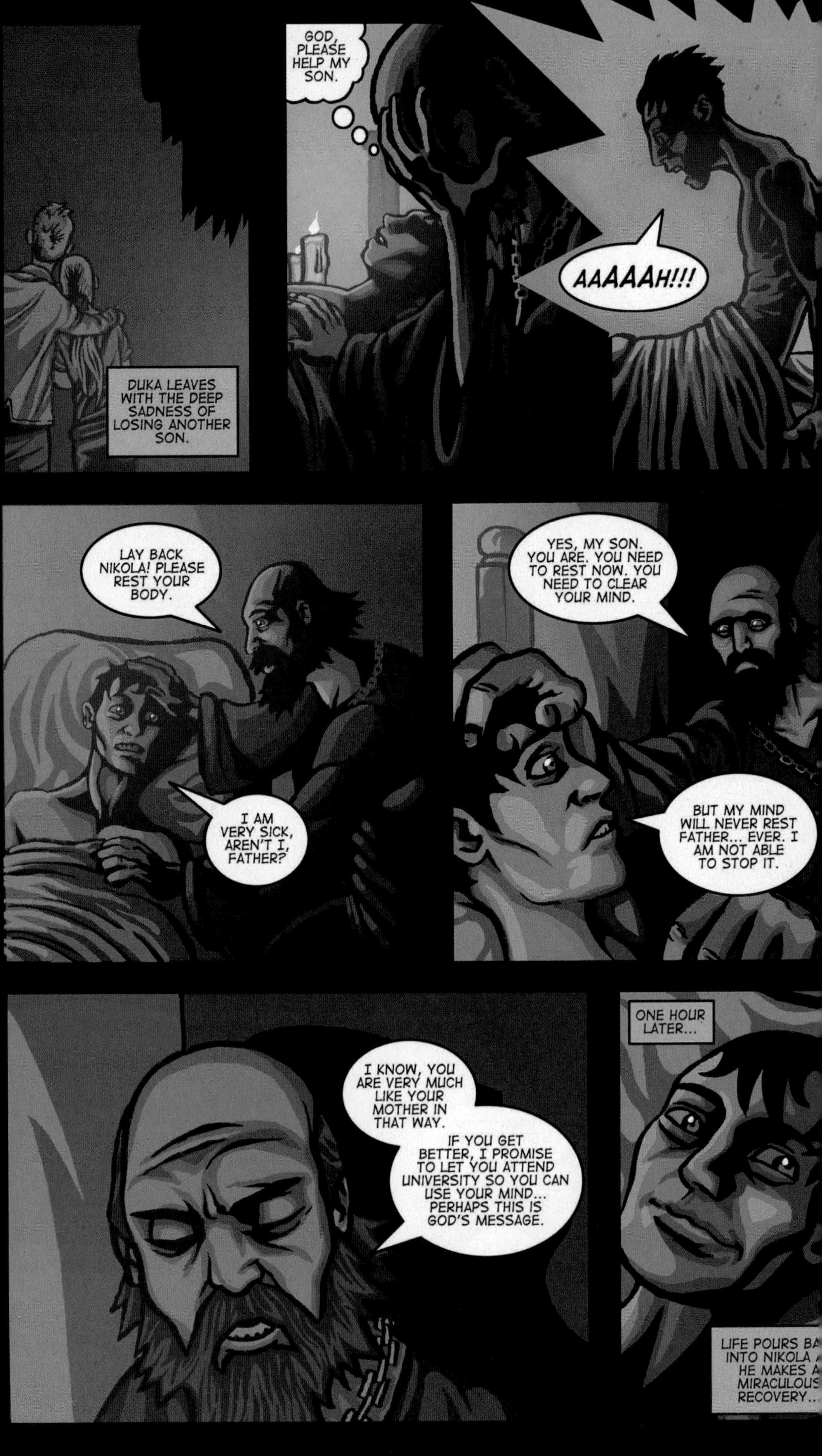
DUKA LEAVES WITH THE DEEP SADNESS OF LOSING ANOTHER SON.
GOD, PLEASE HELP MY SON.
AAAAAH!!!
LAY BACK NIKOLA! PLEASE REST YOUR BODY.
I AM VERY SICK, AREN'T I, FATHER?
YES, MY SON. YOU ARE. YOU NEED TO REST NOW. YOU NEED TO CLEAR YOUR MIND.
BUT MY MIND WILL NEVER REST FATHER... EVER. I AM NOT ABLE TO STOP IT.
I KNOW, YOU ARE VERY MUCH LIKE YOUR MOTHER IN THAT WAY.
IF YOU GET BETTER, I PROMISE TO LET YOU ATTEND UNIVERSITY SO YOU CAN USE YOUR MIND... PERHAPS THIS IS GOD'S MESSAGE.
ONE HOUR LATER...
LIFE POURS BA
INTO NIKOLA
HE MAKES A
MIRACULOUS
RECOVERY...

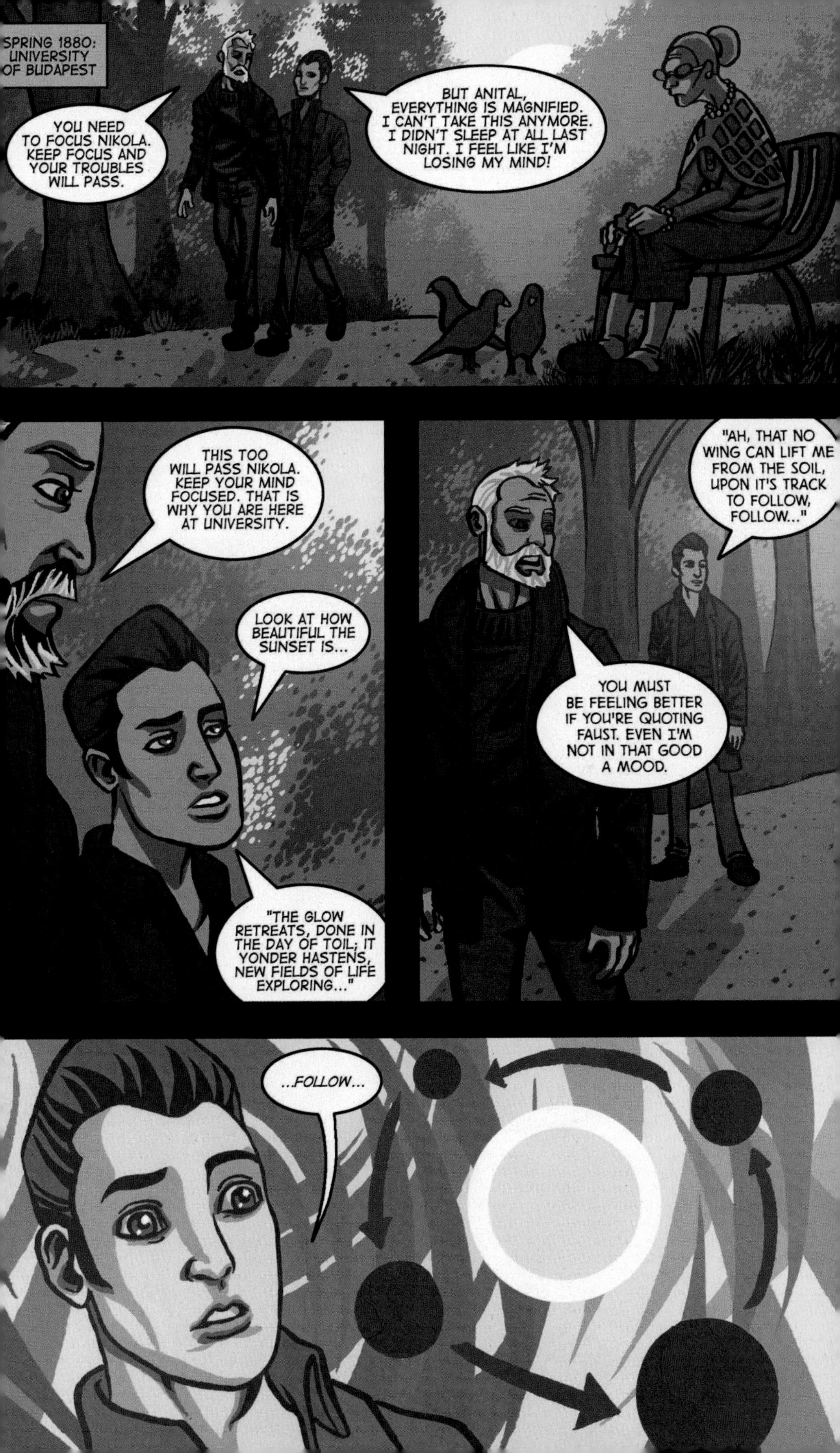
SPRING 1880: UNIVERSITY OF BUDAPEST
YOU NEED TO FOCUS NIKOLA. KEEP FOCUS AND YOUR TROUBLES WILL PASS.
BUT ANITAL, EVERYTHING IS MAGNIFIED. I CAN'T TAKE THIS ANYMORE. I DIDN'T SLEEP AT ALL LAST NIGHT. I FEEL LIKE I'M LOSING MY MIND!
THIS TOO WILL PASS NIKOLA. KEEP YOUR MIND FOCUSED. THAT IS WHY YOU ARE HERE AT UNIVERSITY.
LOOK AT HOW BEAUTIFUL THE SUNSET IS...
"THE GLOW RETREATS, DONE IN THE DAY OF TOIL; IT YONDER HASTENS, NEW FIELDS OF LIFE EXPLORING..."
"AH, THAT NO WING CAN LIFT ME FROM THE SOIL, UPON IT'S TRACK TO FOLLOW, FOLLOW..."
YOU MUST BE FEELING BETTER IF YOU'RE QUOTING FAUST. EVEN I'M NOT IN THAT GOOD A MOOD.
...FOLLOW...

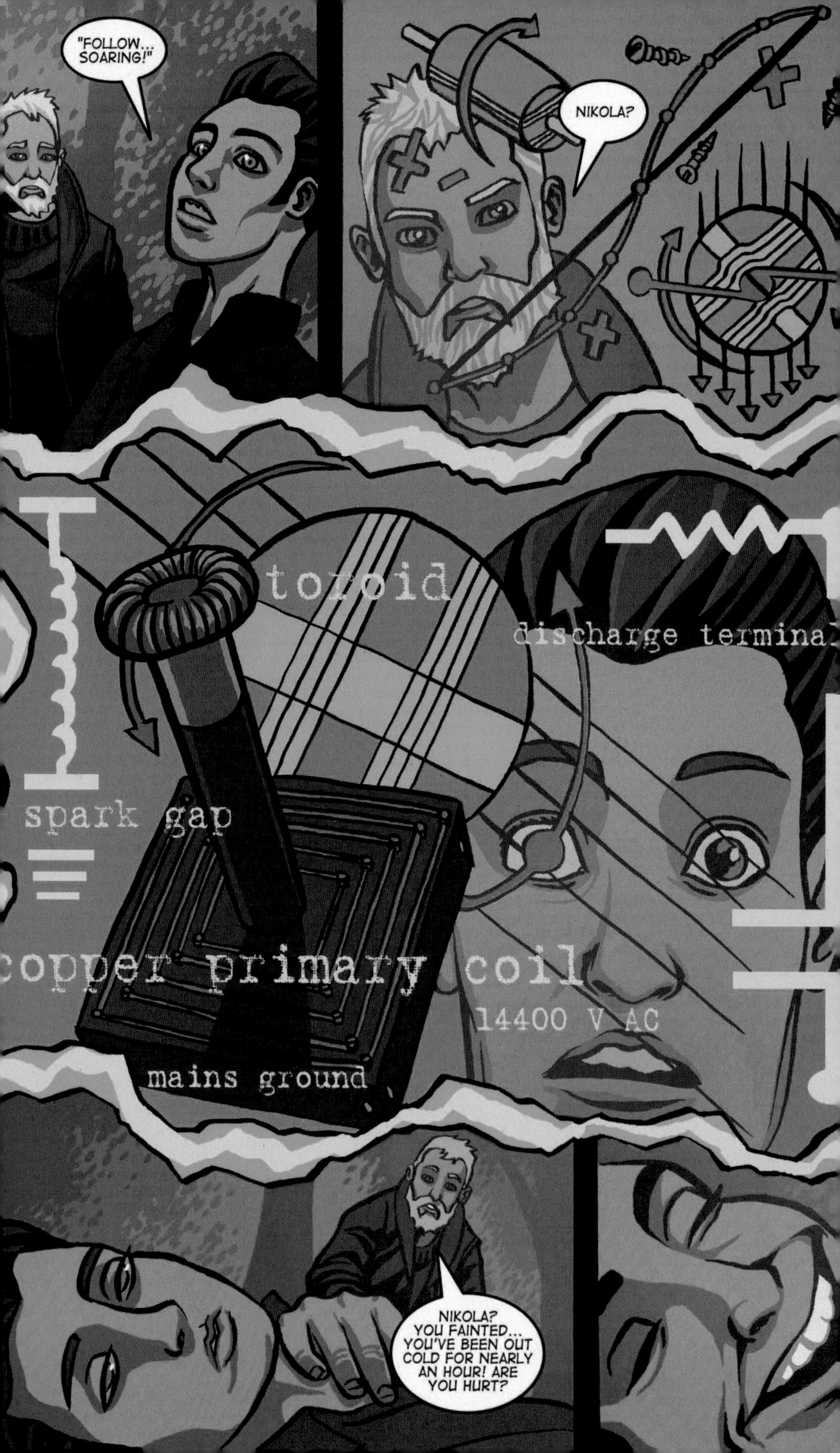
"FOLLOW... SOARING!"
NIKOLA?
toroid
discharge terminal
spark gap
copper primary coil
14400 V AC
mains ground
NIKOLA? YOU FAINTED... YOU'VE BEEN OUT COLD FOR NEARLY AN HOUR! ARE YOU HURT?

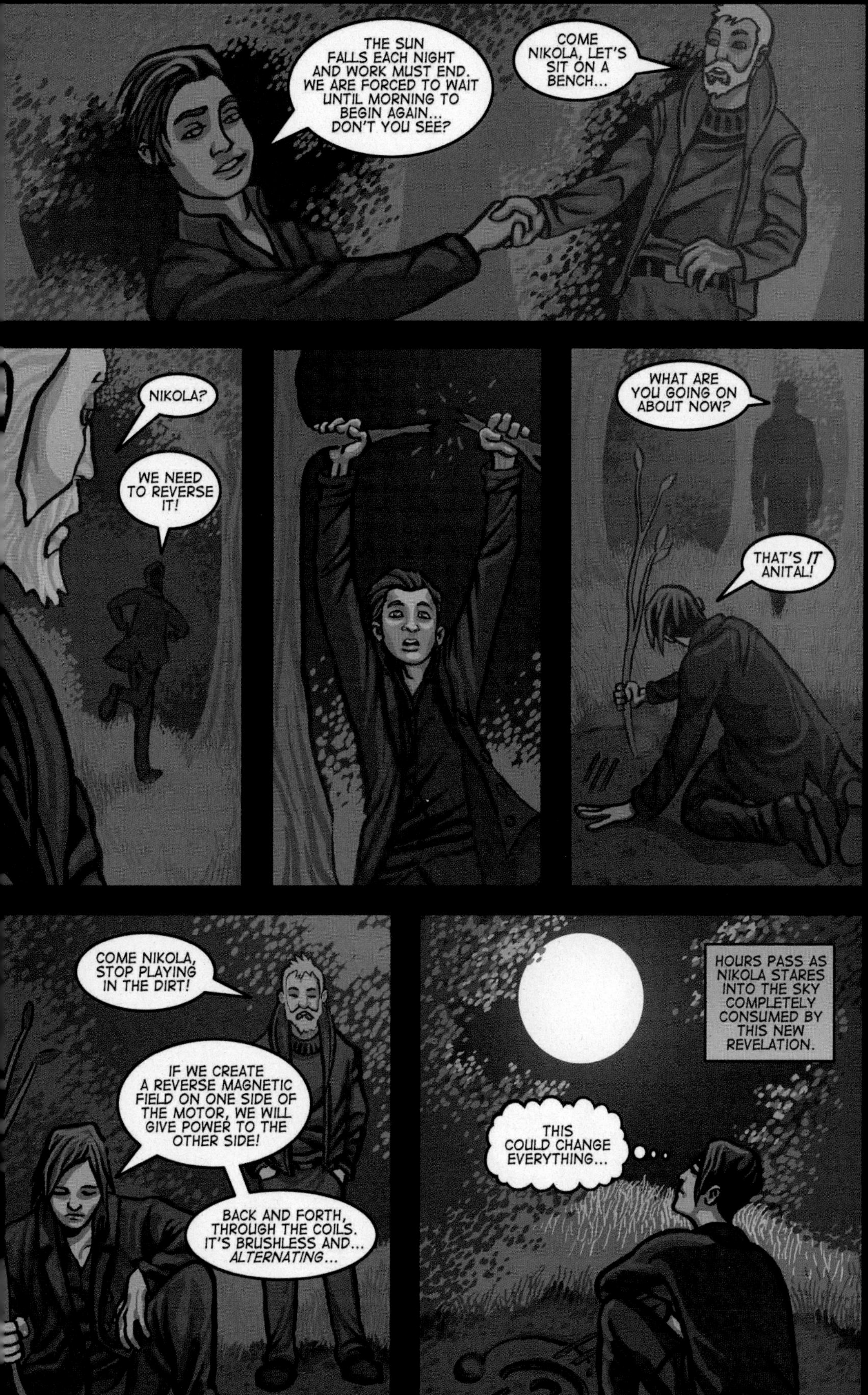
THE SUN FALLS EACH NIGHT AND WORK MUST END. WE ARE FORCED TO WAIT UNTIL MORNING TO BEGIN AGAIN... DON'T YOU SEE?
COME NIKOLA, LET'S SIT ON A BENCH...
NIKOLA?
WE NEED TO REVERSE IT!
WHAT ARE YOU GOING ON ABOUT NOW?
THAT'S *IT* ANITAL!
COME NIKOLA, STOP PLAYING IN THE DIRT!
IF WE CREATE A REVERSE MAGNETIC FIELD ON ONE SIDE OF THE MOTOR, WE WILL GIVE POWER TO THE OTHER SIDE!
BACK AND FORTH, THROUGH THE COILS. IT'S BRUSHLESS AND... *ALTERNATING*...
HOURS PASS AS NIKOLA STARES INTO THE SKY COMPLETELY CONSUMED BY THIS NEW REVELATION.
THIS COULD CHANGE EVERYTHING...

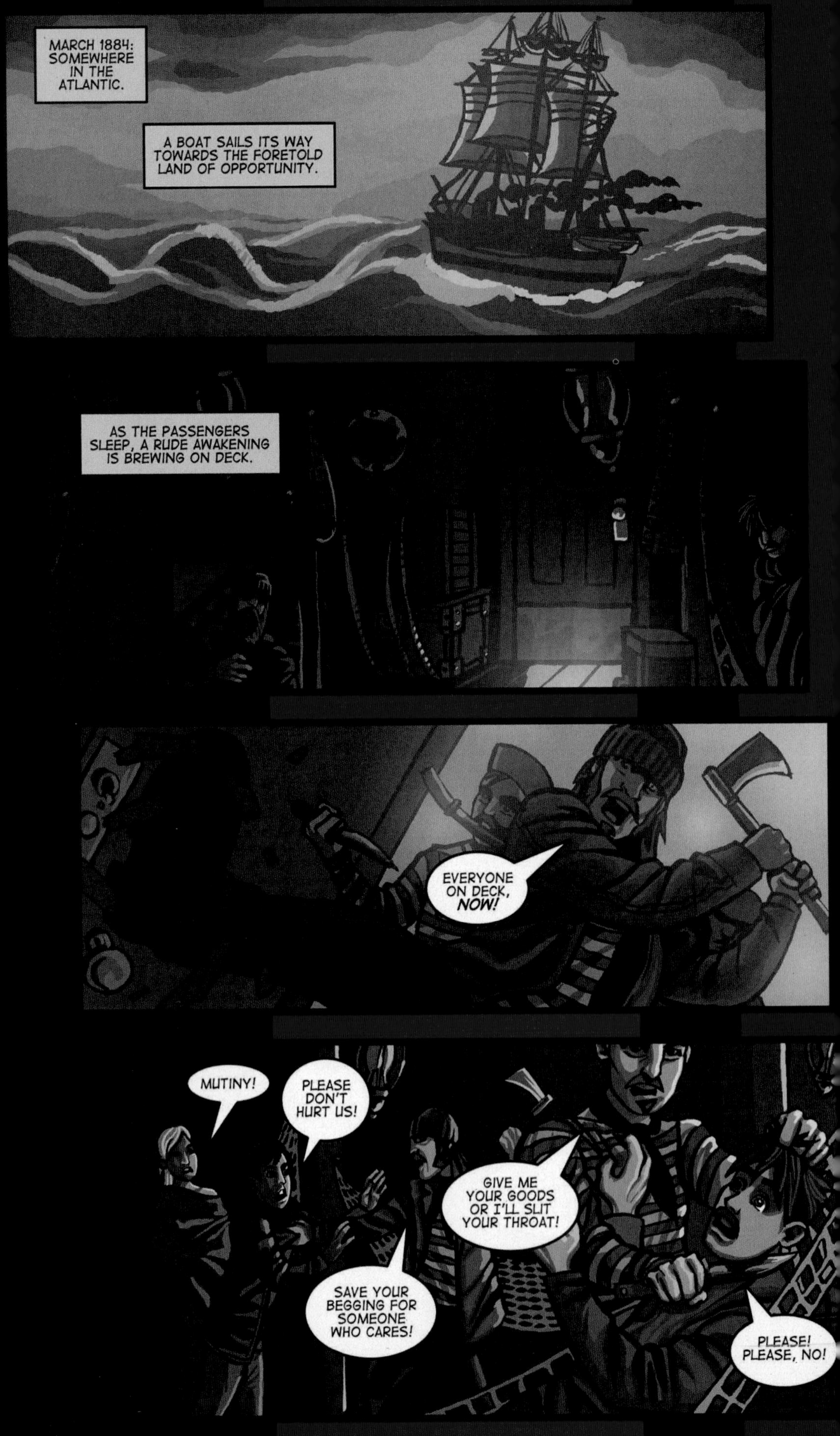
MARCH 1884: SOMEWHERE IN THE ATLANTIC.
A BOAT SAILS ITS WAY TOWARDS THE FORETOLD LAND OF OPPORTUNITY.
AS THE PASSENGERS SLEEP, A RUDE AWAKENING IS BREWING ON DECK.
EVERYONE ON DECK, *NOW!*
MUTINY!
PLEASE DON'T HURT US!
GIVE ME YOUR GOODS OR I'LL SLIT YOUR THROAT!
SAVE YOUR BEGGING FOR SOMEONE WHO CARES!
PLEASE! PLEASE, NO!

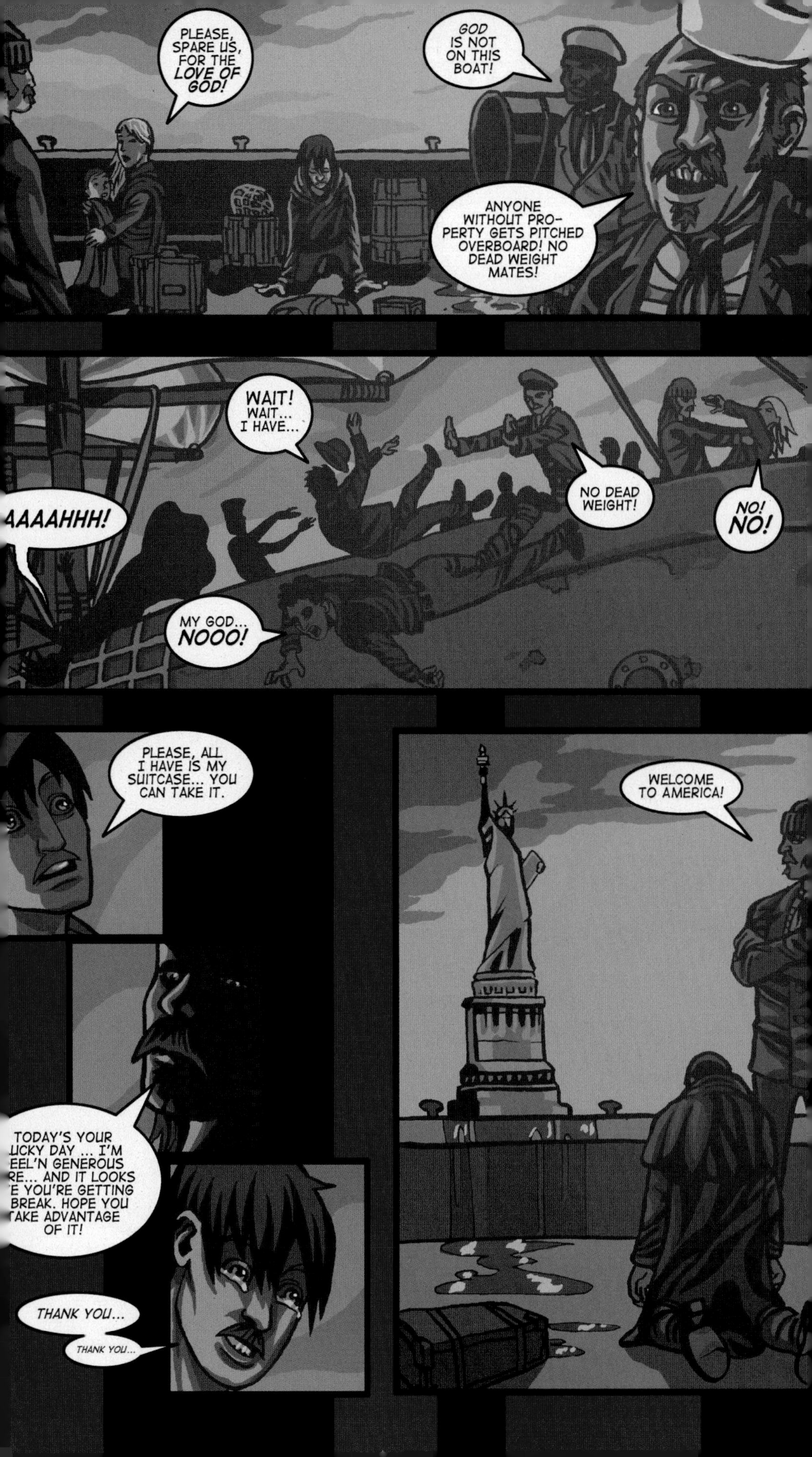

PLEASE, SPARE US, FOR THE *LOVE OF GOD!*
GOD IS NOT ON THIS BOAT!
ANYONE WITHOUT PRO-PERTY GETS PITCHED OVERBOARD! NO DEAD WEIGHT MATES!
AAAAHHH!
WAIT! WAIT... I HAVE...
NO DEAD WEIGHT!
NO! NO!
MY GOD... **NOOO!**
PLEASE, ALL I HAVE IS MY SUITCASE... YOU CAN TAKE IT.
TODAY'S YOUR UCKY DAY ... I'M EEL'N GENEROUS RE... AND IT LOOKS E YOU'RE GETTING BREAK. HOPE YOU TAKE ADVANTAGE OF IT!
THANK YOU...
THANK YOU...
WELCOME TO AMERICA!

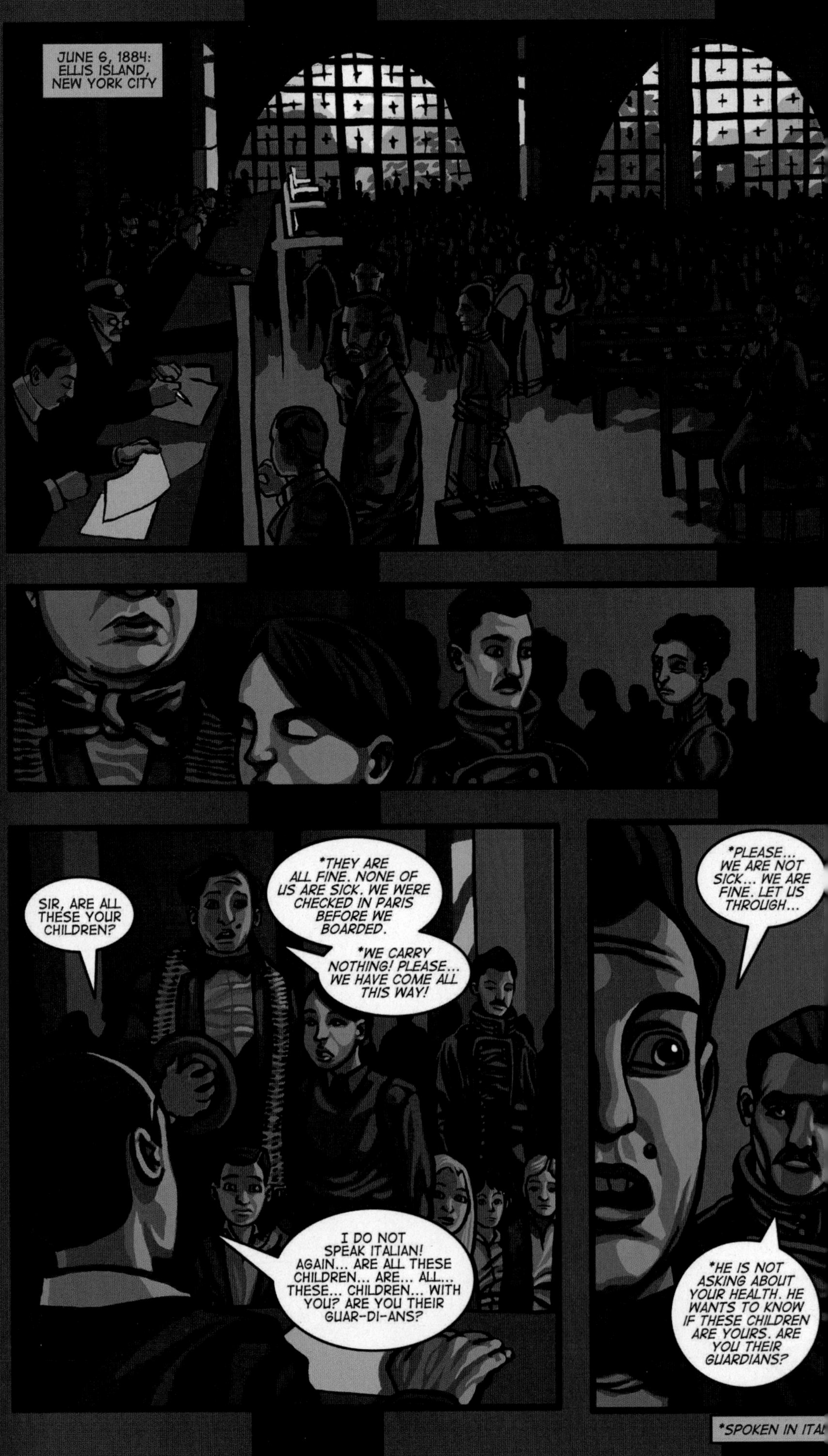
JUNE 6, 1884: ELLIS ISLAND, NEW YORK CITY
SIR, ARE ALL THESE YOUR CHILDREN?
*THEY ARE ALL FINE. NONE OF US ARE SICK. WE WERE CHECKED IN PARIS BEFORE WE BOARDED.
*WE CARRY NOTHING! PLEASE... WE HAVE COME ALL THIS WAY!
I DO NOT SPEAK ITALIAN! AGAIN... ARE ALL THESE CHILDREN... ARE... ALL... THESE... CHILDREN... WITH YOU? ARE YOU THEIR GUAR-DI-ANS?
*PLEASE... WE ARE NOT SICK... WE ARE FINE. LET US THROUGH...
*HE IS NOT ASKING ABOUT YOUR HEALTH. HE WANTS TO KNOW IF THESE CHILDREN ARE YOURS. ARE YOU THEIR GUARDIANS?
*SPOKEN IN ITAL

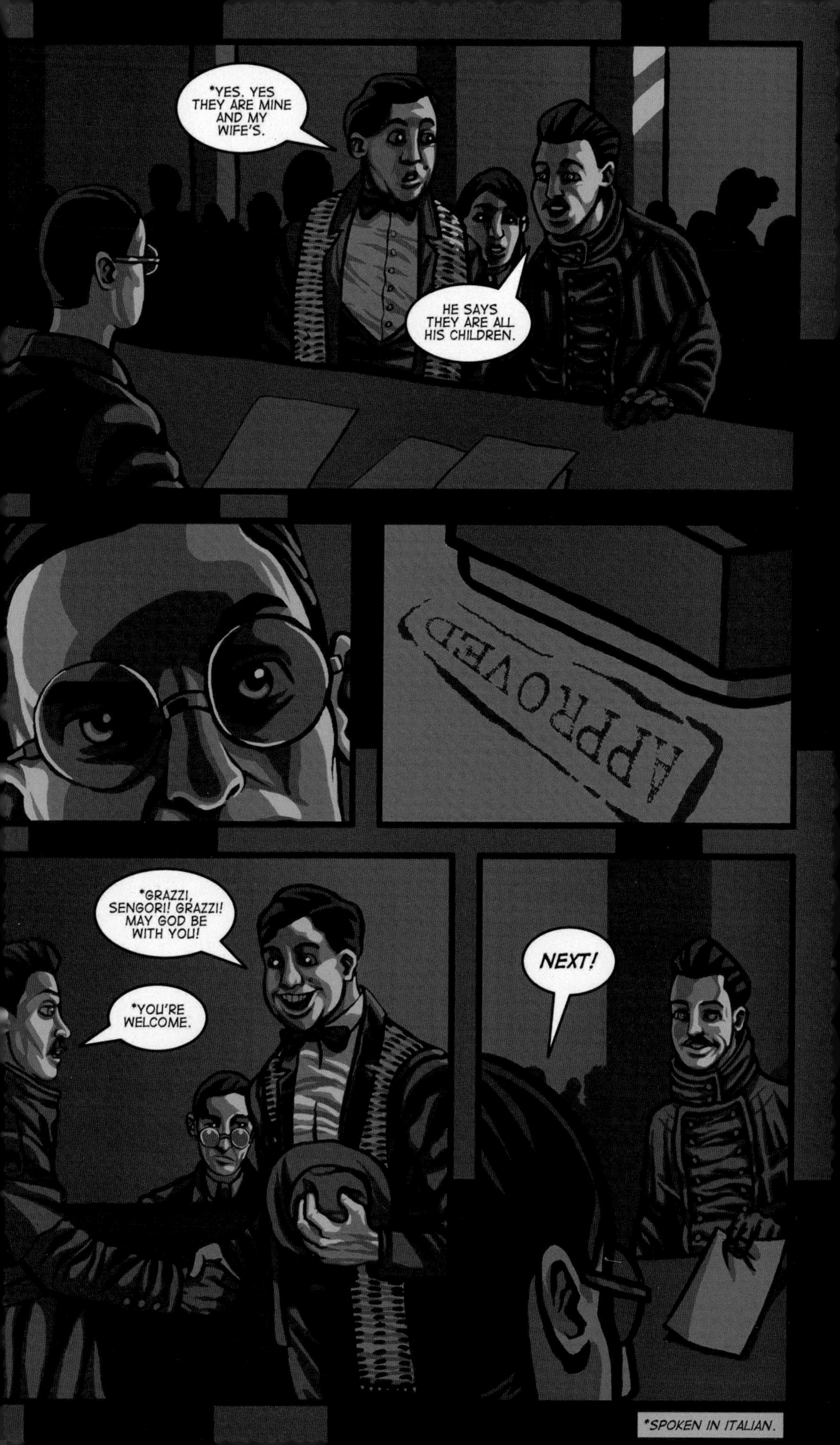
*YES. YES THEY ARE MINE AND MY WIFE'S.
HE SAYS THEY ARE ALL HIS CHILDREN.
APPROVED
*GRAZZI, SENGORI! GRAZZI! MAY GOD BE WITH YOU!
*YOU'RE WELCOME.
NEXT!
*SPOKEN IN ITALIAN.

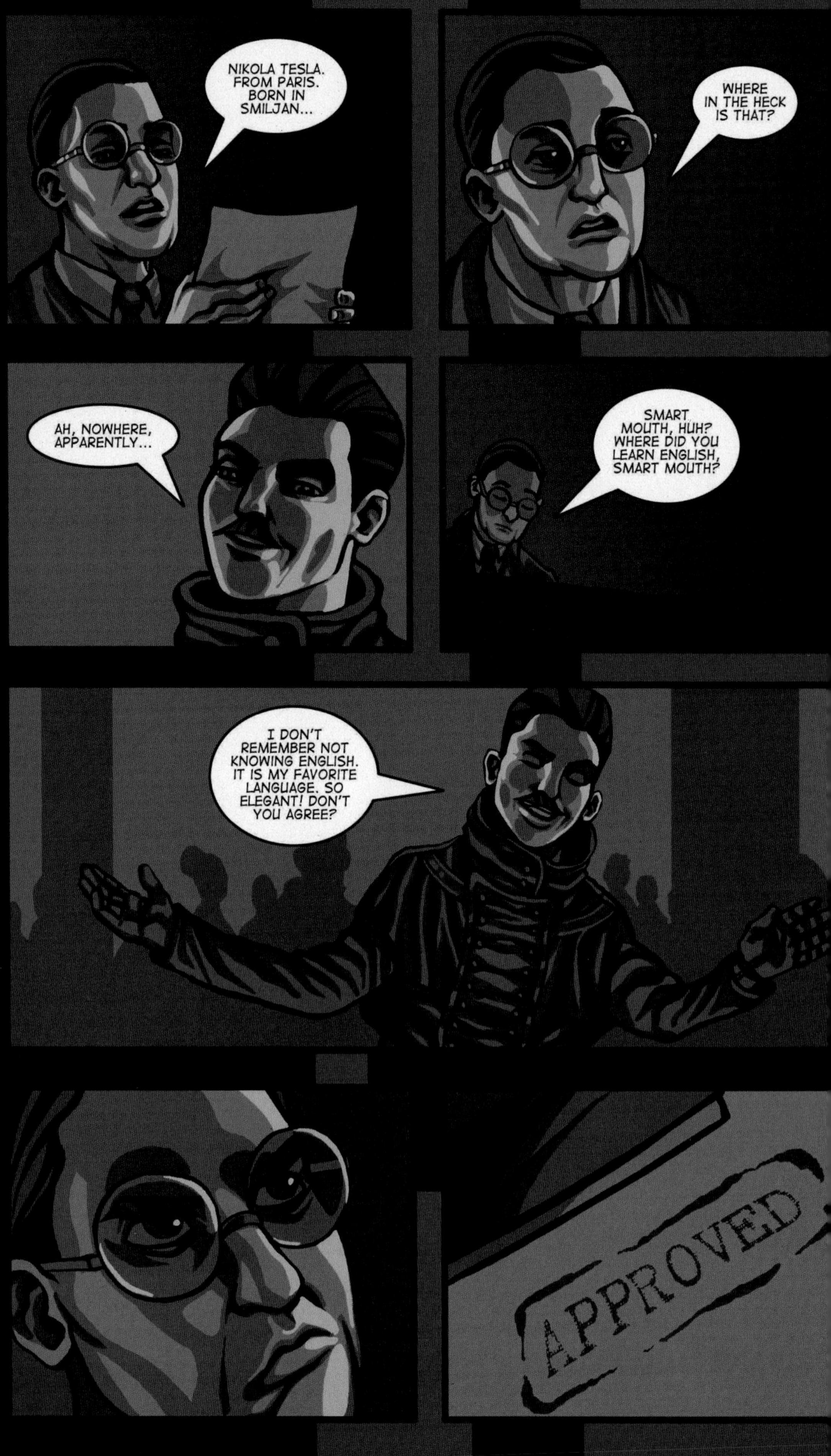
NIKOLA TESLA. FROM PARIS. BORN IN SMILJAN...
WHERE IN THE HECK IS THAT?
AH, NOWHERE, APPARENTLY...
SMART MOUTH, HUH? WHERE DID YOU LEARN ENGLISH, SMART MOUTH?
I DON'T REMEMBER NOT KNOWING ENGLISH. IT IS MY FAVORITE LANGUAGE. SO ELEGANT! DON'T YOU AGREE?
APPROVED

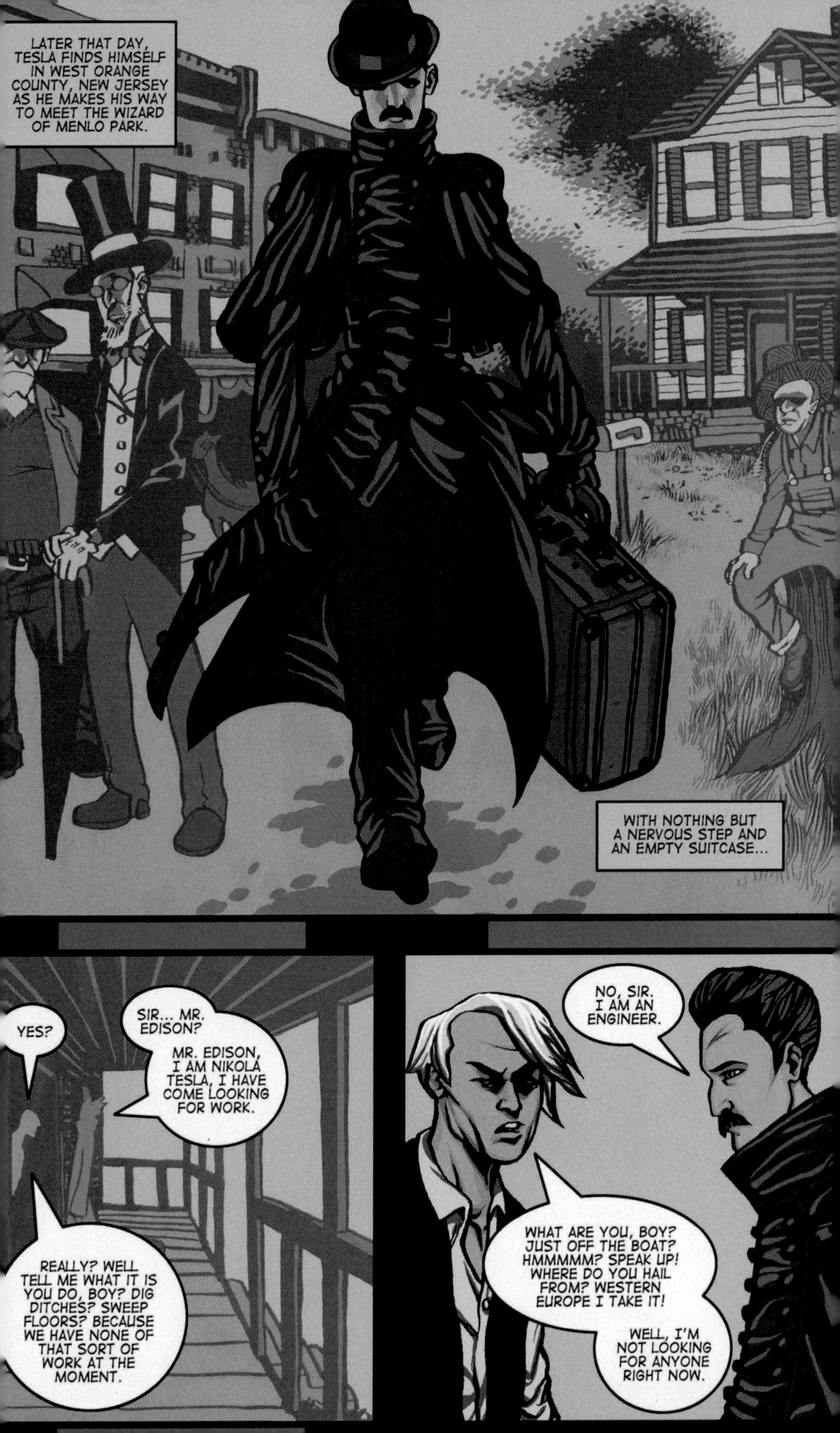
LATER THAT DAY, TESLA FINDS HIMSELF IN WEST ORANGE COUNTY, NEW JERSEY AS HE MAKES HIS WAY TO MEET THE WIZARD OF MENLO PARK.
WITH NOTHING BUT A NERVOUS STEP AND AN EMPTY SUITCASE...
YES?
SIR... MR. EDISON?
MR. EDISON, I AM NIKOLA TESLA, I HAVE COME LOOKING FOR WORK.
REALLY? WELL TELL ME WHAT IT IS YOU DO, BOY? DIG DITCHES? SWEEP FLOORS? BECAUSE WE HAVE NONE OF THAT SORT OF WORK AT THE MOMENT.
NO, SIR. I AM AN ENGINEER.
WHAT ARE YOU, BOY? JUST OFF THE BOAT? HMMMMM? SPEAK UP! WHERE DO YOU HAIL FROM? WESTERN EUROPE I TAKE IT!
WELL, I'M NOT LOOKING FOR ANYONE RIGHT NOW.

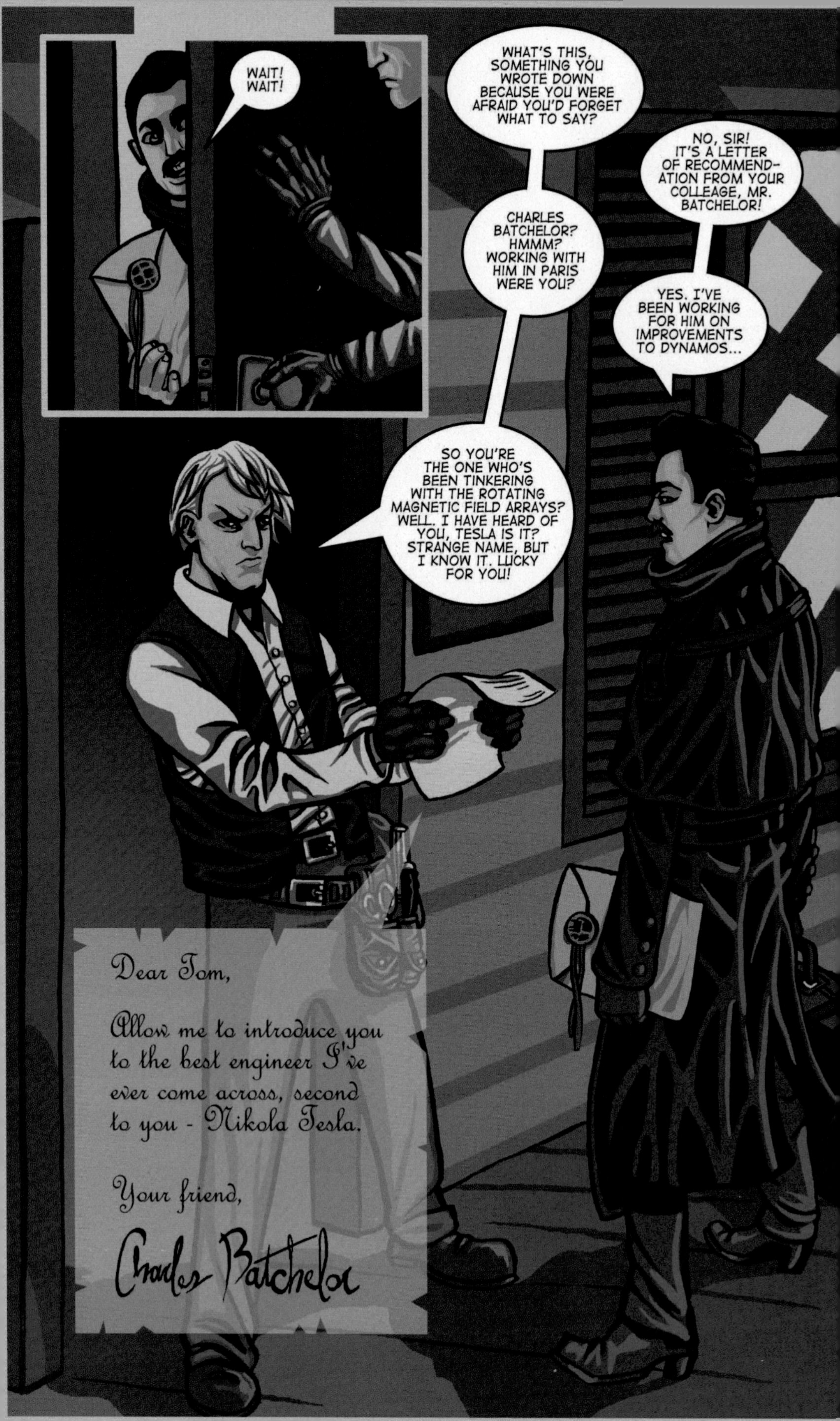
WAIT! WAIT!
WHAT'S THIS, SOMETHING YOU WROTE DOWN BECAUSE YOU WERE AFRAID YOU'D FORGET WHAT TO SAY?
NO, SIR! IT'S A LETTER OF RECOMMENDATION FROM YOUR COLLEAGE, MR. BATCHELOR!
CHARLES BATCHELOR? HMMM? WORKING WITH HIM IN PARIS WERE YOU?
YES. I'VE BEEN WORKING FOR HIM ON IMPROVEMENTS TO DYNAMOS...
SO YOU'RE THE ONE WHO'S BEEN TINKERING WITH THE ROTATING MAGNETIC FIELD ARRAYS? WELL. I HAVE HEARD OF YOU, TESLA IS IT? STRANGE NAME, BUT I KNOW IT. LUCKY FOR YOU!
Dear Tom,
Allow me to introduce you to the best engineer I've ever come across, second to you - Nikola Tesla.
Your friend,
Charles Batchelor

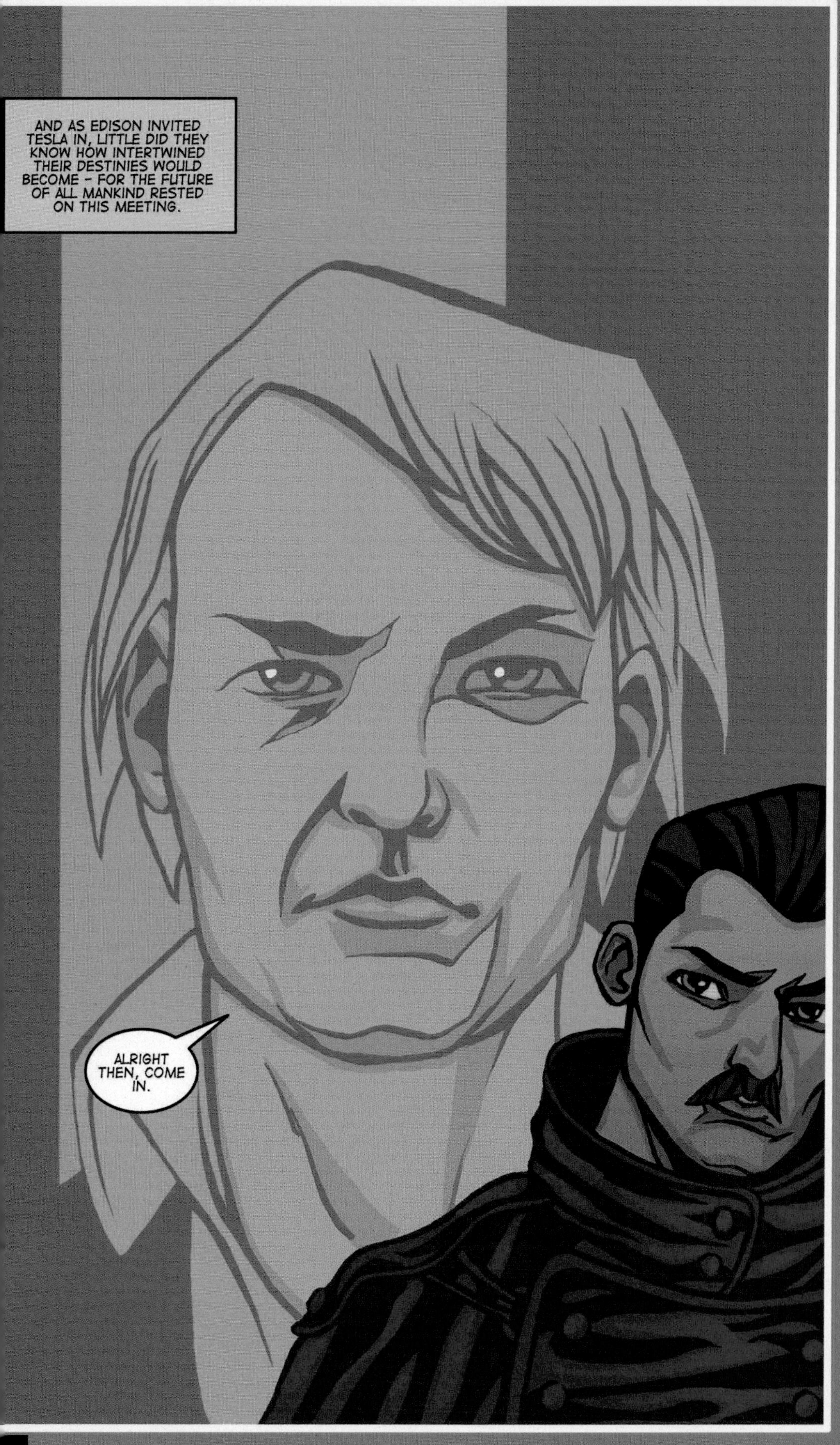
AND AS EDISON INVITED TESLA IN, LITTLE DID THEY KNOW HOW INTERTWINED THEIR DESTINIES WOULD BECOME - FOR THE FUTURE OF ALL MANKIND RESTED ON THIS MEETING.
ALRIGHT THEN, COME IN.

"THE PROGRESSIVE DEVELOPMENT OF MAN IS VITALLY DEPENDENT ON INVENTION. IT IS THE MOST IMPORTANT PRODUCT OF HIS CREATIVE BRAIN. ITS ULTIMATE PURPOSE IS THE COMPLETE MASTERY OF MIND OVER THE MATERIAL WORLD, THE HARNESSING OF THE FORCES OF NATURE TO HUMAN NEEDS."

- NIKOLA TESLA (1856-1943)

CHAPTER 2

SENSORY OVERLOAD

AT LONG LAST, TESLA GAINS ENTRY INTO THE WIZARD'S DEN AS EDISON INTRODUCES HIM TO HIS KINGDOM OF CONCEPTION. IN A PLACE WHERE ONE'S SOLE PURPOSE IS TO 'THINK AND CREATE', TESLA QUICKLY LEARNS WHAT IT TAKES TO MANIFEST THE TENORS OF HIS IMAGINATION INTO THE REAL WORLD...THE PRECEPTS OF BEING AN INVENTOR.

YET EDISON'S MOST VALUABLE TEACHINGS FOR HIS PROTÉGÉ IS NOT OF ENGINEERING NOR SCIENCE, BUT OF THE HUMAN EGO.

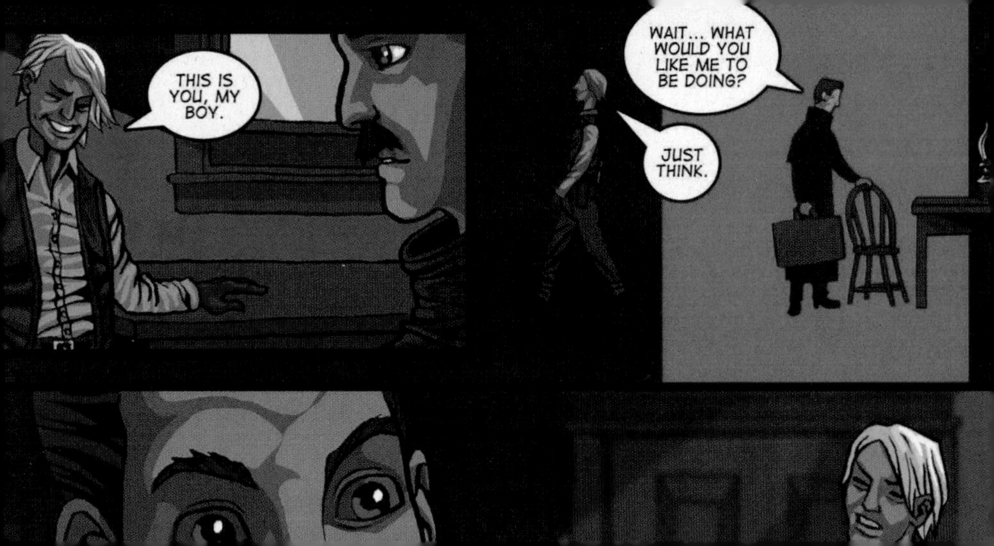
THIS IS YOU, MY BOY.
WAIT... WHAT WOULD YOU LIKE ME TO BE DOING?
JUST THINK.

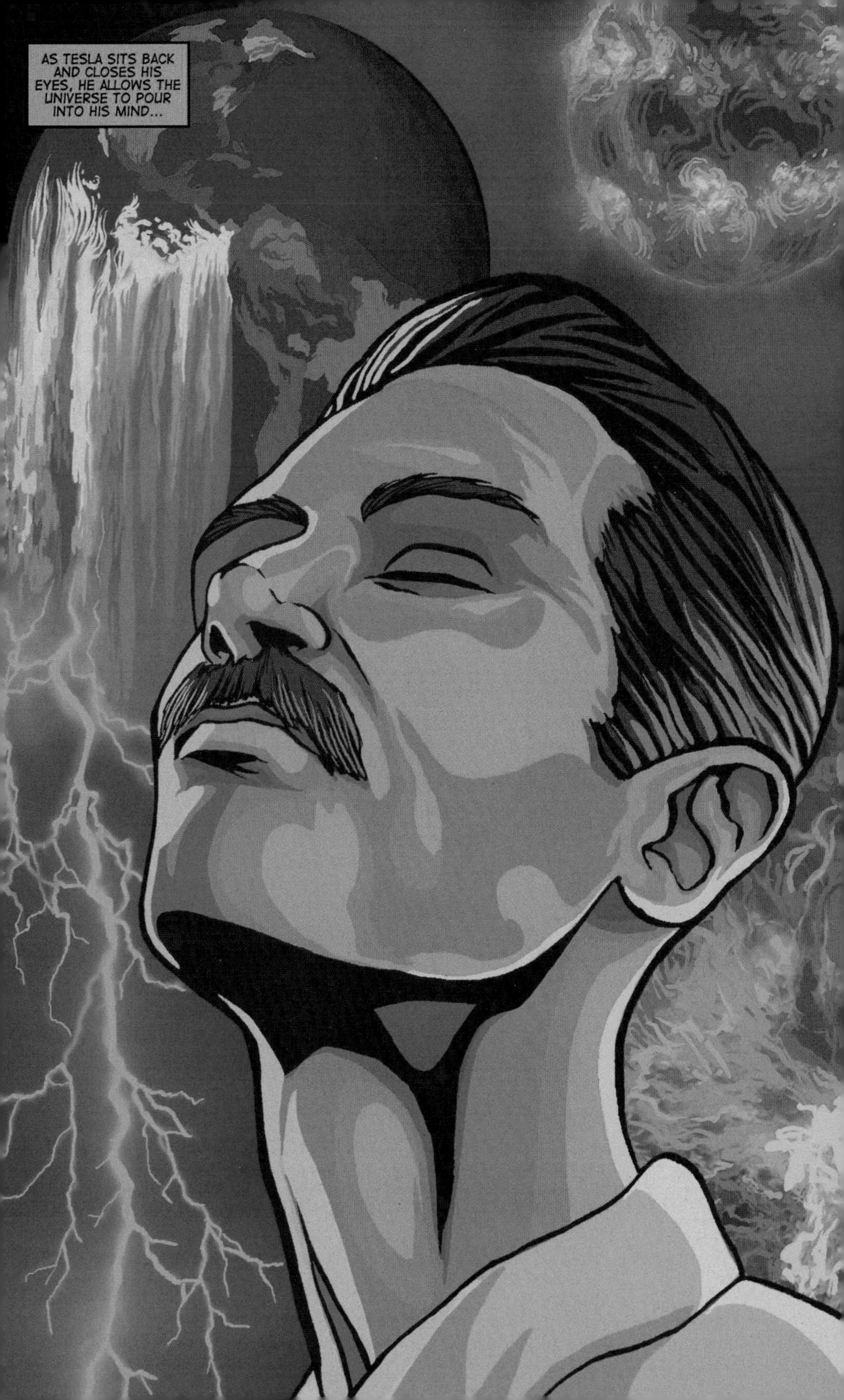
AS TESLA SITS BACK AND CLOSES HIS EYES, HE ALLOWS THE UNIVERSE TO POUR INTO HIS MIND...

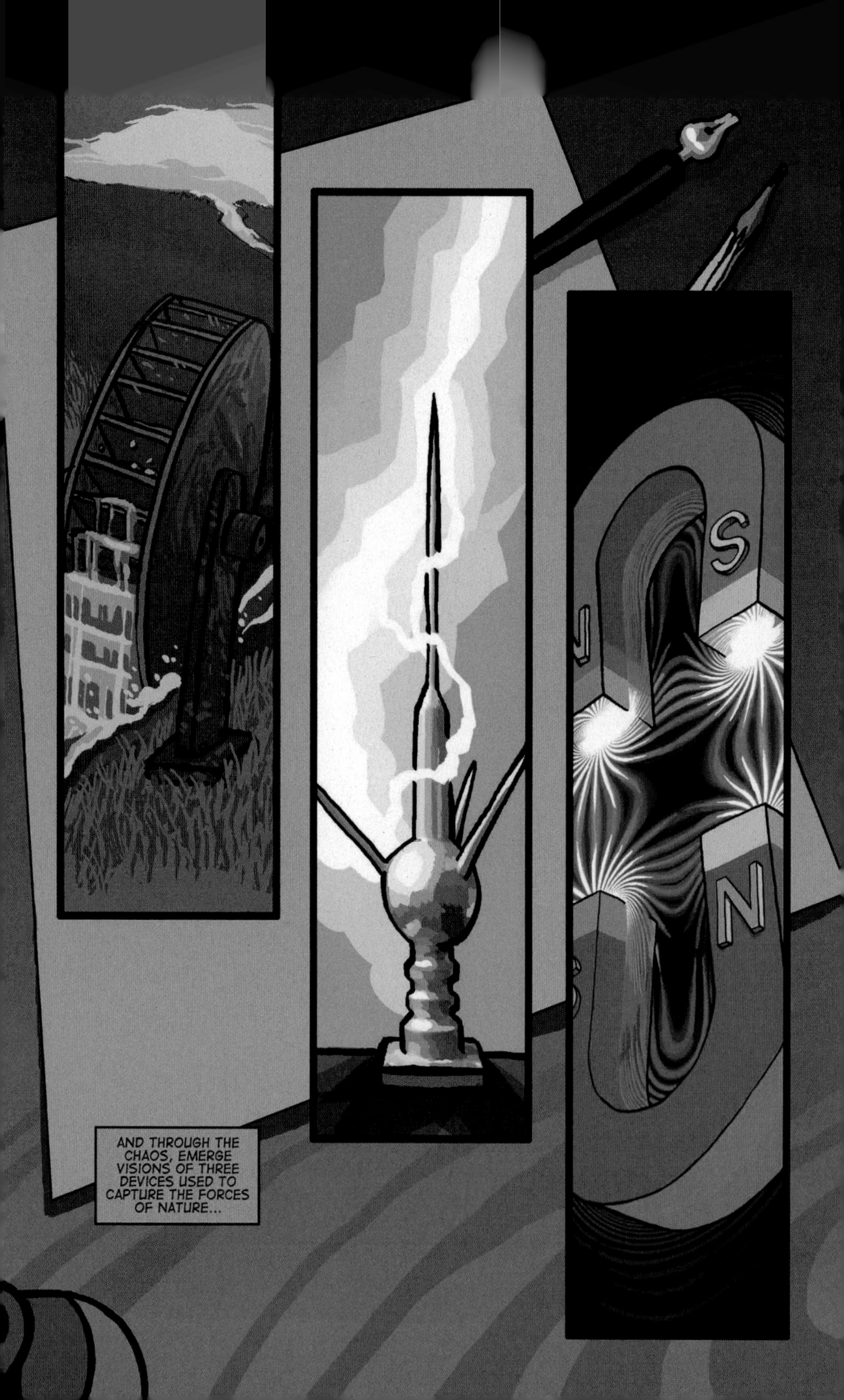
AND THROUGH THE CHAOS, EMERGE VISIONS OF THREE DEVICES USED TO CAPTURE THE FORCES OF NATURE...
S
N

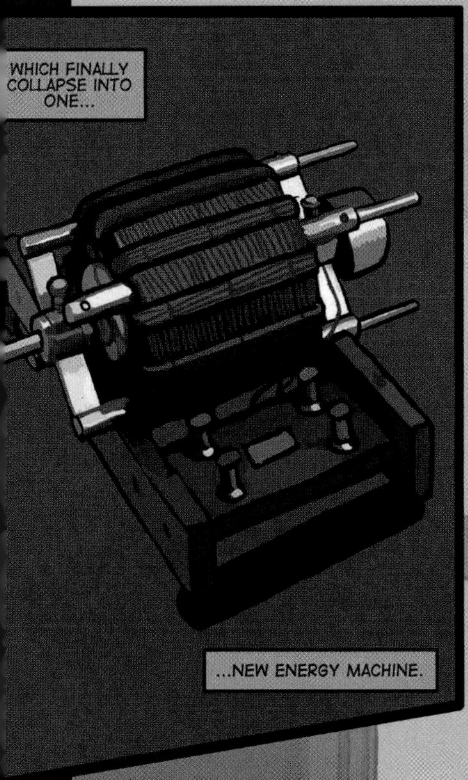
WHICH FINALLY COLLAPSE INTO ONE...
...NEW ENERGY MACHINE.

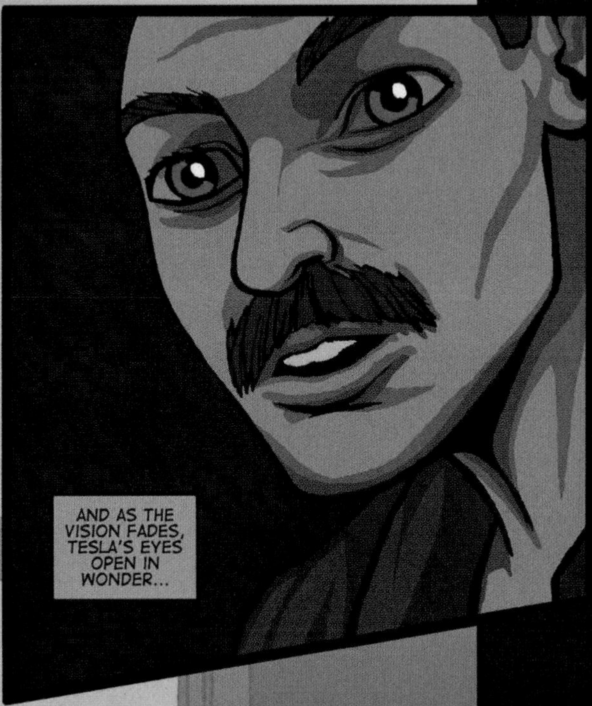
AND AS THE VISION FADES, TESLA'S EYES OPEN IN WONDER...

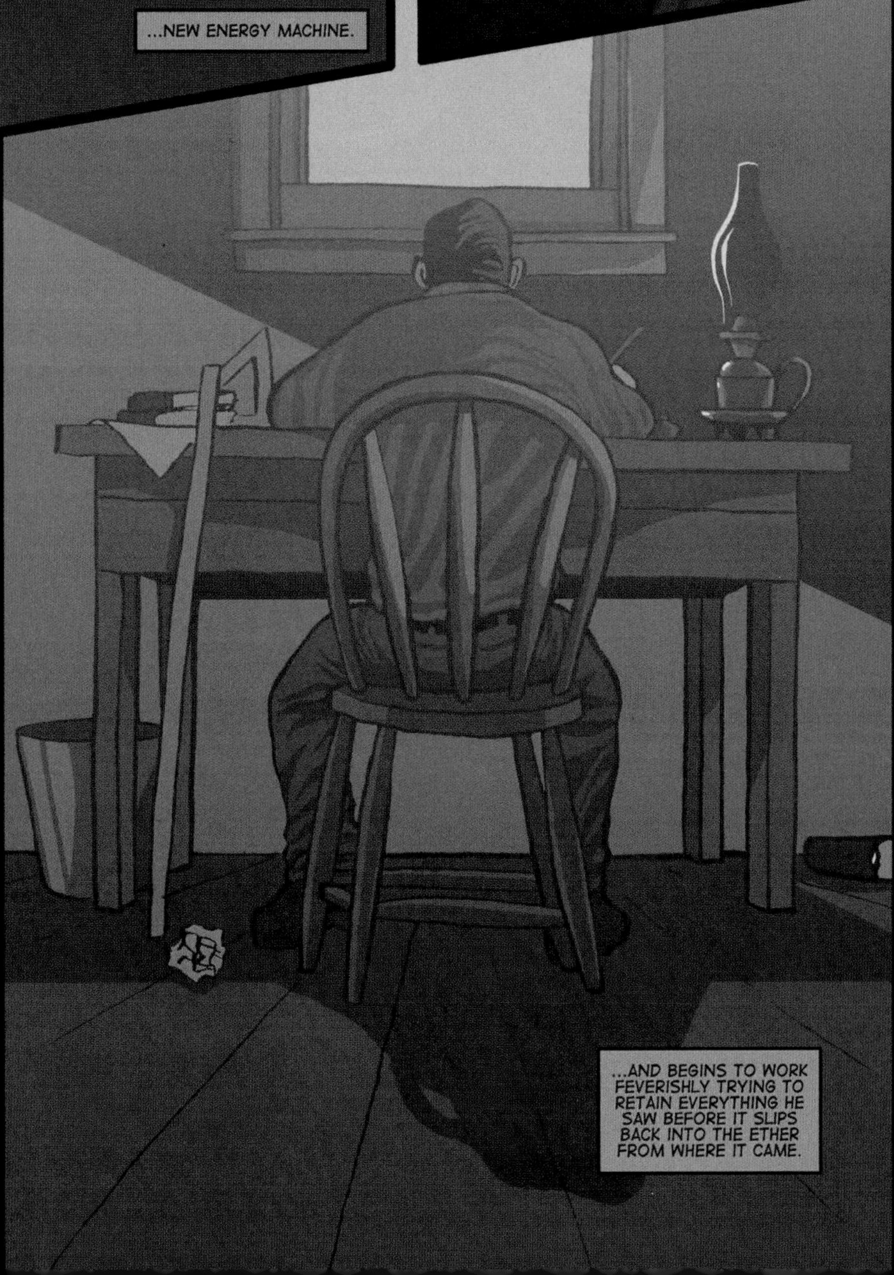
...AND BEGINS TO WORK FEVERISHLY TRYING TO RETAIN EVERYTHING HE SAW BEFORE IT SLIPS BACK INTO THE ETHER FROM WHERE IT CAME.

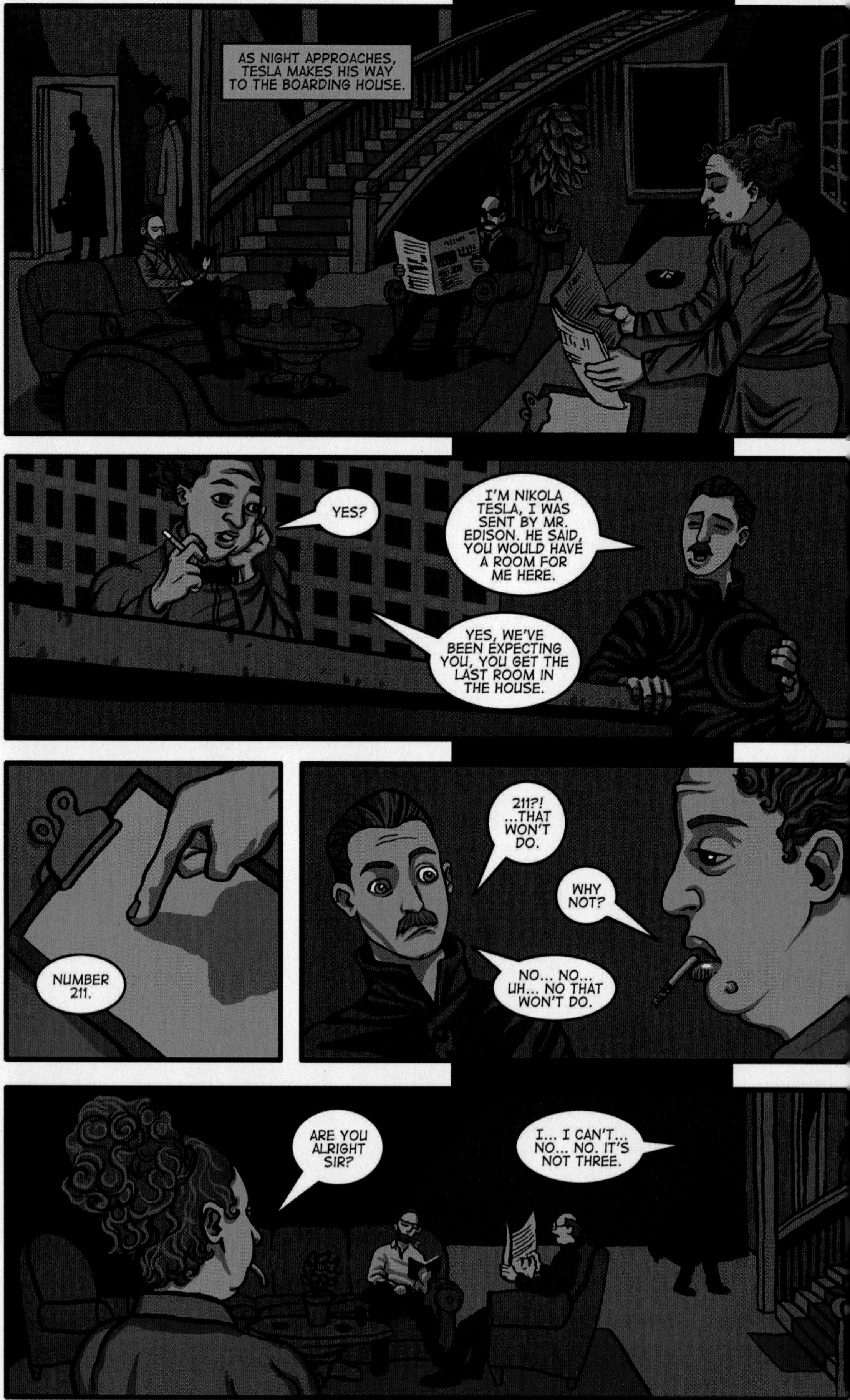
AS NIGHT APPROACHES, TESLA MAKES HIS WAY TO THE BOARDING HOUSE.
YES?
I'M NIKOLA TESLA, I WAS SENT BY MR. EDISON. HE SAID, YOU WOULD HAVE A ROOM FOR ME HERE.
YES, WE'VE BEEN EXPECTING YOU, YOU GET THE LAST ROOM IN THE HOUSE.
NUMBER 211.
211?! ...THAT WON'T DO.
WHY NOT?
NO... NO... UH... NO THAT WON'T DO.
ARE YOU ALRIGHT SIR?
I... I CAN'T... NO... NO. IT'S NOT THREE.

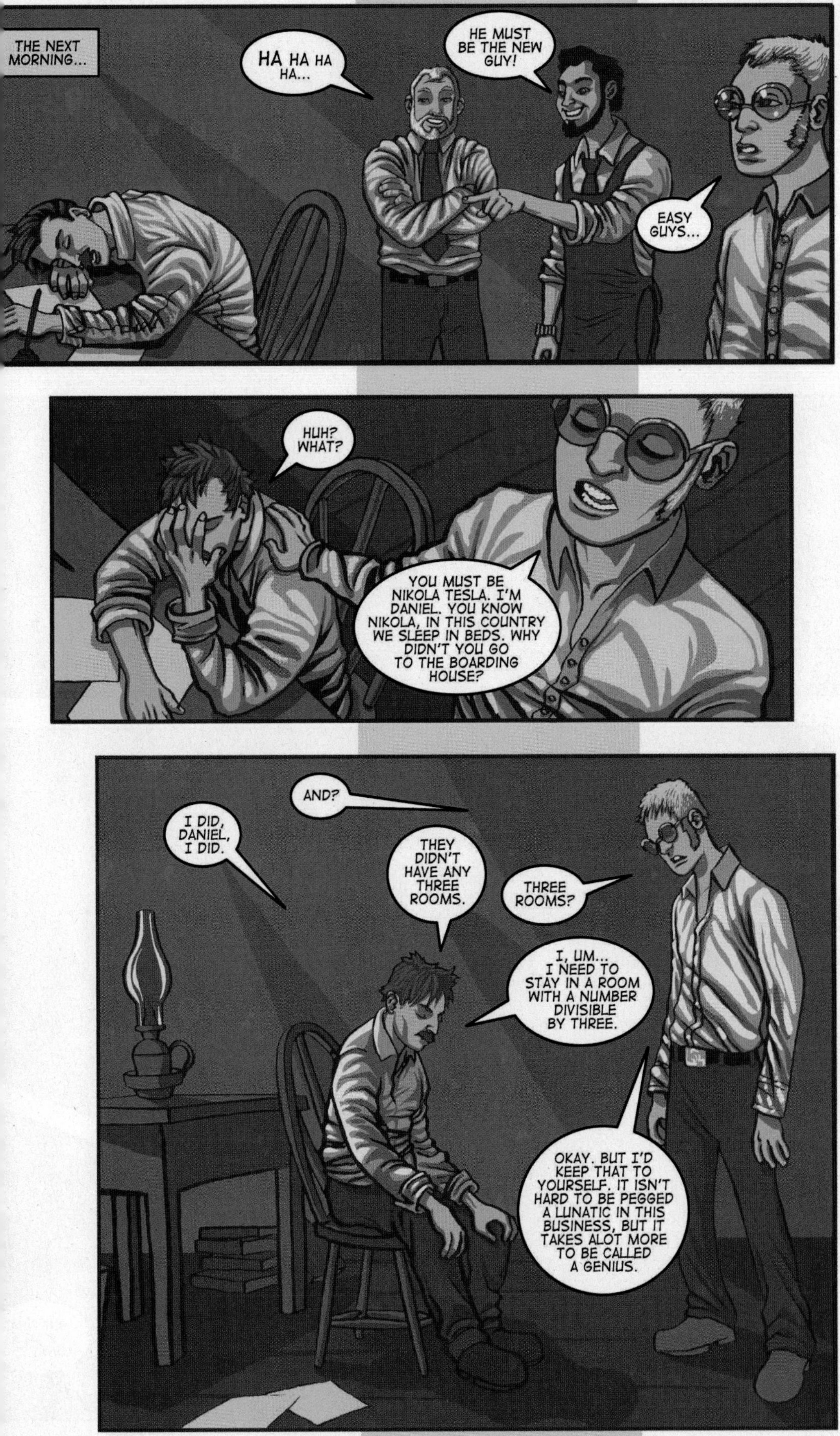
THE NEXT MORNING...
HA HA HA HA...
HE MUST BE THE NEW GUY!
EASY GUYS...
HUH? WHAT?
YOU MUST BE NIKOLA TESLA. I'M DANIEL. YOU KNOW NIKOLA, IN THIS COUNTRY WE SLEEP IN BEDS. WHY DIDN'T YOU GO TO THE BOARDING HOUSE?
AND?
I DID, DANIEL, I DID.
THEY DIDN'T HAVE ANY THREE ROOMS.
THREE ROOMS?
I, UM... I NEED TO STAY IN A ROOM WITH A NUMBER DIVISIBLE BY THREE.
OKAY. BUT I'D KEEP THAT TO YOURSELF. IT ISN'T HARD TO BE PEGGED A LUNATIC IN THIS BUSINESS, BUT IT TAKES ALOT MORE TO BE CALLED A GENIUS.

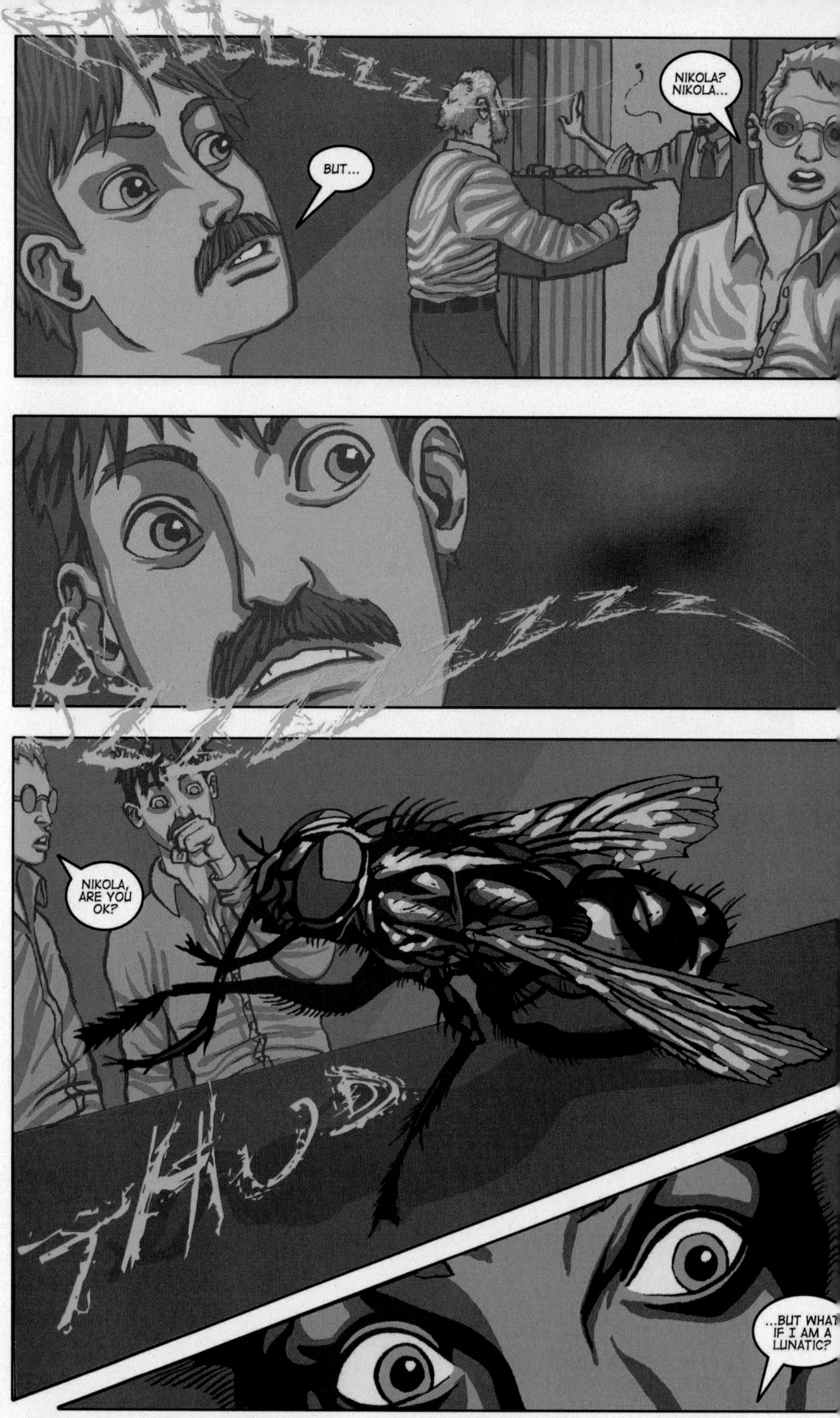
BUT...
NIKOLA? NIKOLA...
NIKOLA, ARE YOU OK?
THUD
...BUT WHAT IF I AM A LUNATIC?

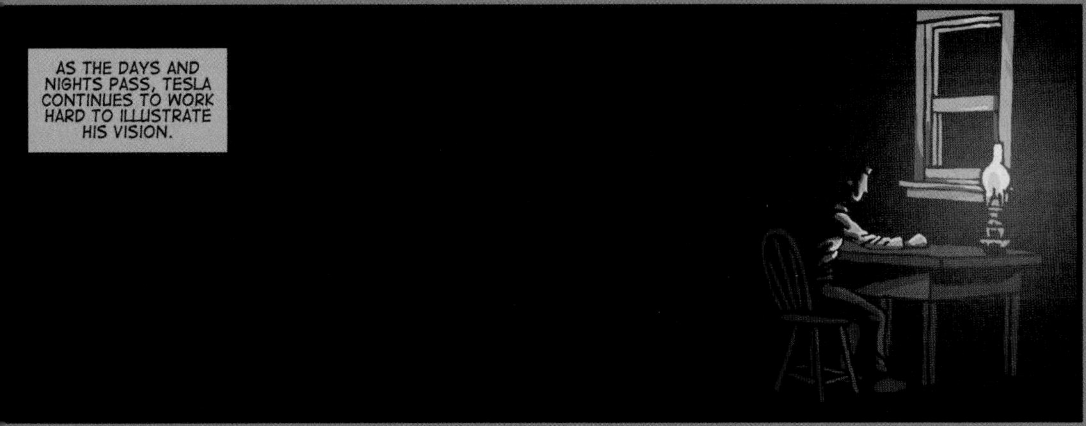
AS THE DAYS AND NIGHTS PASS, TESLA CONTINUES TO WORK HARD TO ILLUSTRATE HIS VISION.

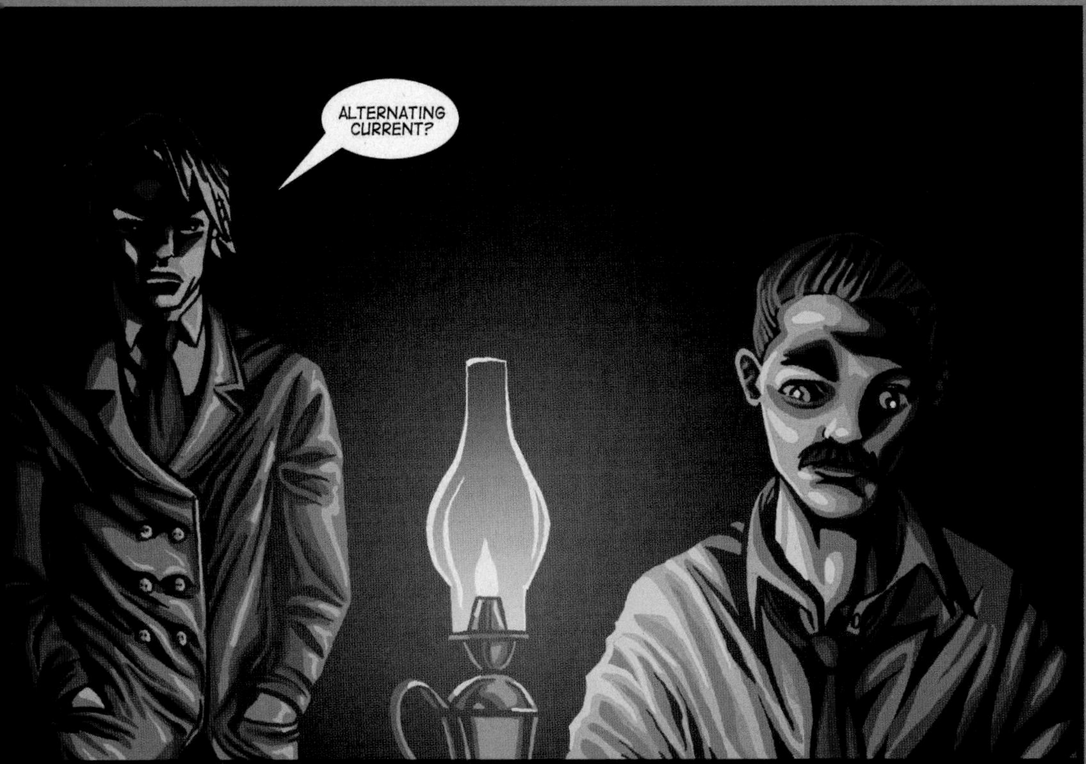
ALTERNATING CURRENT?

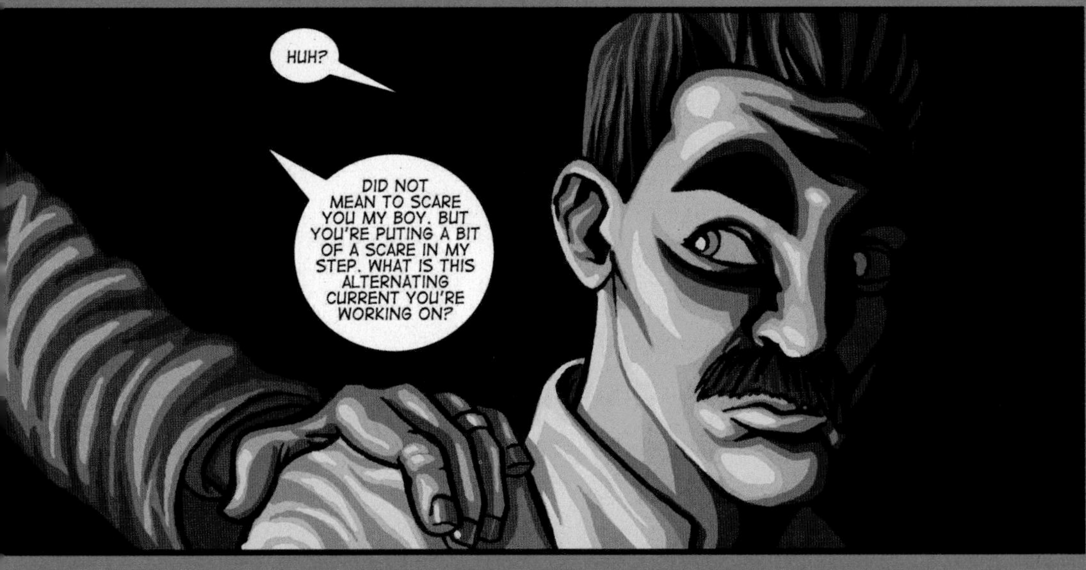
HUH?
DID NOT MEAN TO SCARE YOU MY BOY. BUT YOU'RE PUTING A BIT OF A SCARE IN MY STEP. WHAT IS THIS ALTERNATING CURRENT YOU'RE WORKING ON?

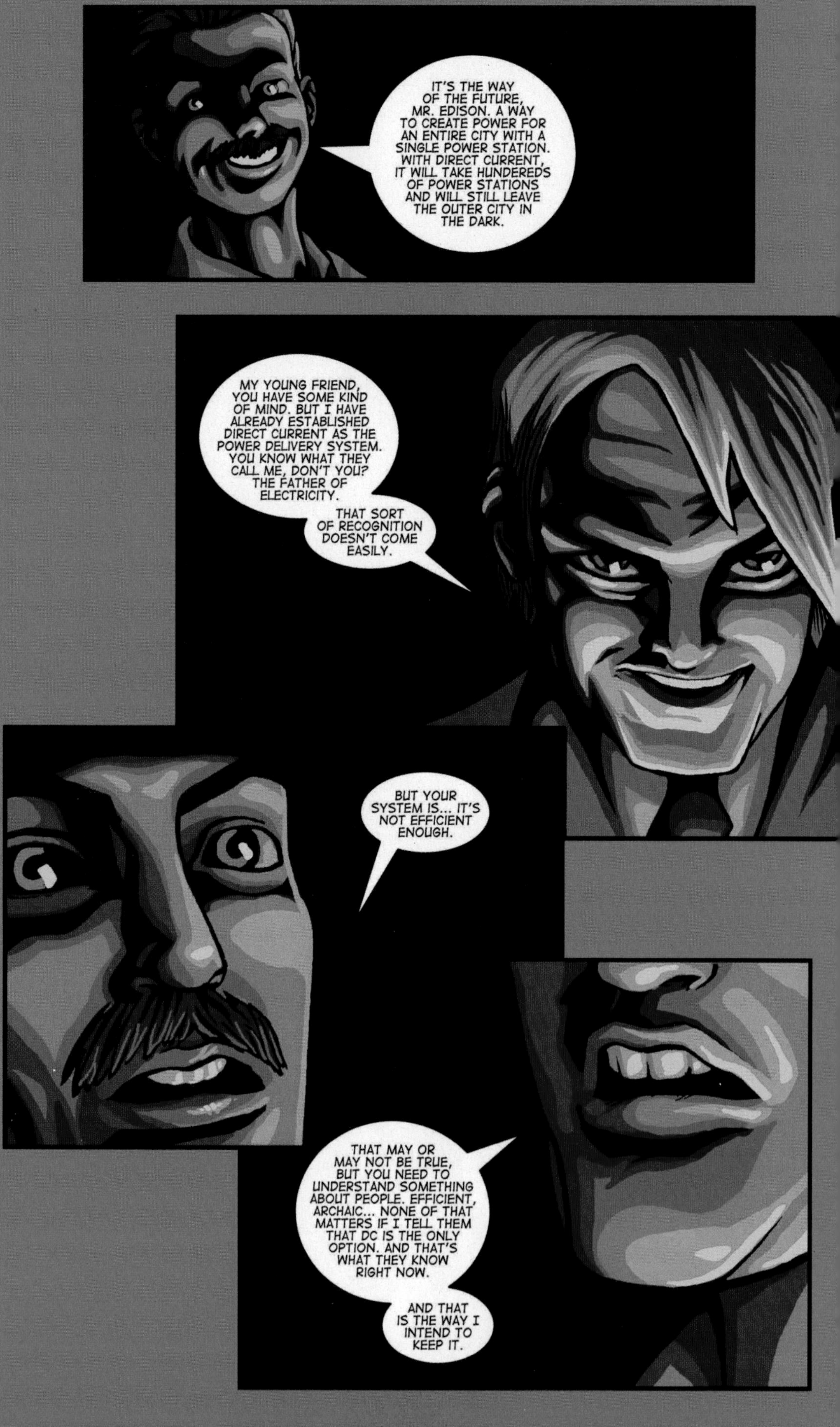
IT'S THE WAY OF THE FUTURE, MR. EDISON. A WAY TO CREATE POWER FOR AN ENTIRE CITY WITH A SINGLE POWER STATION. WITH DIRECT CURRENT, IT WILL TAKE HUNDEREDS OF POWER STATIONS AND WILL STILL LEAVE THE OUTER CITY IN THE DARK.
MY YOUNG FRIEND, YOU HAVE SOME KIND OF MIND. BUT I HAVE ALREADY ESTABLISHED DIRECT CURRENT AS THE POWER DELIVERY SYSTEM. YOU KNOW WHAT THEY CALL ME, DON'T YOU? THE FATHER OF ELECTRICITY.
THAT SORT OF RECOGNITION DOESN'T COME EASILY.
BUT YOUR SYSTEM IS... IT'S NOT EFFICIENT ENOUGH.
THAT MAY OR MAY NOT BE TRUE, BUT YOU NEED TO UNDERSTAND SOMETHING ABOUT PEOPLE. EFFICIENT, ARCHAIC... NONE OF THAT MATTERS IF I TELL THEM THAT DC IS THE ONLY OPTION. AND THAT'S WHAT THEY KNOW RIGHT NOW.
AND THAT IS THE WAY I INTEND TO KEEP IT.

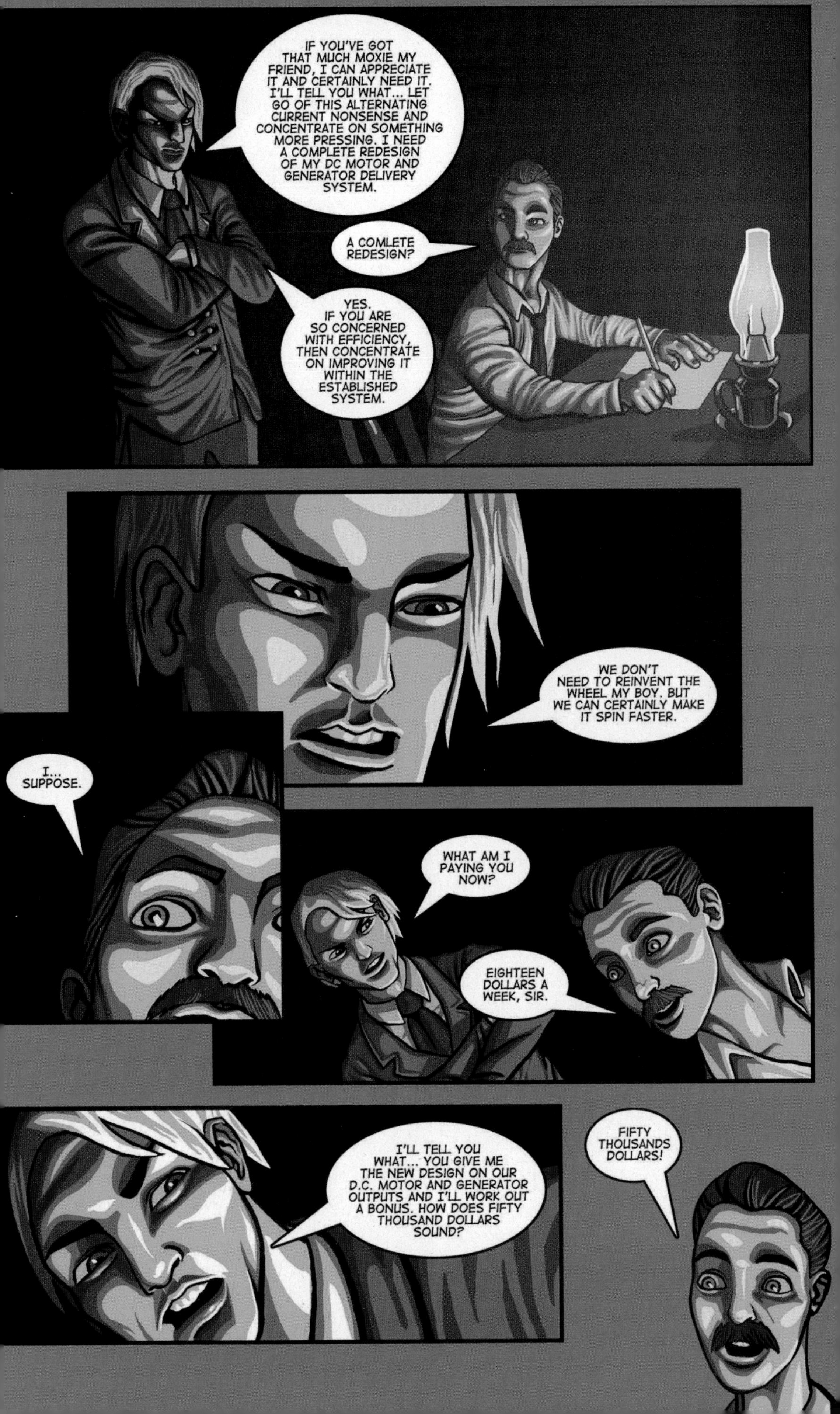
IF YOU'VE GOT THAT MUCH MOXIE MY FRIEND, I CAN APPRECIATE IT AND CERTAINLY NEED IT. I'LL TELL YOU WHAT... LET GO OF THIS ALTERNATING CURRENT NONSENSE AND CONCENTRATE ON SOMETHING MORE PRESSING. I NEED A COMPLETE REDESIGN OF MY DC MOTOR AND GENERATOR DELIVERY SYSTEM.
A COMLETE REDESIGN?
YES. IF YOU ARE SO CONCERNED WITH EFFICIENCY, THEN CONCENTRATE ON IMPROVING IT WITHIN THE ESTABLISHED SYSTEM.
WE DON'T NEED TO REINVENT THE WHEEL MY BOY. BUT WE CAN CERTAINLY MAKE IT SPIN FASTER.
I... SUPPOSE.
WHAT AM I PAYING YOU NOW?
EIGHTEEN DOLLARS A WEEK, SIR.
I'LL TELL YOU WHAT... YOU GIVE ME THE NEW DESIGN ON OUR D.C. MOTOR AND GENERATOR OUTPUTS AND I'LL WORK OUT A BONUS. HOW DOES FIFTY THOUSAND DOLLARS SOUND?
FIFTY THOUSANDS DOLLARS!

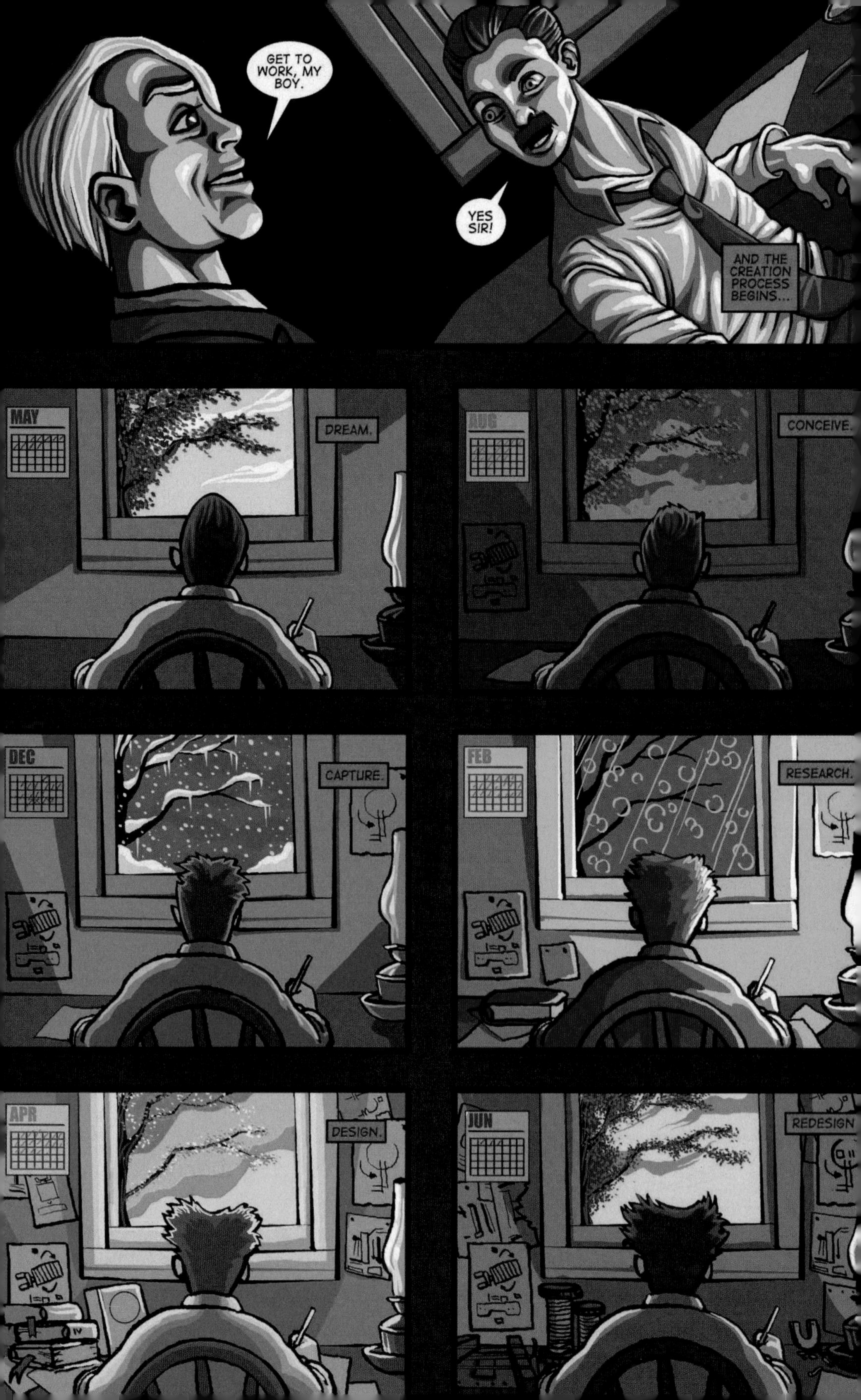
GET TO WORK, MY BOY.
YES SIR!
AND THE CREATION PROCESS BEGINS...
MAY
DREAM.
AUG
CONCEIVE.
DEC
CAPTURE.
FEB
RESEARCH.
APR
DESIGN.
JUN
REDESIGN

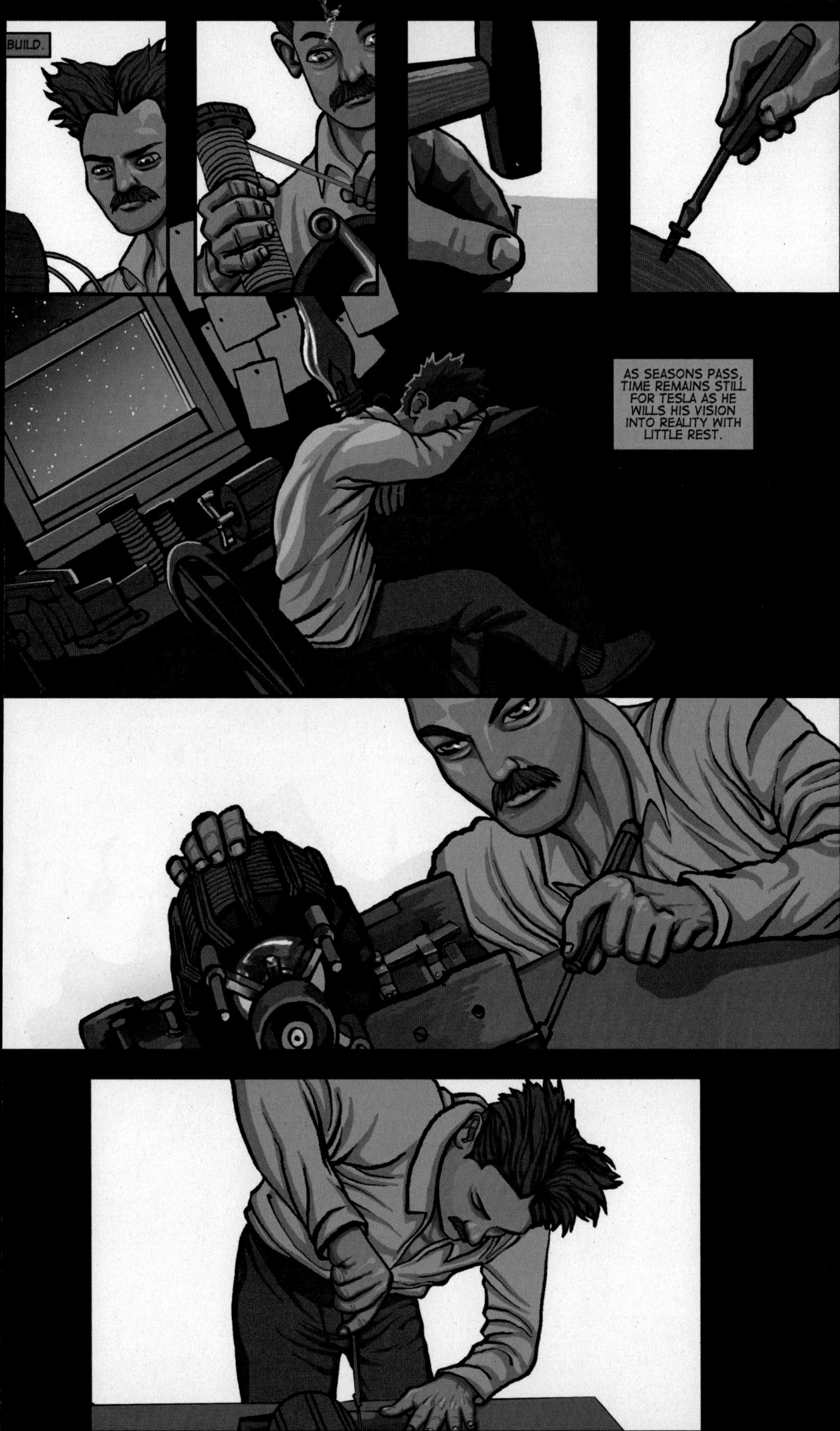
BUILD.
AS SEASONS PASS, TIME REMAINS STILL FOR TESLA AS HE WILLS HIS VISION INTO REALITY WITH LITTLE REST.

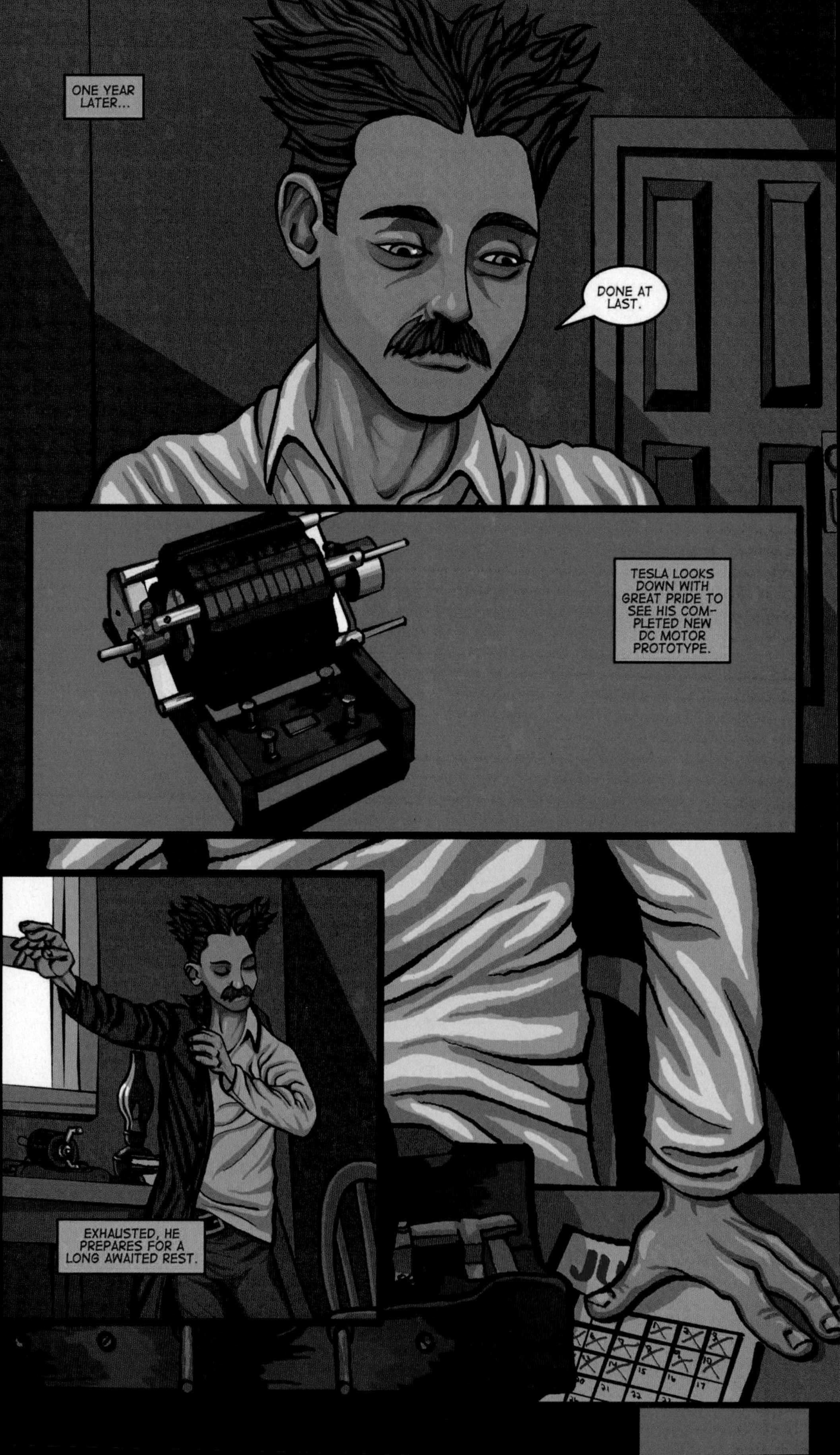
ONE YEAR LATER...
DONE AT LAST.
TESLA LOOKS DOWN WITH GREAT PRIDE TO SEE HIS COMPLETED NEW DC MOTOR PROTOTYPE.
EXHAUSTED, HE PREPARES FOR A LONG AWAITED REST.

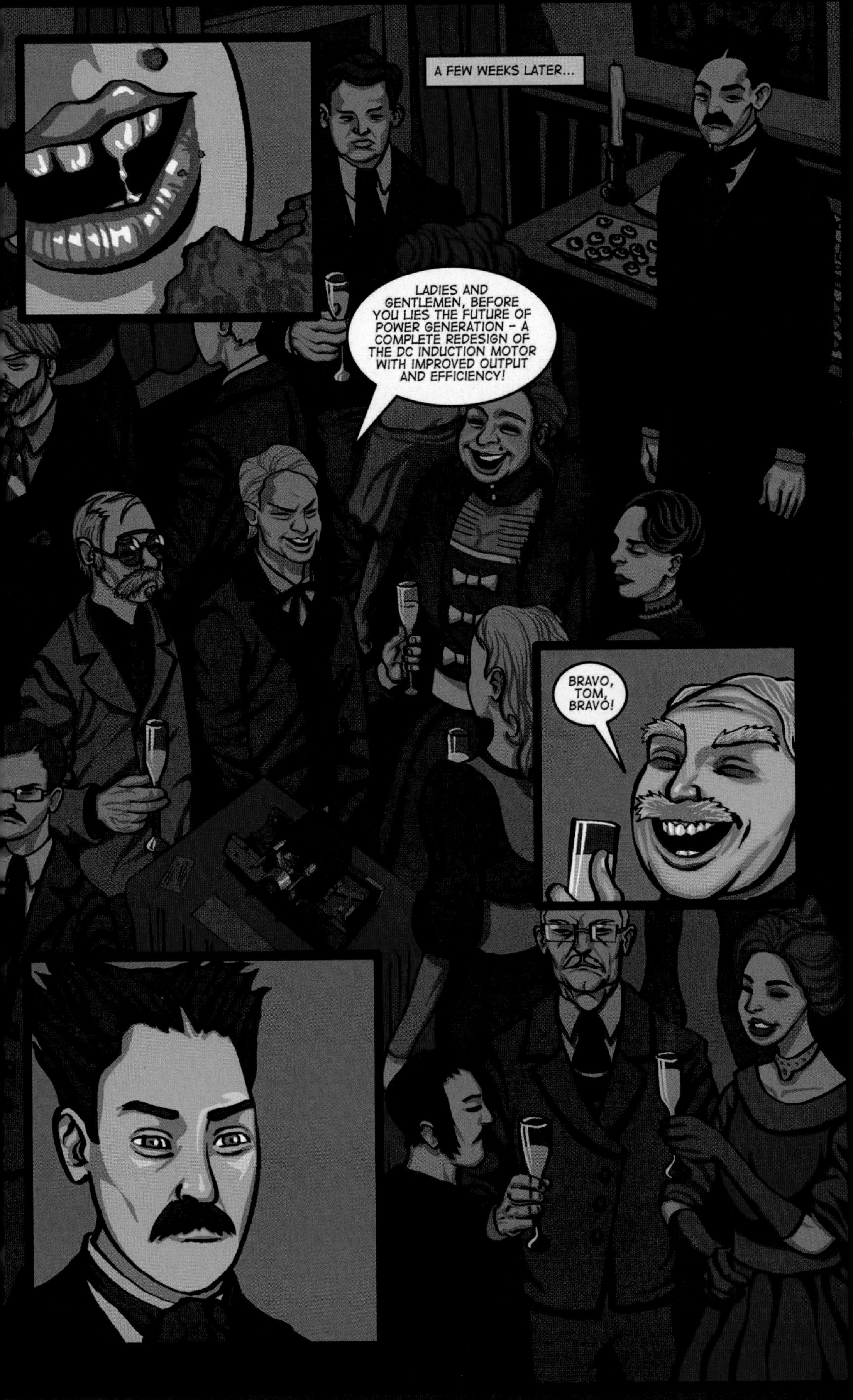
A FEW WEEKS LATER...
LADIES AND GENTLEMEN, BEFORE YOU LIES THE FUTURE OF POWER GENERATION - A COMPLETE REDESIGN OF THE DC INDUCTION MOTOR WITH IMPROVED OUTPUT AND EFFICIENCY!
BRAVO, TOM, BRAVO!

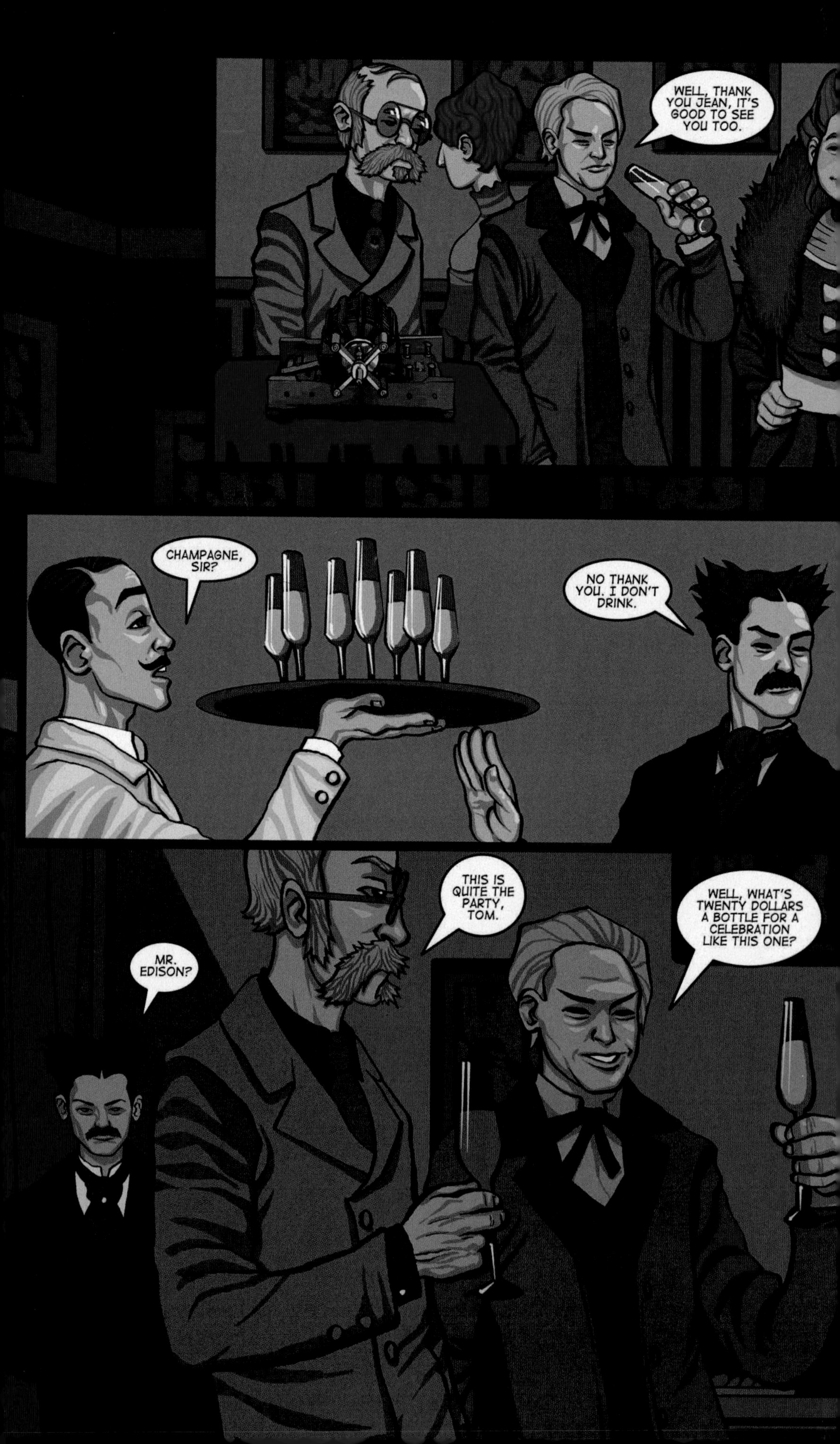
WELL, THANK YOU JEAN, IT'S GOOD TO SEE YOU TOO.
CHAMPAGNE, SIR?
NO THANK YOU. I DON'T DRINK.
MR. EDISON?
THIS IS QUITE THE PARTY, TOM.
WELL, WHAT'S TWENTY DOLLARS A BOTTLE FOR A CELEBRATION LIKE THIS ONE?

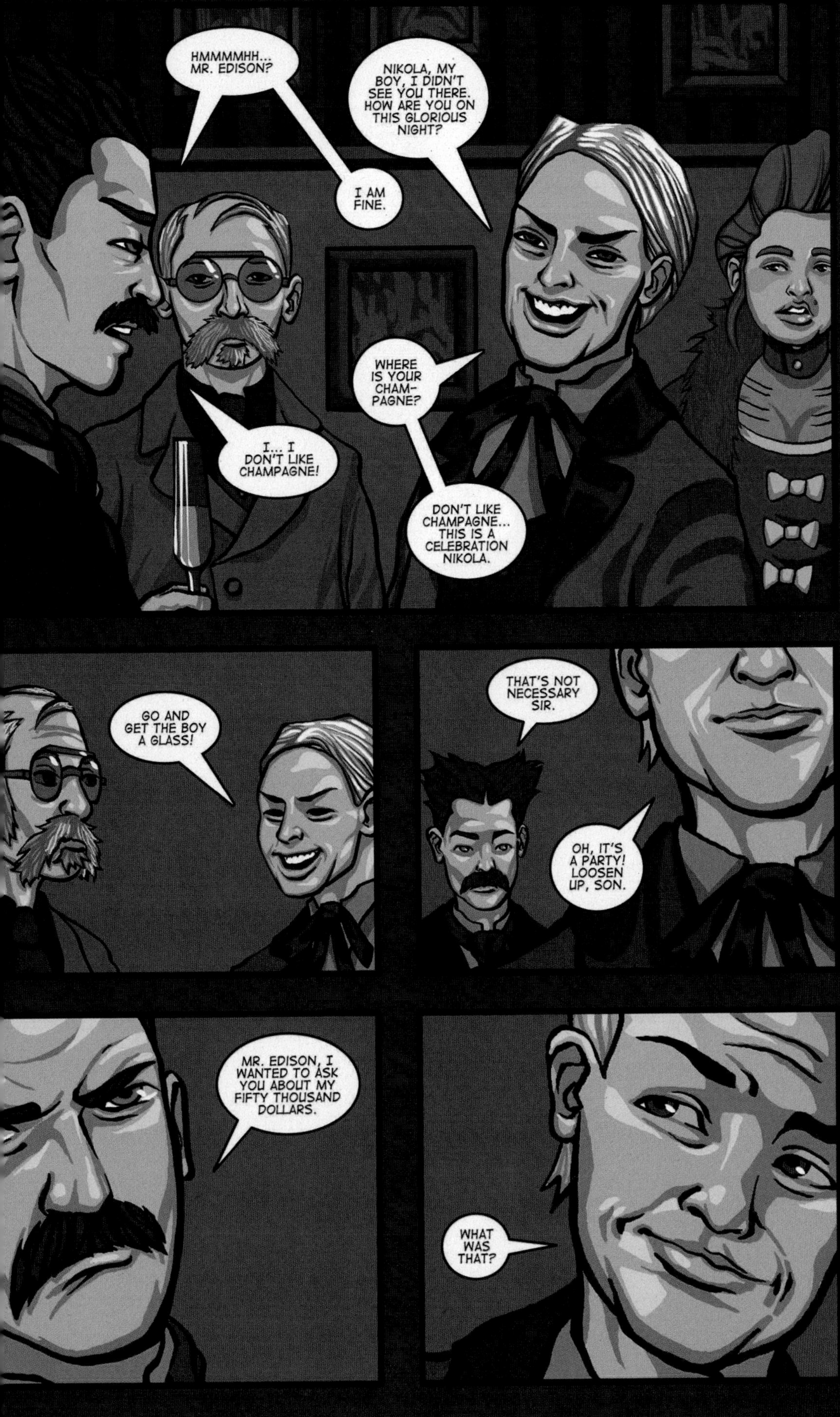
HMMMMHH... MR. EDISON?
NIKOLA, MY BOY, I DIDN'T SEE YOU THERE. HOW ARE YOU ON THIS GLORIOUS NIGHT?
I AM FINE.
WHERE IS YOUR CHAM-PAGNE?
I... I DON'T LIKE CHAMPAGNE!
DON'T LIKE CHAMPAGNE... THIS IS A CELEBRATION NIKOLA.
GO AND GET THE BOY A GLASS!
THAT'S NOT NECESSARY SIR.
OH, IT'S A PARTY! LOOSEN UP, SON.
MR. EDISON, I WANTED TO ASK YOU ABOUT MY FIFTY THOUSAND DOLLARS.
WHAT WAS THAT?

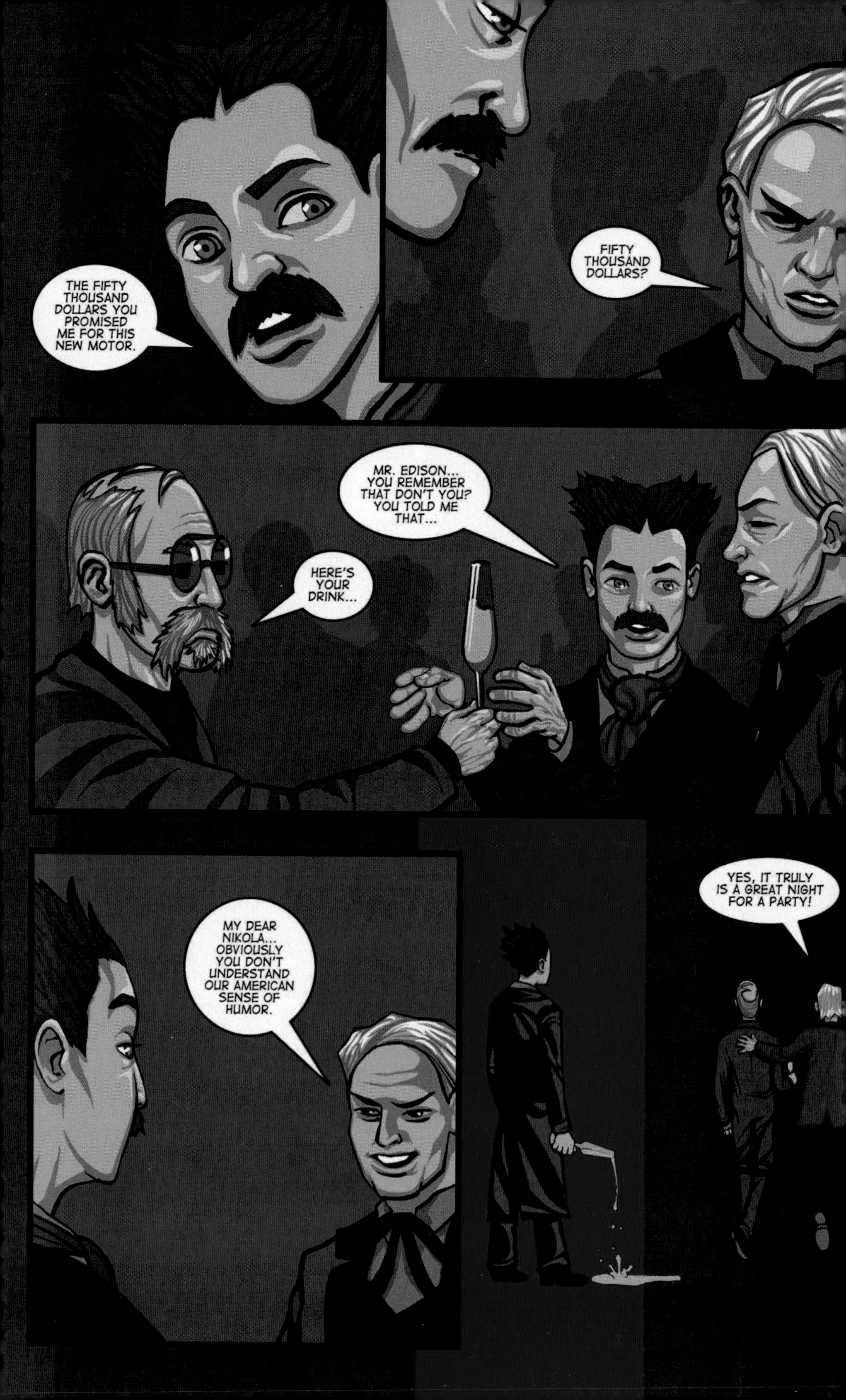
THE FIFTY THOUSAND DOLLARS YOU PROMISED ME FOR THIS NEW MOTOR.
FIFTY THOUSAND DOLLARS?
MR. EDISON... YOU REMEMBER THAT DON'T YOU? YOU TOLD ME THAT...
HERE'S YOUR DRINK...
MY DEAR NIKOLA... OBVIOUSLY YOU DON'T UNDERSTAND OUR AMERICAN SENSE OF HUMOR.
YES, IT TRULY IS A GREAT NIGHT FOR A PARTY!

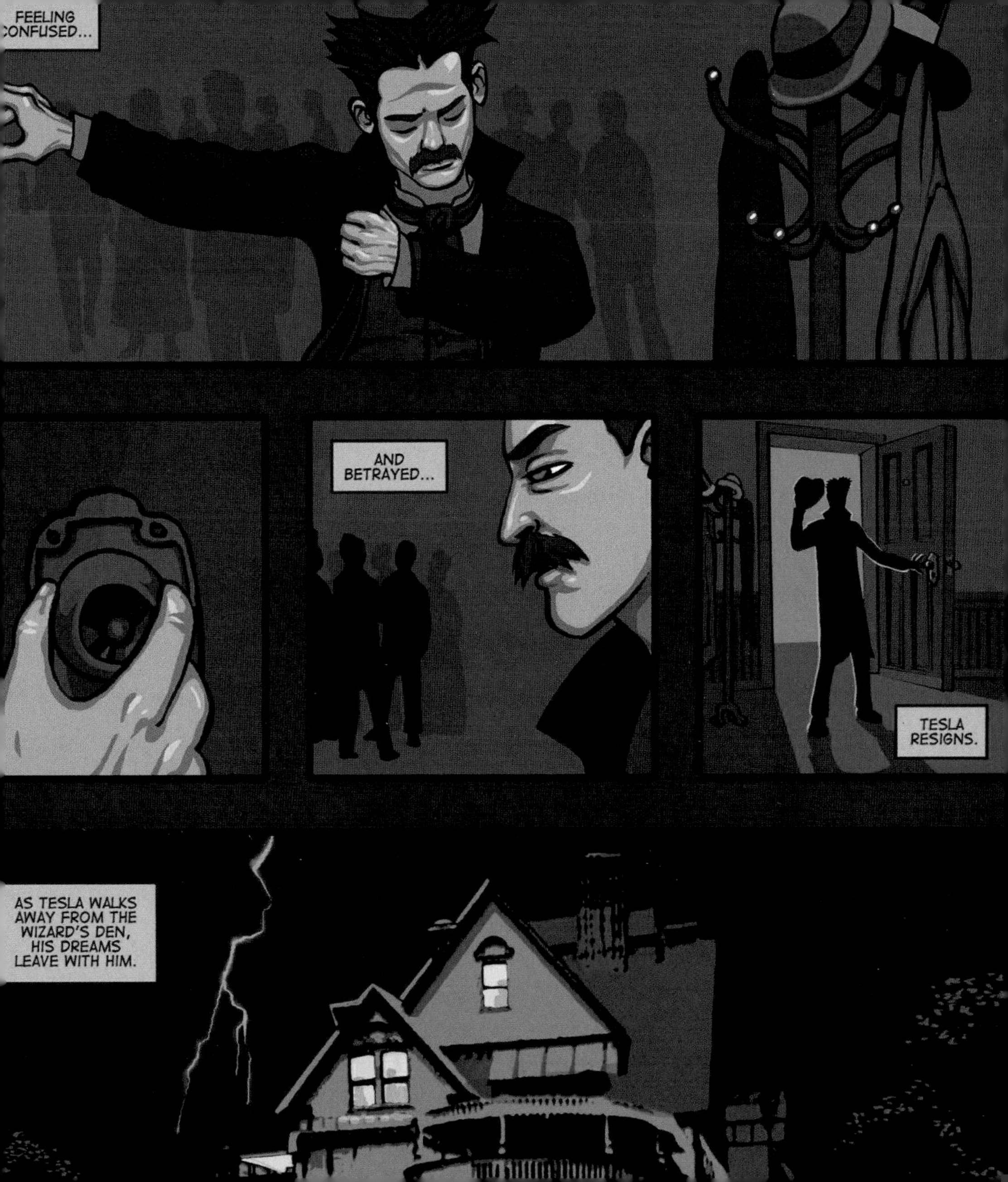
FEELING CONFUSED...
AND BETRAYED...
TESLA RESIGNS.
AS TESLA WALKS AWAY FROM THE WIZARD'S DEN, HIS DREAMS LEAVE WITH HIM.

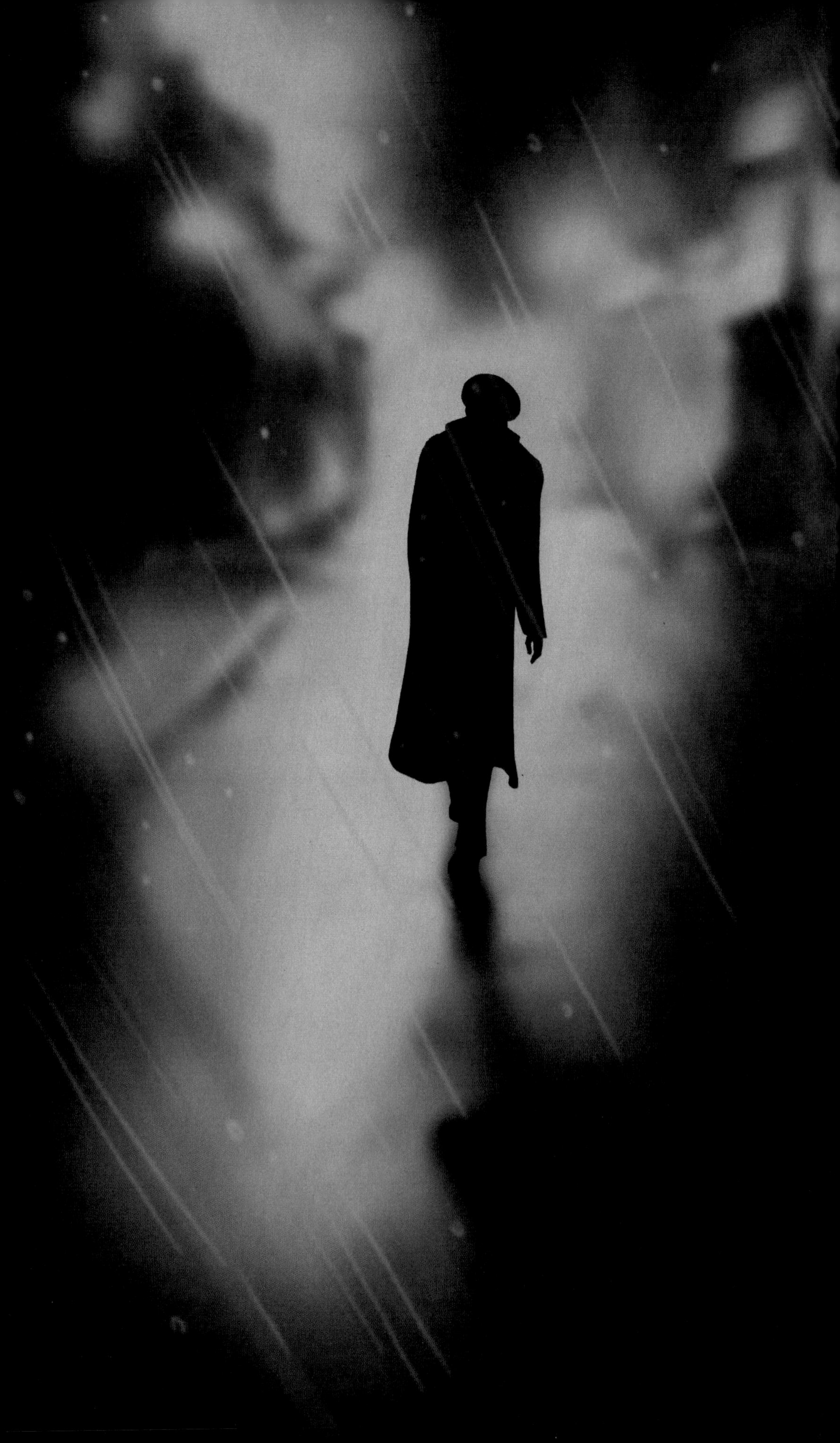

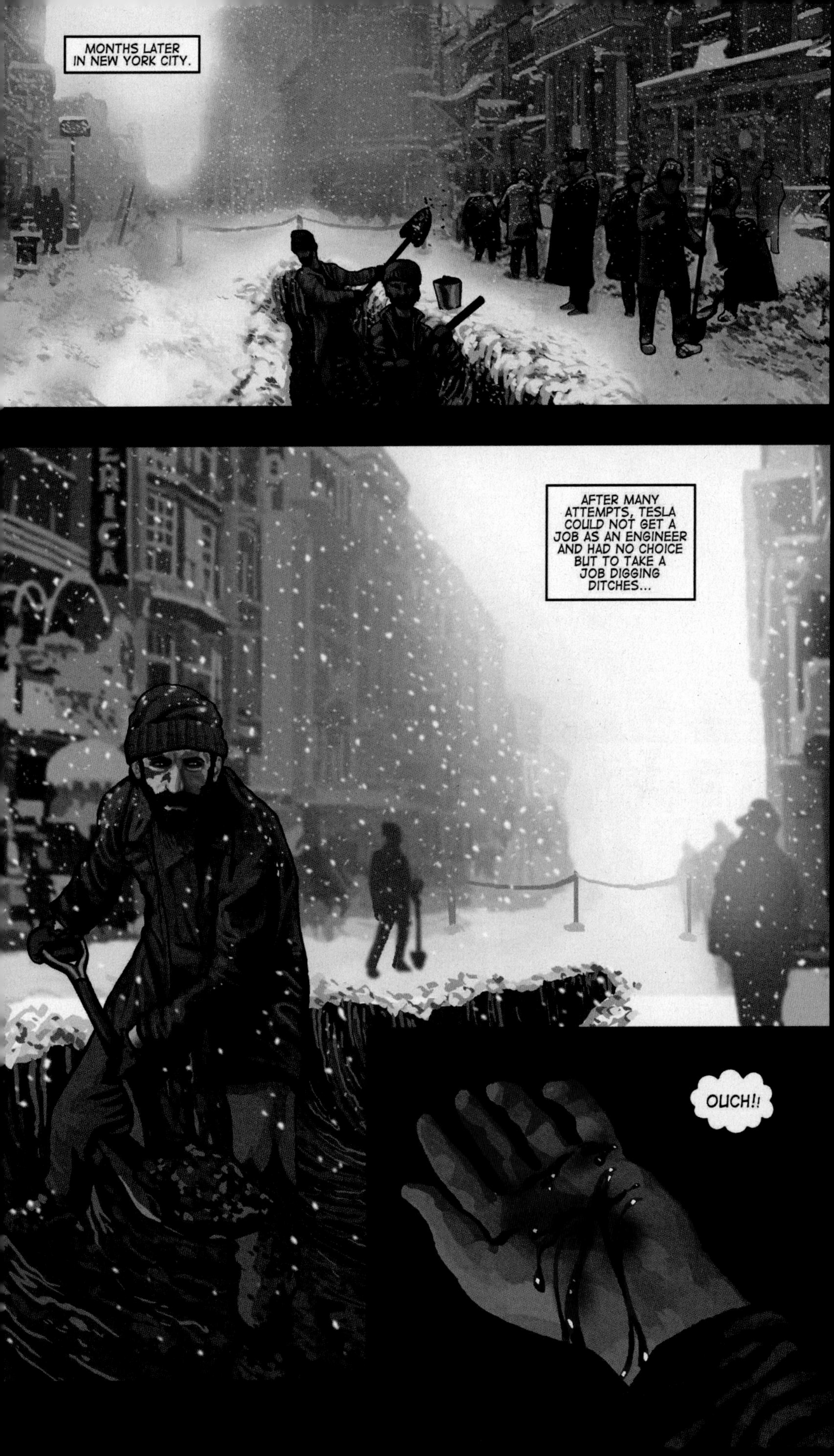
MONTHS LATER IN NEW YORK CITY.
AFTER MANY ATTEMPTS, TESLA COULD NOT GET A JOB AS AN ENGINEER AND HAD NO CHOICE BUT TO TAKE A JOB DIGGING DITCHES...
OUCH!!

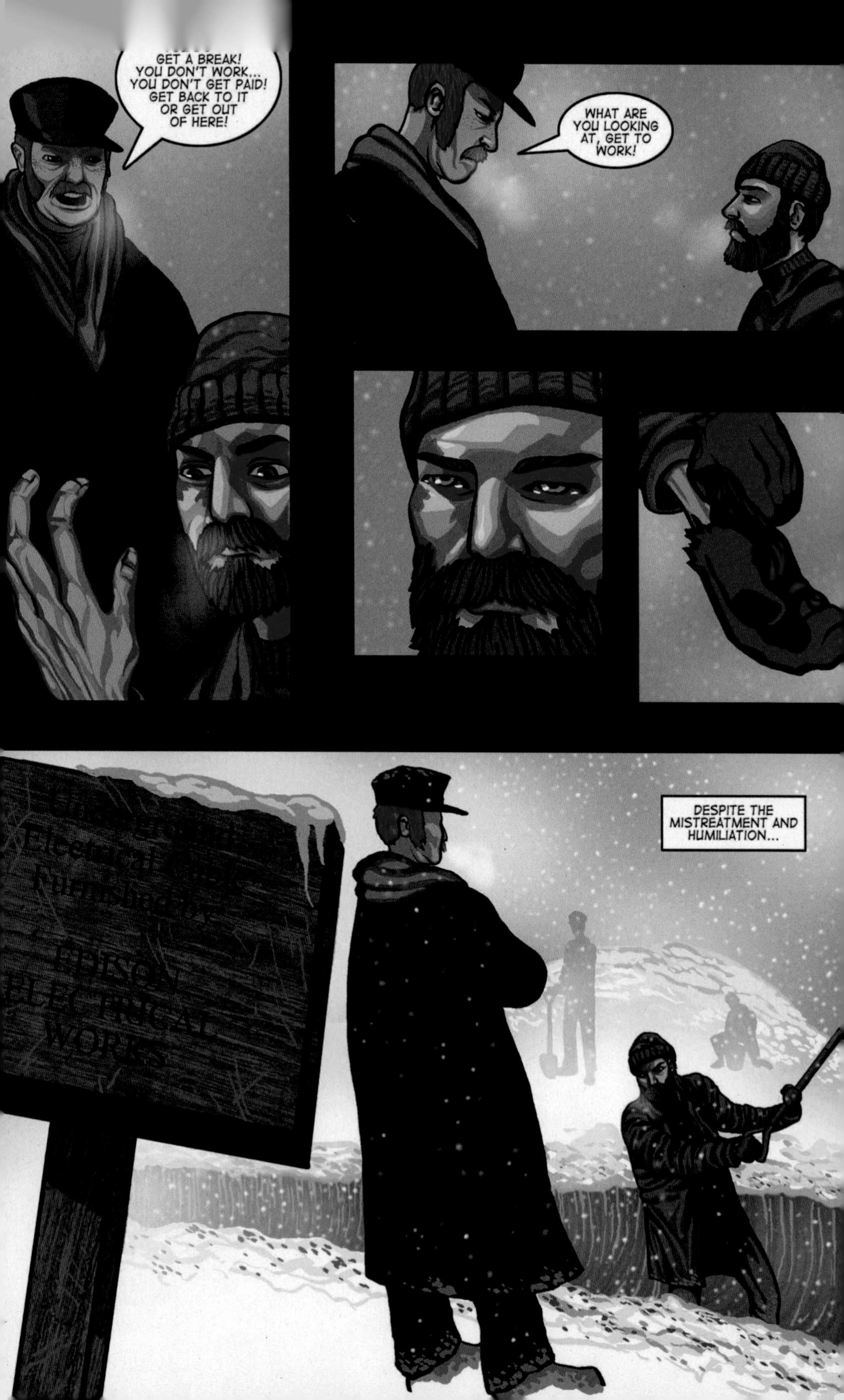
GET A BREAK! YOU DON'T WORK... YOU DON'T GET PAID! GET BACK TO IT OR GET OUT OF HERE!
WHAT ARE YOU LOOKING AT, GET TO WORK!
EDISON
DESPITE THE MISTREATMENT AND HUMILIATION...

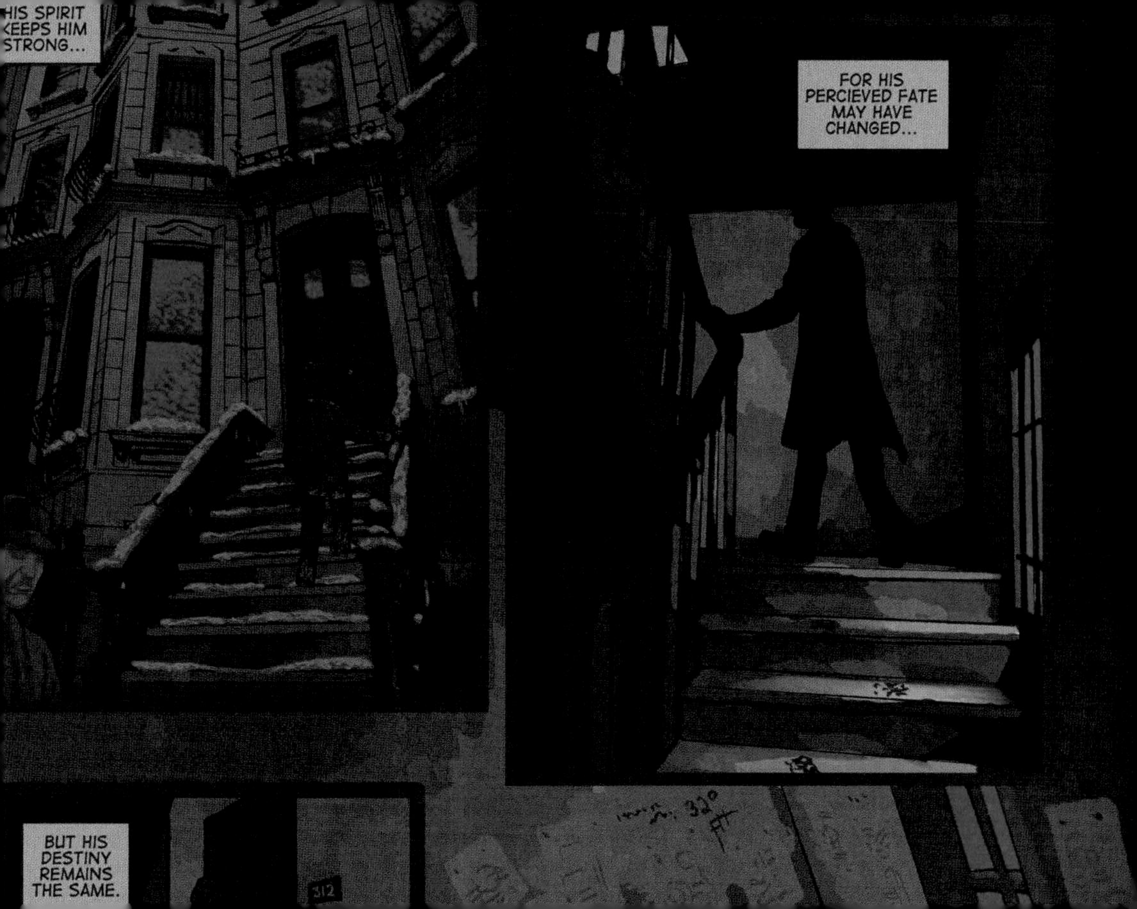
HIS SPIRIT KEEPS HIM STRONG...
FOR HIS PERCIEVED FATE MAY HAVE CHANGED...
BUT HIS DESTINY REMAINS THE SAME.

"ALL THAT WAS GREAT IN THE PAST WAS RIDICULED, CONDEMNED, COMBATED, SUPPRESSED-
ONLY TO EMERGE ALL THE MORE POWERFULLY, ALL THE MORE TRIUMPHANTLY FROM THE
STRUGGLE. LET THE FUTURE TELL THE TRUTH AND EVALUATE EACH ONE ACCORDING TO HIS
WORK AND ACCOMPLISHMENTS. THE PRESENT IS THEIRS; THE FUTURE, FOR WHICH I REALLY
WORKED, IS MINE."

- NIKOLA TESLA (1856-1943)

CHAPTER 3
SHOCK THERAPY

THE HOUR APPROACHES AS TESLA REVEALS HIS NEW INVENTION THAT WILL CHANGE THE COURSE OF HUMANITY YET HE SOON LEARNS THAT SCIENCE AND INTENTION ALONE IS NOT ENOUGH TO NAVIGATE THE WORLD OF MAN. AS TESLA BRINGS THE FORCES OF NATURE TO HUMANITY'S DOORSTEP, EDISON UNLEASHES THE FORCES OF HUMAN NATURE...

AND SO BEGINS THE WAR OF THE CURRENTS.

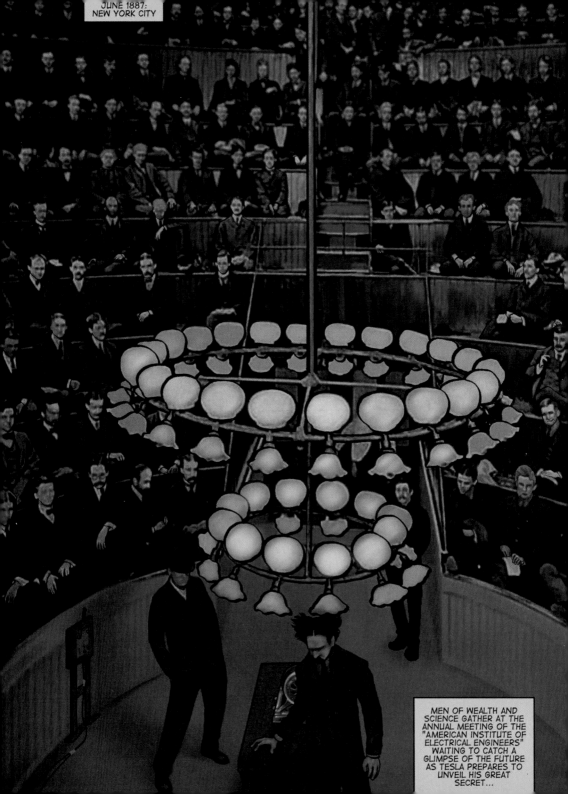

JUNE 1887:
NEW YORK CITY

MEN OF WEALTH AND
SCIENCE GATHER AT THE
ANNUAL MEETING OF THE
"AMERICAN INSTITUTE OF
ELECTRICAL ENGINEERS"
WAITING TO CATCH A
GLIMPSE OF THE FUTURE
AS TESLA PREPARES TO
UNVEIL HIS GREAT
SECRET...

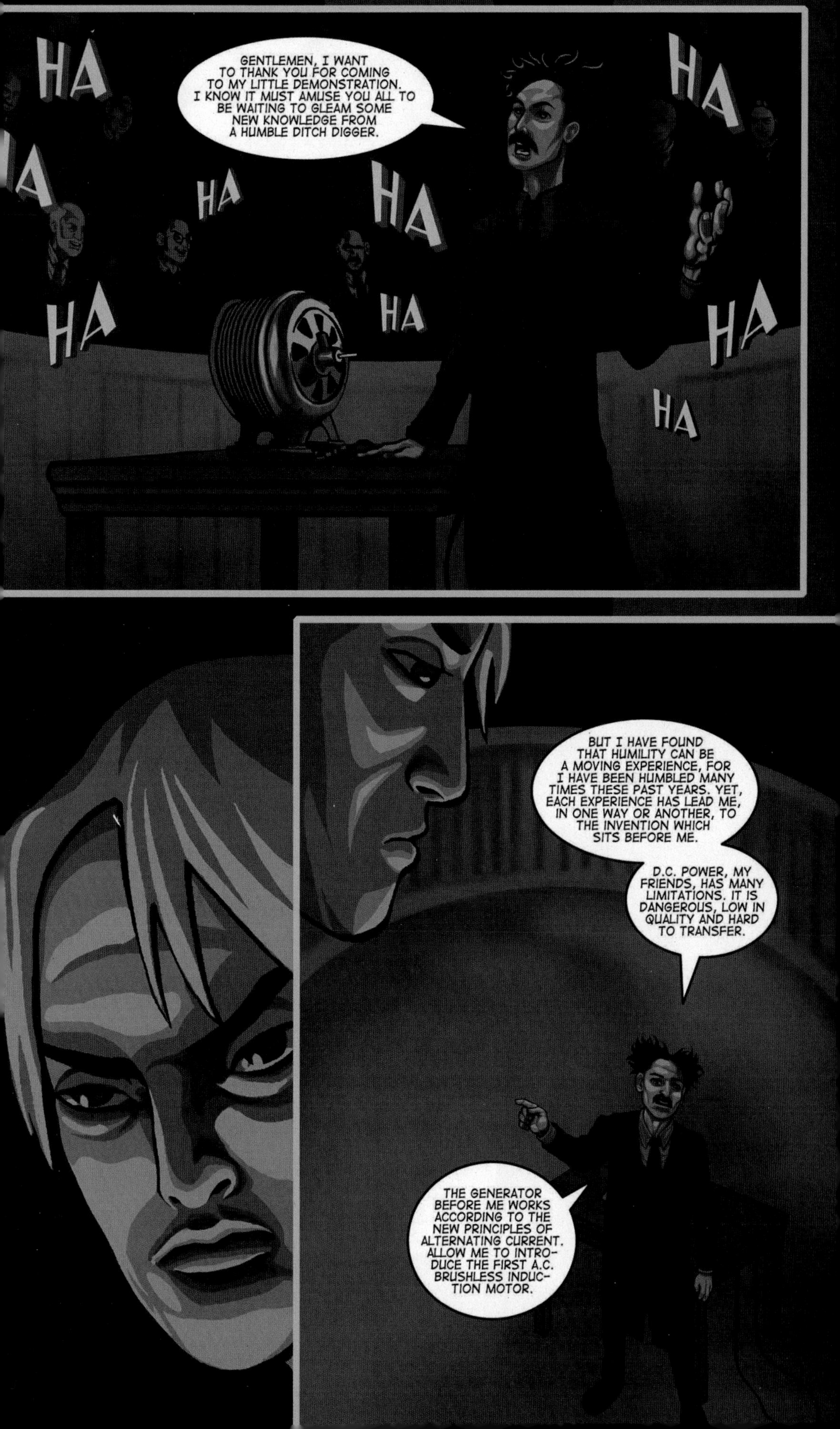

HA
HA
GENTLEMEN, I WANT TO THANK YOU FOR COMING TO MY LITTLE DEMONSTRATION. I KNOW IT MUST AMUSE YOU ALL TO BE WAITING TO GLEAM SOME NEW KNOWLEDGE FROM A HUMBLE DITCH DIGGER.
HA
HA
HA
HA
HA
HA
HA
BUT I HAVE FOUND THAT HUMILITY CAN BE A MOVING EXPERIENCE, FOR I HAVE BEEN HUMBLED MANY TIMES THESE PAST YEARS. YET, EACH EXPERIENCE HAS LEAD ME, IN ONE WAY OR ANOTHER, TO THE INVENTION WHICH SITS BEFORE ME.
D.C. POWER, MY FRIENDS, HAS MANY LIMITATIONS. IT IS DANGEROUS, LOW IN QUALITY AND HARD TO TRANSFER.
THE GENERATOR BEFORE ME WORKS ACCORDING TO THE NEW PRINCIPLES OF ALTERNATING CURRENT. ALLOW ME TO INTRODUCE THE FIRST A.C. BRUSHLESS INDUCTION MOTOR.

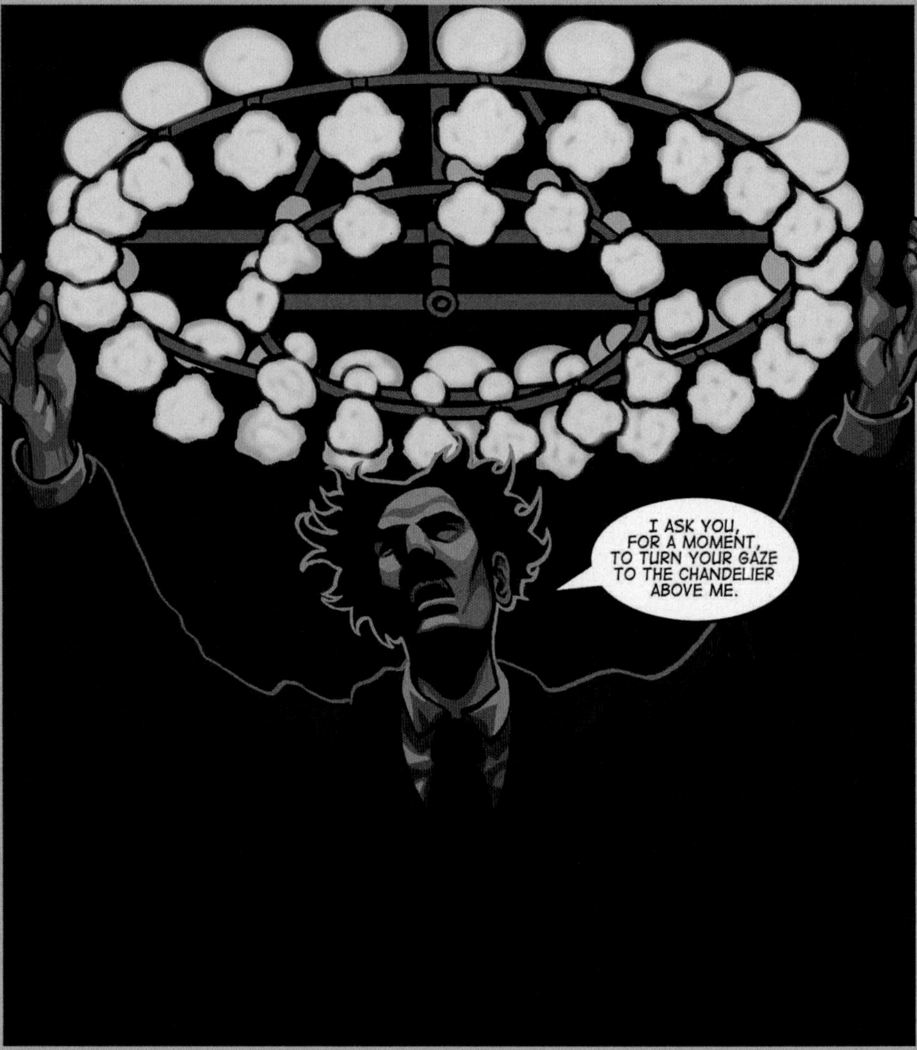
I ASK YOU, FOR A MOMENT, TO TURN YOUR GAZE TO THE CHANDELIER ABOVE ME.

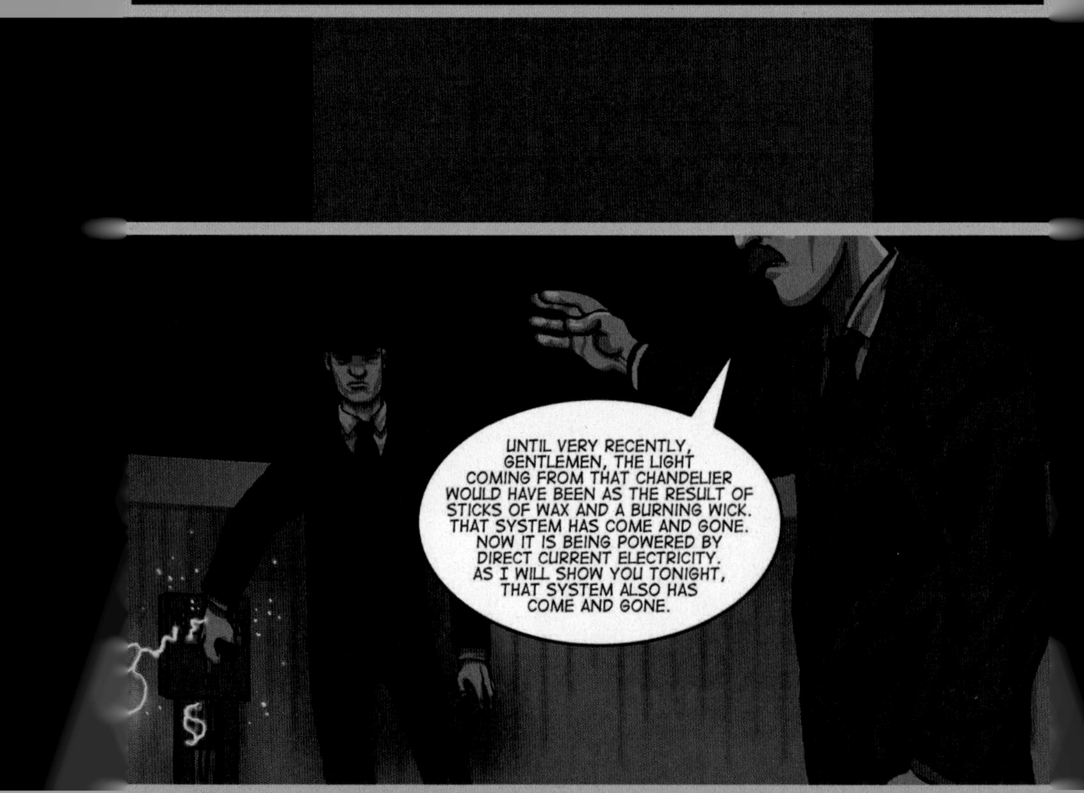
UNTIL VERY RECENTLY, GENTLEMEN, THE LIGHT COMING FROM THAT CHANDELIER WOULD HAVE BEEN AS THE RESULT OF STICKS OF WAX AND A BURNING WICK. THAT SYSTEM HAS COME AND GONE. NOW IT IS BEING POWERED BY DIRECT CURRENT ELECTRICITY. AS I WILL SHOW YOU TONIGHT, THAT SYSTEM ALSO HAS COME AND GONE.

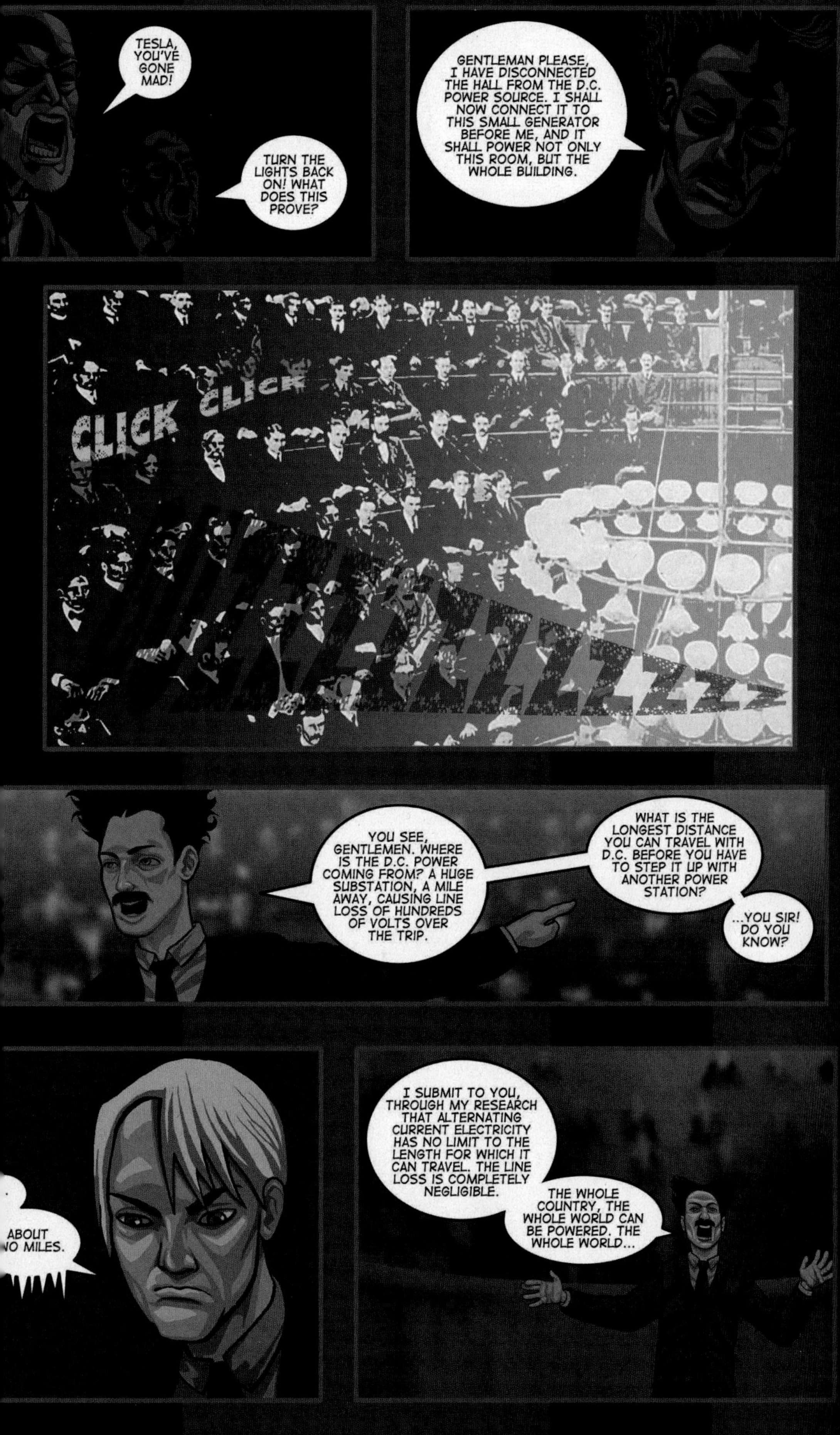
TESLA, YOU'VE GONE MAD!
TURN THE LIGHTS BACK ON! WHAT DOES THIS PROVE?
GENTLEMAN PLEASE, I HAVE DISCONNECTED THE HALL FROM THE D.C. POWER SOURCE. I SHALL NOW CONNECT IT TO THIS SMALL GENERATOR BEFORE ME, AND IT SHALL POWER NOT ONLY THIS ROOM, BUT THE WHOLE BUILDING.
CLICK CLICK
YOU SEE, GENTLEMEN. WHERE IS THE D.C. POWER COMING FROM? A HUGE SUBSTATION, A MILE AWAY, CAUSING LINE LOSS OF HUNDREDS OF VOLTS OVER THE TRIP.
WHAT IS THE LONGEST DISTANCE YOU CAN TRAVEL WITH D.C. BEFORE YOU HAVE TO STEP IT UP WITH ANOTHER POWER STATION?
...YOU SIR! DO YOU KNOW?
ABOUT
O MILES.
I SUBMIT TO YOU, THROUGH MY RESEARCH THAT ALTERNATING CURRENT ELECTRICITY HAS NO LIMIT TO THE LENGTH FOR WHICH IT CAN TRAVEL. THE LINE LOSS IS COMPLETELY NEGLIGIBLE.
THE WHOLE COUNTRY, THE WHOLE WORLD CAN BE POWERED. THE WHOLE WORLD...

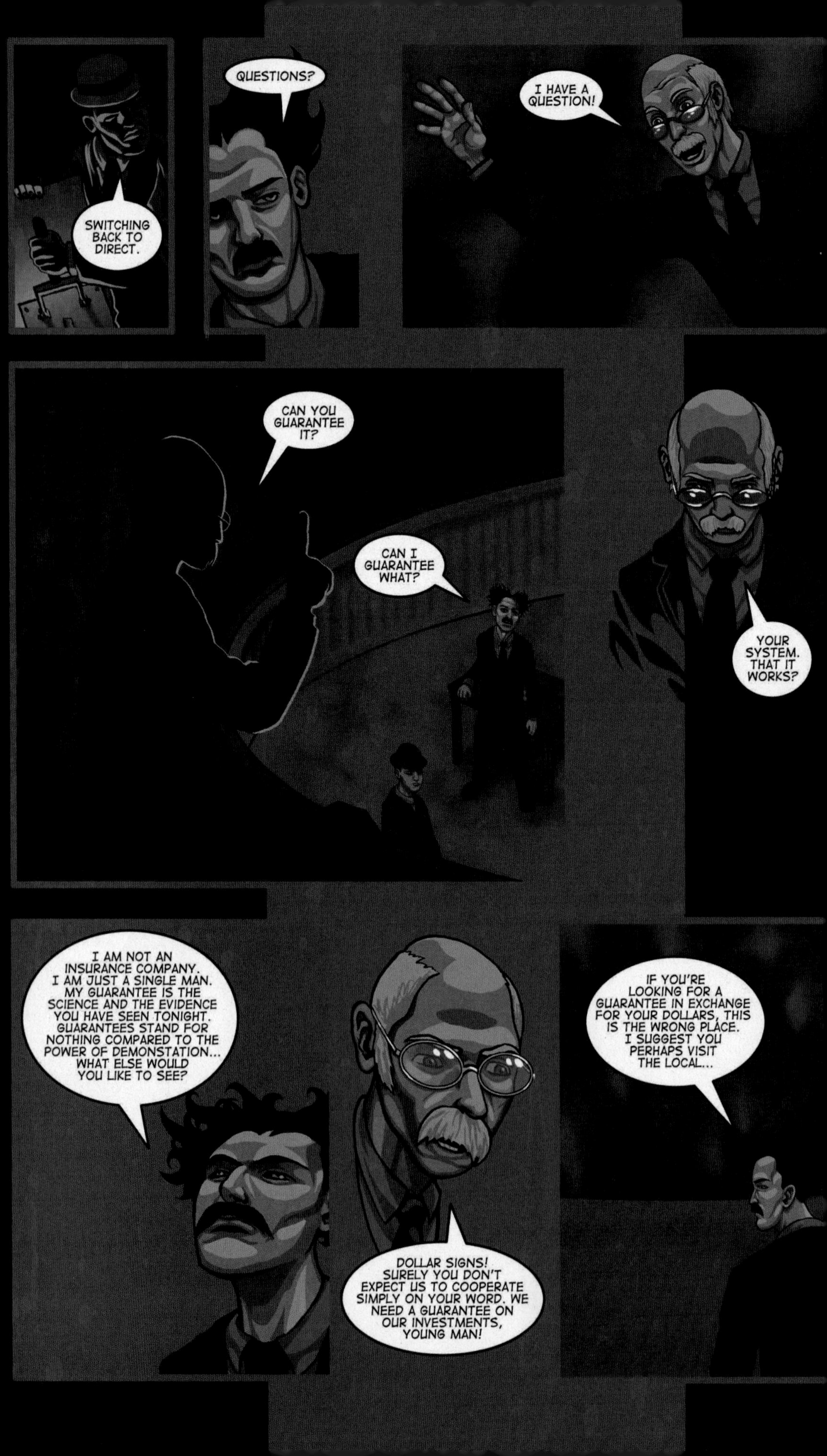
SWITCHING BACK TO DIRECT.
QUESTIONS?
I HAVE A QUESTION!
CAN YOU GUARANTEE IT?
CAN I GUARANTEE WHAT?
YOUR SYSTEM. THAT IT WORKS?
I AM NOT AN INSURANCE COMPANY. I AM JUST A SINGLE MAN. MY GUARANTEE IS THE SCIENCE AND THE EVIDENCE YOU HAVE SEEN TONIGHT. GUARANTEES STAND FOR NOTHING COMPARED TO THE POWER OF DEMONSTATION... WHAT ELSE WOULD YOU LIKE TO SEE?
DOLLAR SIGNS! SURELY YOU DON'T EXPECT US TO COOPERATE SIMPLY ON YOUR WORD. WE NEED A GUARANTEE ON OUR INVESTMENTS, YOUNG MAN!
IF YOU'RE LOOKING FOR A GUARANTEE IN EXCHANGE FOR YOUR DOLLARS, THIS IS THE WRONG PLACE. I SUGGEST YOU PERHAPS VISIT THE LOCAL...

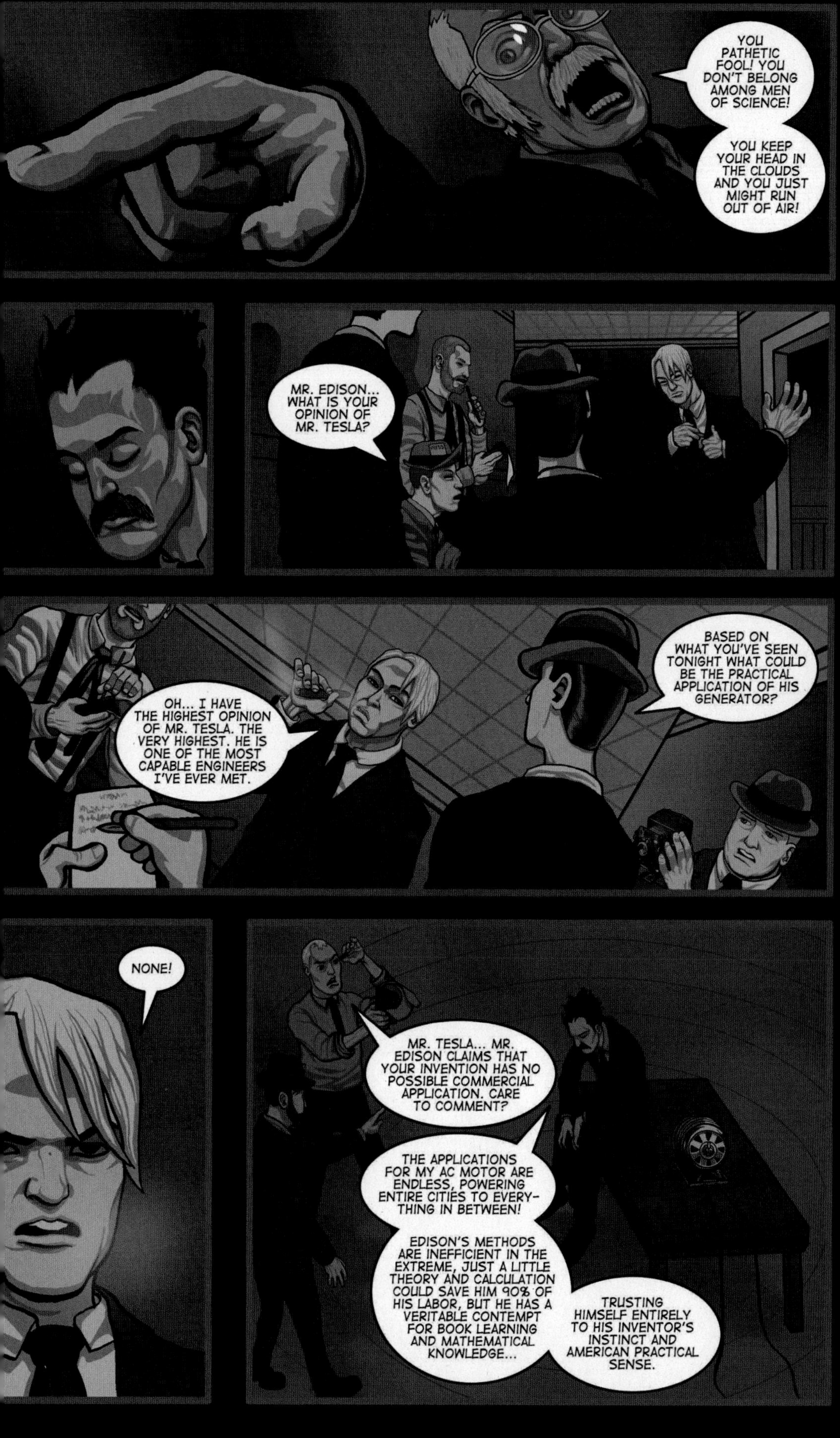
YOU PATHETIC FOOL! YOU DON'T BELONG AMONG MEN OF SCIENCE!
YOU KEEP YOUR HEAD IN THE CLOUDS AND YOU JUST MIGHT RUN OUT OF AIR!
MR. EDISON... WHAT IS YOUR OPINION OF MR. TESLA?
BASED ON WHAT YOU'VE SEEN TONIGHT WHAT COULD BE THE PRACTICAL APPLICATION OF HIS GENERATOR?
OH... I HAVE THE HIGHEST OPINION OF MR. TESLA. THE VERY HIGHEST. HE IS ONE OF THE MOST CAPABLE ENGINEERS I'VE EVER MET.
NONE!
MR. TESLA... MR. EDISON CLAIMS THAT YOUR INVENTION HAS NO POSSIBLE COMMERCIAL APPLICATION. CARE TO COMMENT?
THE APPLICATIONS FOR MY AC MOTOR ARE ENDLESS, POWERING ENTIRE CITIES TO EVERY-THING IN BETWEEN!
EDISON'S METHODS ARE INEFFICIENT IN THE EXTREME, JUST A LITTLE THEORY AND CALCULATION COULD SAVE HIM 90% OF HIS LABOR, BUT HE HAS A VERITABLE CONTEMPT FOR BOOK LEARNING AND MATHEMATICAL KNOWLEDGE...
TRUSTING HIMSELF ENTIRELY TO HIS INVENTOR'S INSTINCT AND AMERICAN PRACTICAL SENSE.

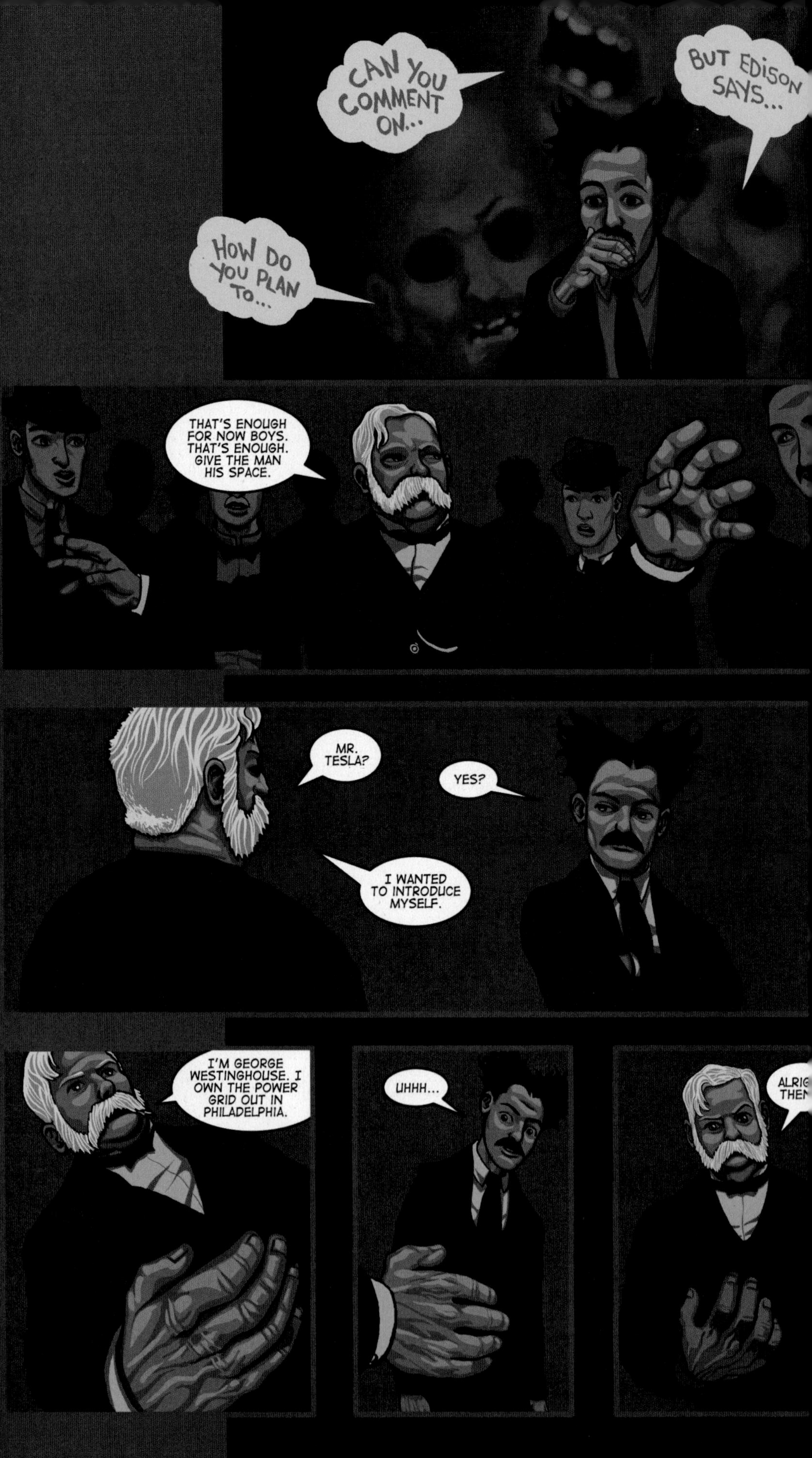
CAN YOU COMMENT ON...
BUT EDISON SAYS...
HOW DO YOU PLAN TO...
THAT'S ENOUGH FOR NOW BOYS. THAT'S ENOUGH. GIVE THE MAN HIS SPACE.
MR. TESLA?
YES?
I WANTED TO INTRODUCE MYSELF.
I'M GEORGE WESTINGHOUSE. I OWN THE POWER GRID OUT IN PHILADELPHIA.
UHHH...
ALRIG THE

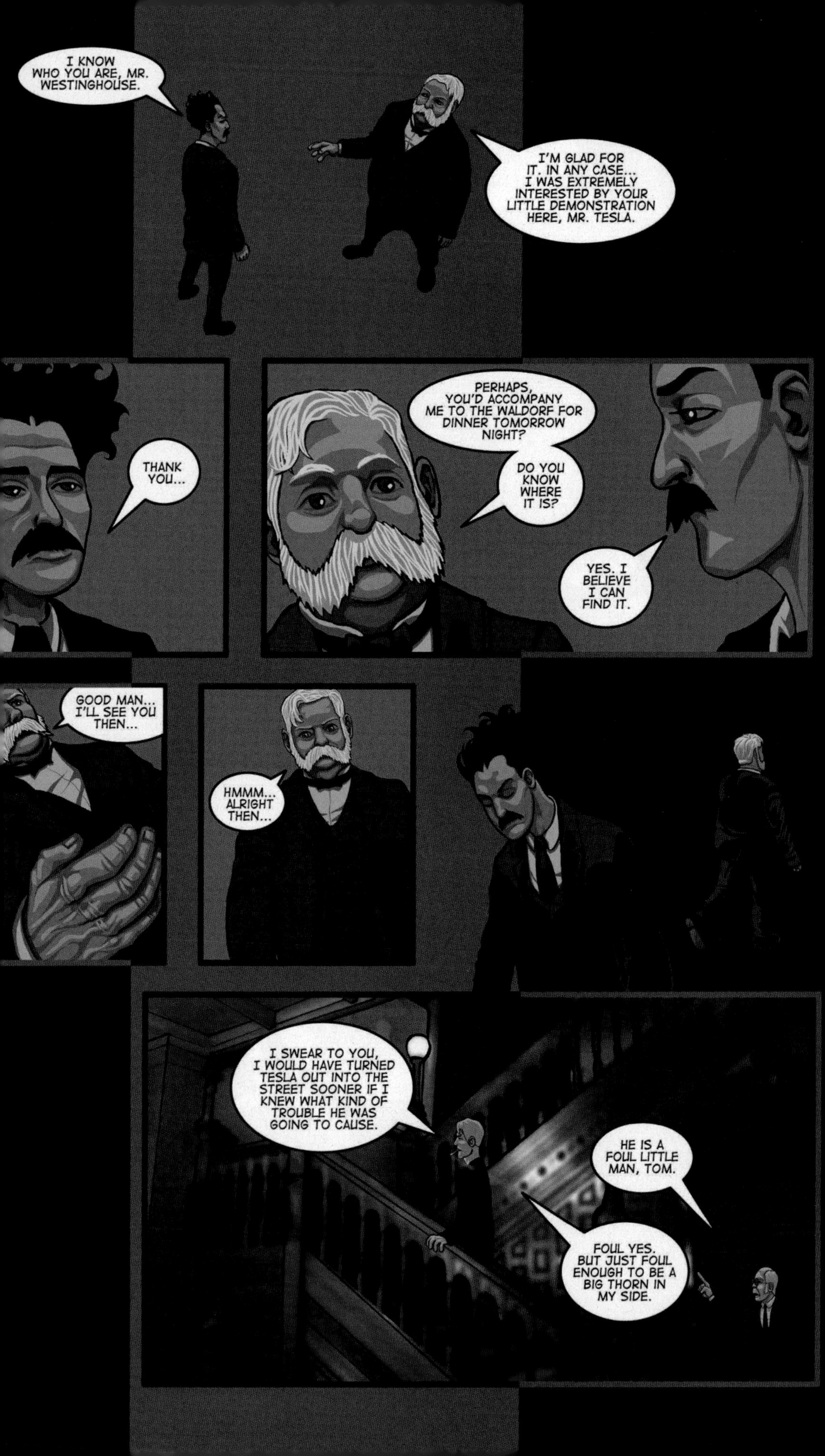
I KNOW WHO YOU ARE, MR. WESTINGHOUSE.
I'M GLAD FOR IT. IN ANY CASE... I WAS EXTREMELY INTERESTED BY YOUR LITTLE DEMONSTRATION HERE, MR. TESLA.
THANK YOU...
PERHAPS, YOU'D ACCOMPANY ME TO THE WALDORF FOR DINNER TOMORROW NIGHT?
DO YOU KNOW WHERE IT IS?
YES. I BELIEVE I CAN FIND IT.
GOOD MAN... I'LL SEE YOU THEN...
HMMM... ALRIGHT THEN...
I SWEAR TO YOU, I WOULD HAVE TURNED TESLA OUT INTO THE STREET SOONER IF I KNEW WHAT KIND OF TROUBLE HE WAS GOING TO CAUSE.
HE IS A FOUL LITTLE MAN, TOM.
FOUL YES. BUT JUST FOUL ENOUGH TO BE A BIG THORN IN MY SIDE.

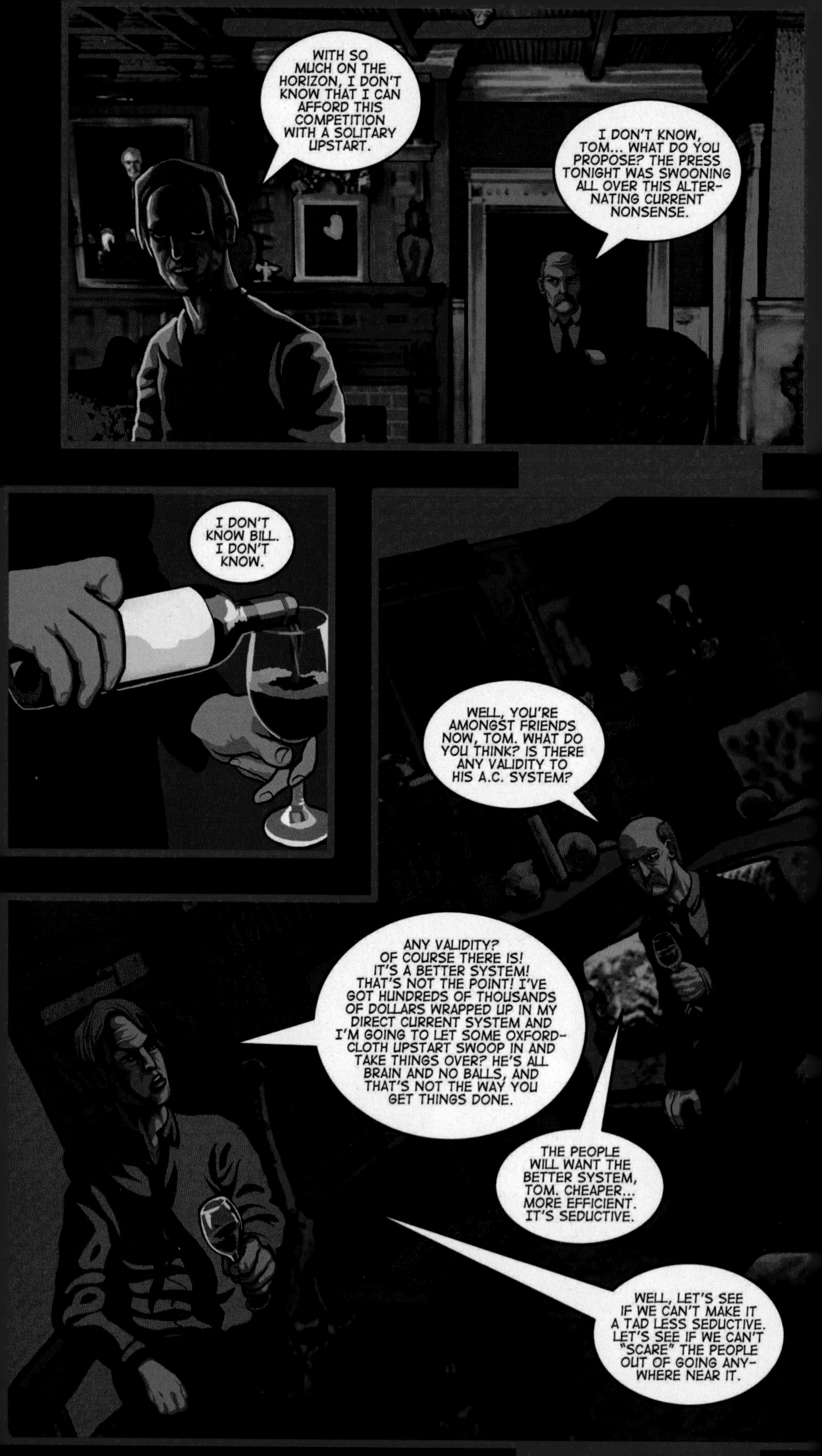
WITH SO MUCH ON THE HORIZON, I DON'T KNOW THAT I CAN AFFORD THIS COMPETITION WITH A SOLITARY UPSTART.
I DON'T KNOW, TOM... WHAT DO YOU PROPOSE? THE PRESS TONIGHT WAS SWOONING ALL OVER THIS ALTER-NATING CURRENT NONSENSE.
I DON'T KNOW BILL. I DON'T KNOW.
WELL, YOU'RE AMONGST FRIENDS NOW, TOM. WHAT DO YOU THINK? IS THERE ANY VALIDITY TO HIS A.C. SYSTEM?
ANY VALIDITY? OF COURSE THERE IS! IT'S A BETTER SYSTEM! THAT'S NOT THE POINT! I'VE GOT HUNDREDS OF THOUSANDS OF DOLLARS WRAPPED UP IN MY DIRECT CURRENT SYSTEM AND I'M GOING TO LET SOME OXFORD-CLOTH UPSTART SWOOP IN AND TAKE THINGS OVER? HE'S ALL BRAIN AND NO BALLS, AND THAT'S NOT THE WAY YOU GET THINGS DONE.
THE PEOPLE WILL WANT THE BETTER SYSTEM, TOM. CHEAPER... MORE EFFICIENT. IT'S SEDUCTIVE.
WELL, LET'S SEE IF WE CAN'T MAKE IT A TAD LESS SEDUCTIVE. LET'S SEE IF WE CAN'T "SCARE" THE PEOPLE OUT OF GOING ANY-WHERE NEAR IT.

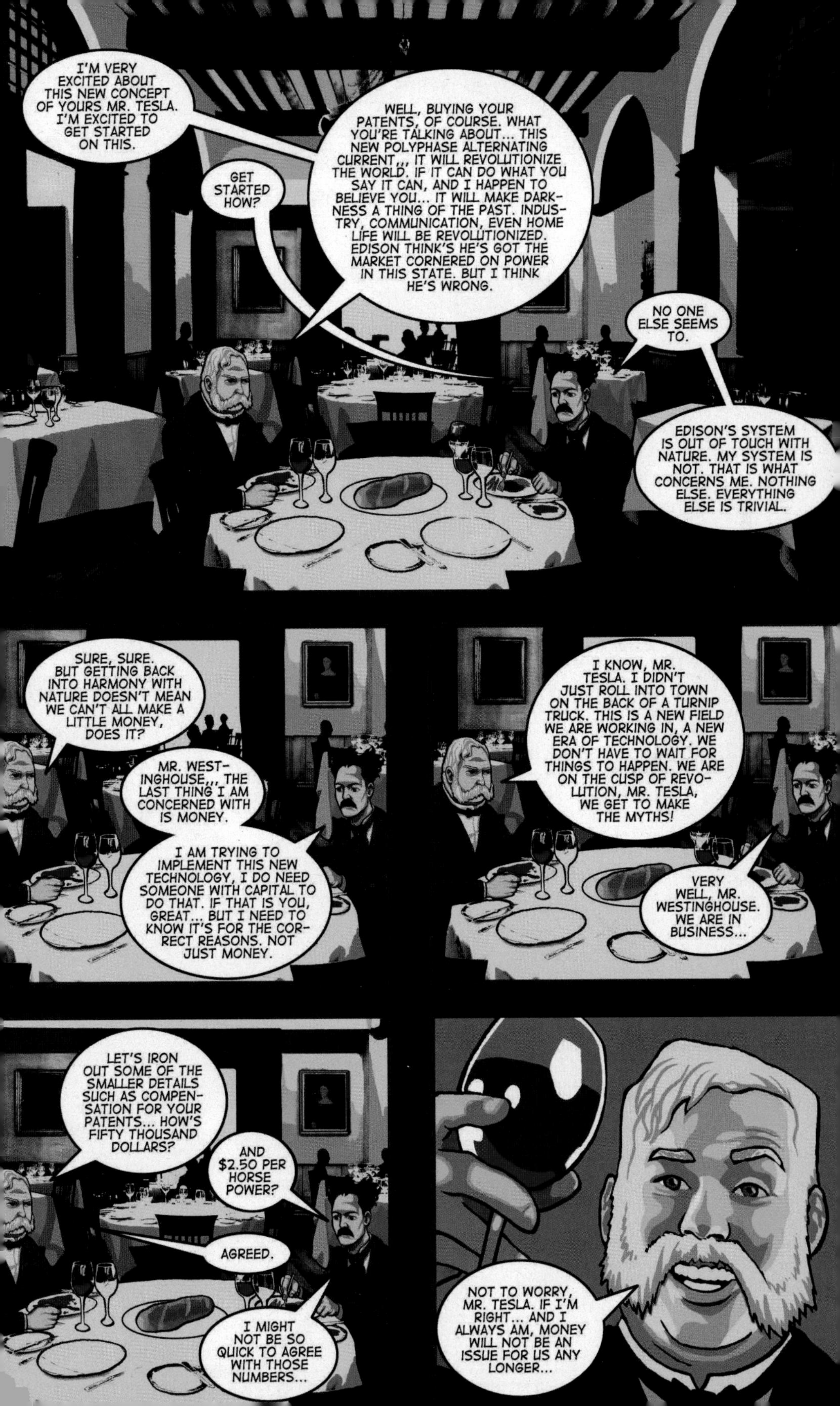
I'M VERY EXCITED ABOUT THIS NEW CONCEPT OF YOURS MR. TESLA. I'M EXCITED TO GET STARTED ON THIS.
GET STARTED HOW?
WELL, BUYING YOUR PATENTS, OF COURSE. WHAT YOU'RE TALKING ABOUT... THIS NEW POLYPHASE ALTERNATING CURRENT,,, IT WILL REVOLUTIONIZE THE WORLD. IF IT CAN DO WHAT YOU SAY IT CAN, AND I HAPPEN TO BELIEVE YOU... IT WILL MAKE DARK-NESS A THING OF THE PAST. INDUS-TRY, COMMUNICATION, EVEN HOME LIFE WILL BE REVOLUTIONIZED. EDISON THINK'S HE'S GOT THE MARKET CORNERED ON POWER IN THIS STATE. BUT I THINK HE'S WRONG.
NO ONE ELSE SEEMS TO.
EDISON'S SYSTEM IS OUT OF TOUCH WITH NATURE. MY SYSTEM IS NOT. THAT IS WHAT CONCERNS ME. NOTHING ELSE. EVERYTHING ELSE IS TRIVIAL.
SURE, SURE. BUT GETTING BACK INTO HARMONY WITH NATURE DOESN'T MEAN WE CAN'T ALL MAKE A LITTLE MONEY, DOES IT?
MR. WEST-INGHOUSE,,, THE LAST THING I AM CONCERNED WITH IS MONEY.
I AM TRYING TO IMPLEMENT THIS NEW TECHNOLOGY, I DO NEED SOMEONE WITH CAPITAL TO DO THAT. IF THAT IS YOU, GREAT... BUT I NEED TO KNOW IT'S FOR THE COR-RECT REASONS. NOT JUST MONEY.
I KNOW, MR. TESLA. I DIDN'T JUST ROLL INTO TOWN ON THE BACK OF A TURNIP TRUCK. THIS IS A NEW FIELD WE ARE WORKING IN, A NEW ERA OF TECHNOLOGY. WE DON'T HAVE TO WAIT FOR THINGS TO HAPPEN. WE ARE ON THE CUSP OF REVO-LUTION, MR. TESLA, WE GET TO MAKE THE MYTHS!
VERY WELL, MR. WESTINGHOUSE. WE ARE IN BUSINESS...
LET'S IRON OUT SOME OF THE SMALLER DETAILS SUCH AS COMPEN-SATION FOR YOUR PATENTS... HOW'S FIFTY THOUSAND DOLLARS?
AND $2.50 PER HORSE POWER?
AGREED.
I MIGHT NOT BE SO QUICK TO AGREE WITH THOSE NUMBERS...
NOT TO WORRY, MR. TESLA. IF I'M RIGHT... AND I ALWAYS AM, MONEY WILL NOT BE AN ISSUE FOR US ANY LONGER...

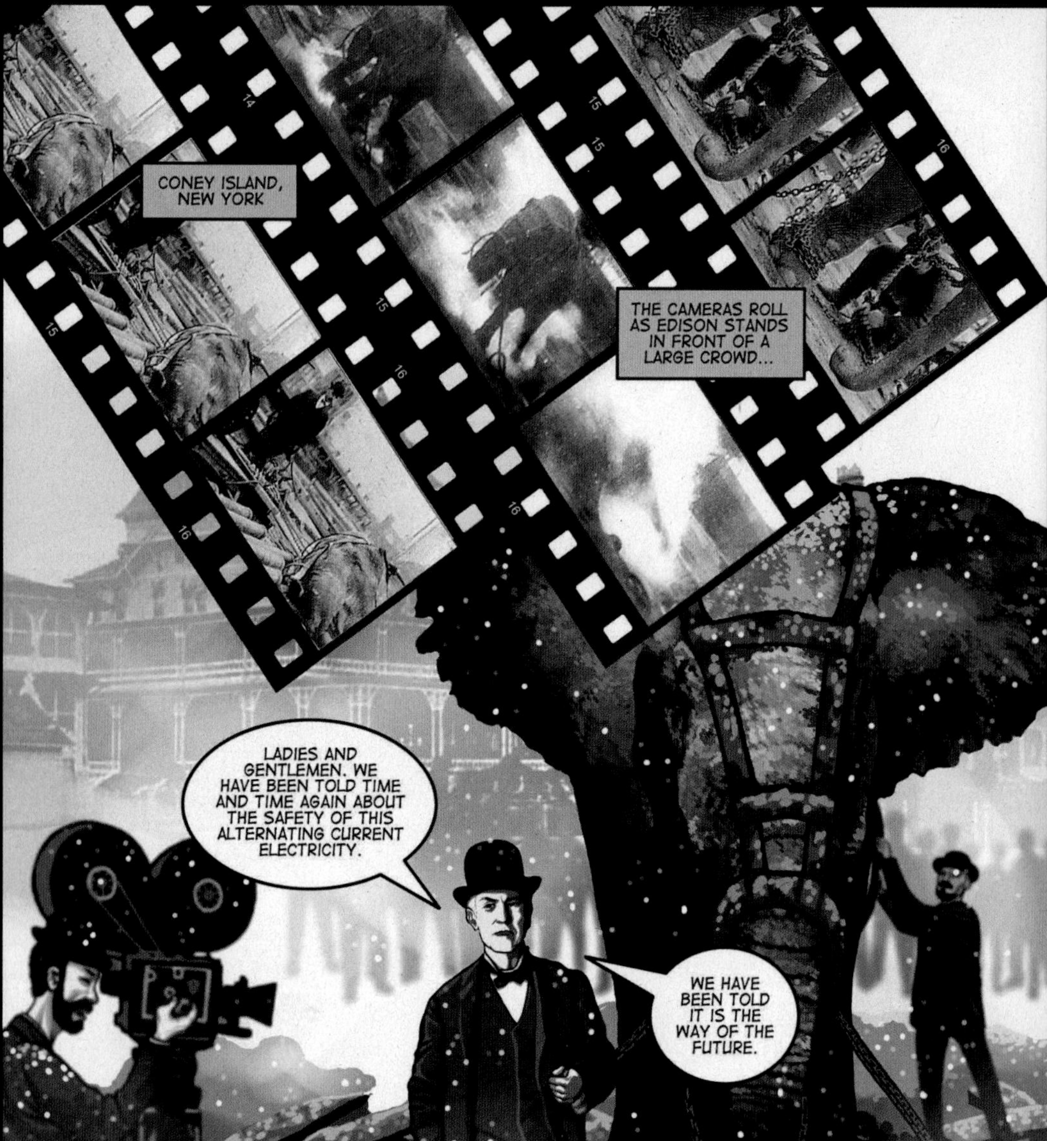
CONEY ISLAND, NEW YORK
THE CAMERAS ROLL AS EDISON STANDS IN FRONT OF A LARGE CROWD...
LADIES AND GENTLEMEN. WE HAVE BEEN TOLD TIME AND TIME AGAIN ABOUT THE SAFETY OF THIS ALTERNATING CURRENT ELECTRICITY.
WE HAVE BEEN TOLD IT IS THE WAY OF THE FUTURE.

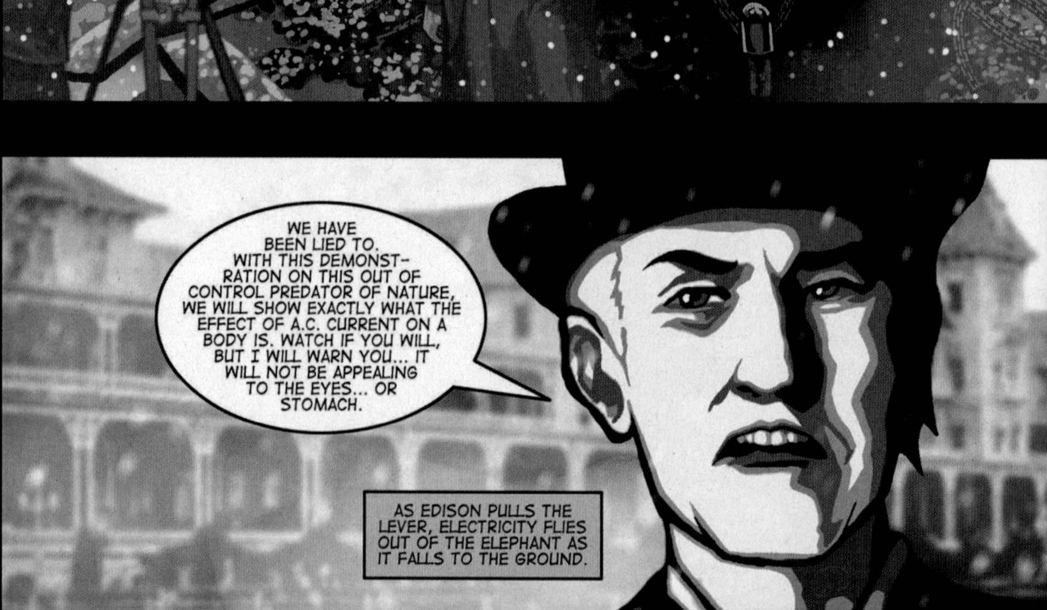
WE HAVE BEEN LIED TO. WITH THIS DEMONSTRATION ON THIS OUT OF CONTROL PREDATOR OF NATURE, WE WILL SHOW EXACTLY WHAT THE EFFECT OF A.C. CURRENT ON A BODY IS. WATCH IF YOU WILL, BUT I WILL WARN YOU... IT WILL NOT BE APPEALING TO THE EYES... OR STOMACH.
AS EDISON PULLS THE LEVER, ELECTRICITY FLIES OUT OF THE ELEPHANT AS IT FALLS TO THE GROUND.

GENTLEMEN, I ASK YOU, IS THIS THE INVENTION YOU WANT YOUR WIFE TO COOK WITH?
HAVE YOU HEARD THE NEWS?
I DOUBT IT GEORGE. SOME OF US ARE WORKING...
EDISON'S DONE IT AGAIN!
WHAT? KILL ANOTHER CHICKEN OR DOG? THOSE MINISCULE DISPLAYS OF THE MISAPPROPRIATION OF MY POWER SYSTEM WILL NOT SCARE OFF PEOPLE OF INTELLIGENCE.
HOW ABOUT AN ELEPHANT?
WHAT!?
HE FRIED A THREE TON ELEPHANT IN FRONT OF TWO THOUSAND PEOPLE ON CONEY ISLAND YESTERDAY, AND HE FILMED IT WITH HIS MOVIE CAMERA.

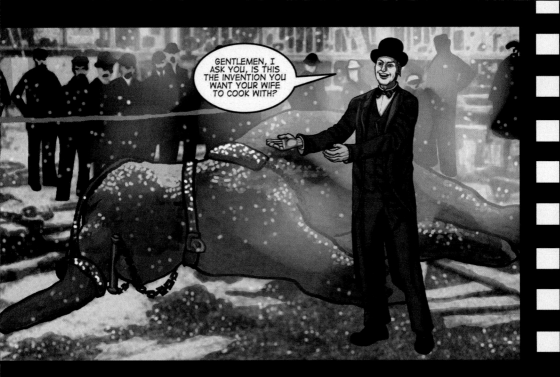

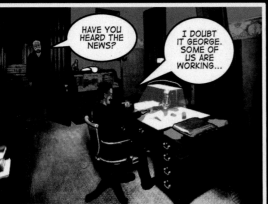

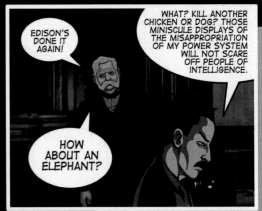

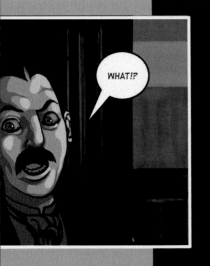

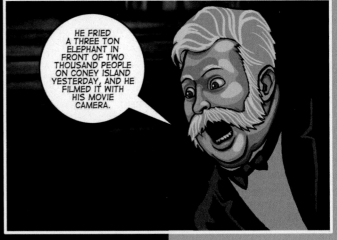

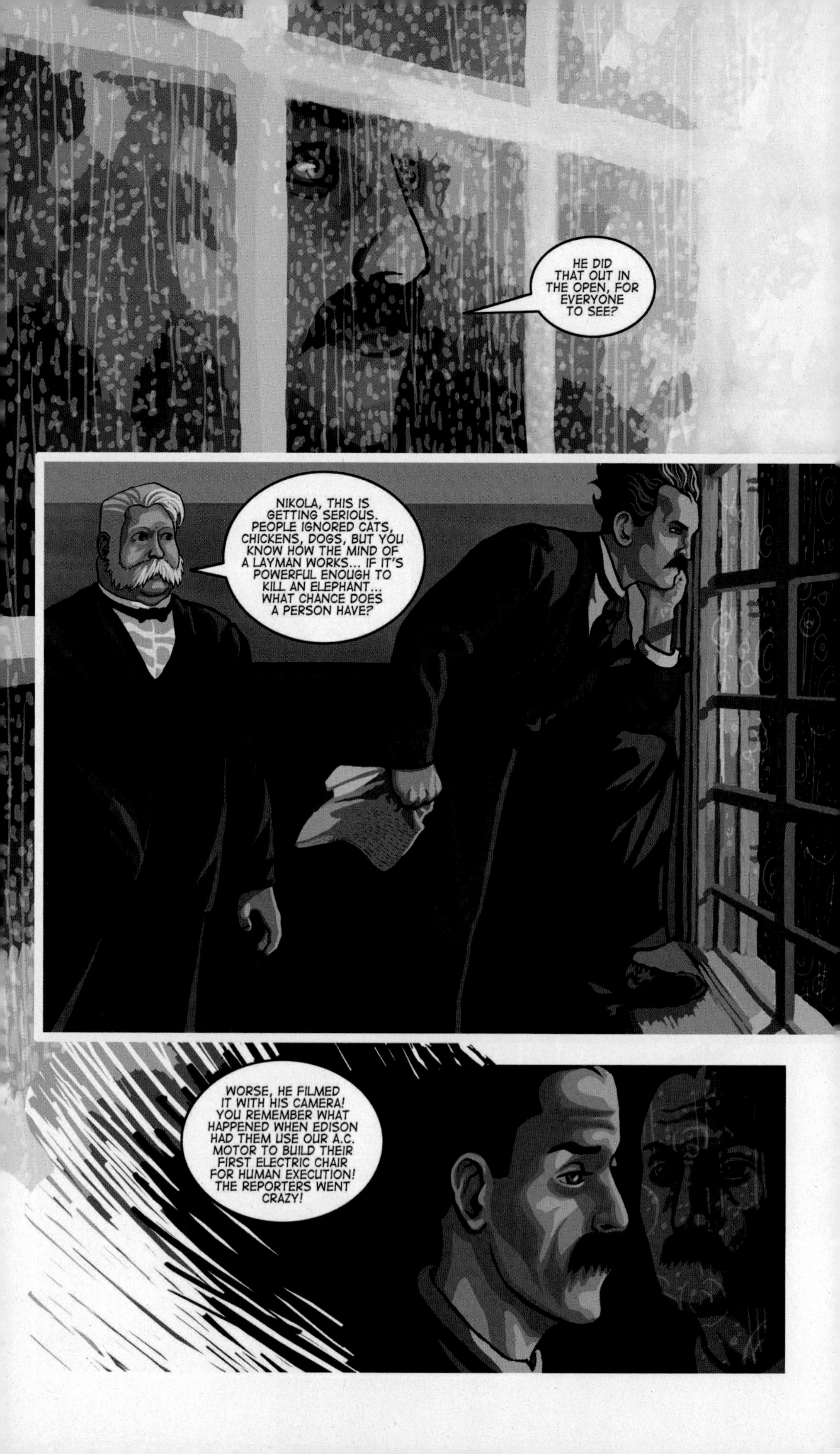
HE DID THAT OUT IN THE OPEN, FOR EVERYONE TO SEE?
NIKOLA, THIS IS GETTING SERIOUS. PEOPLE IGNORED CATS, CHICKENS, DOGS, BUT YOU KNOW HOW THE MIND OF A LAYMAN WORKS... IF IT'S POWERFUL ENOUGH TO KILL AN ELEPHANT... WHAT CHANCE DOES A PERSON HAVE?
WORSE, HE FILMED IT WITH HIS CAMERA! YOU REMEMBER WHAT HAPPENED WHEN EDISON HAD THEM USE OUR A.C. MOTOR TO BUILD THEIR FIRST ELECTRIC CHAIR FOR HUMAN EXECUTION! THE REPORTERS WENT CRAZY!

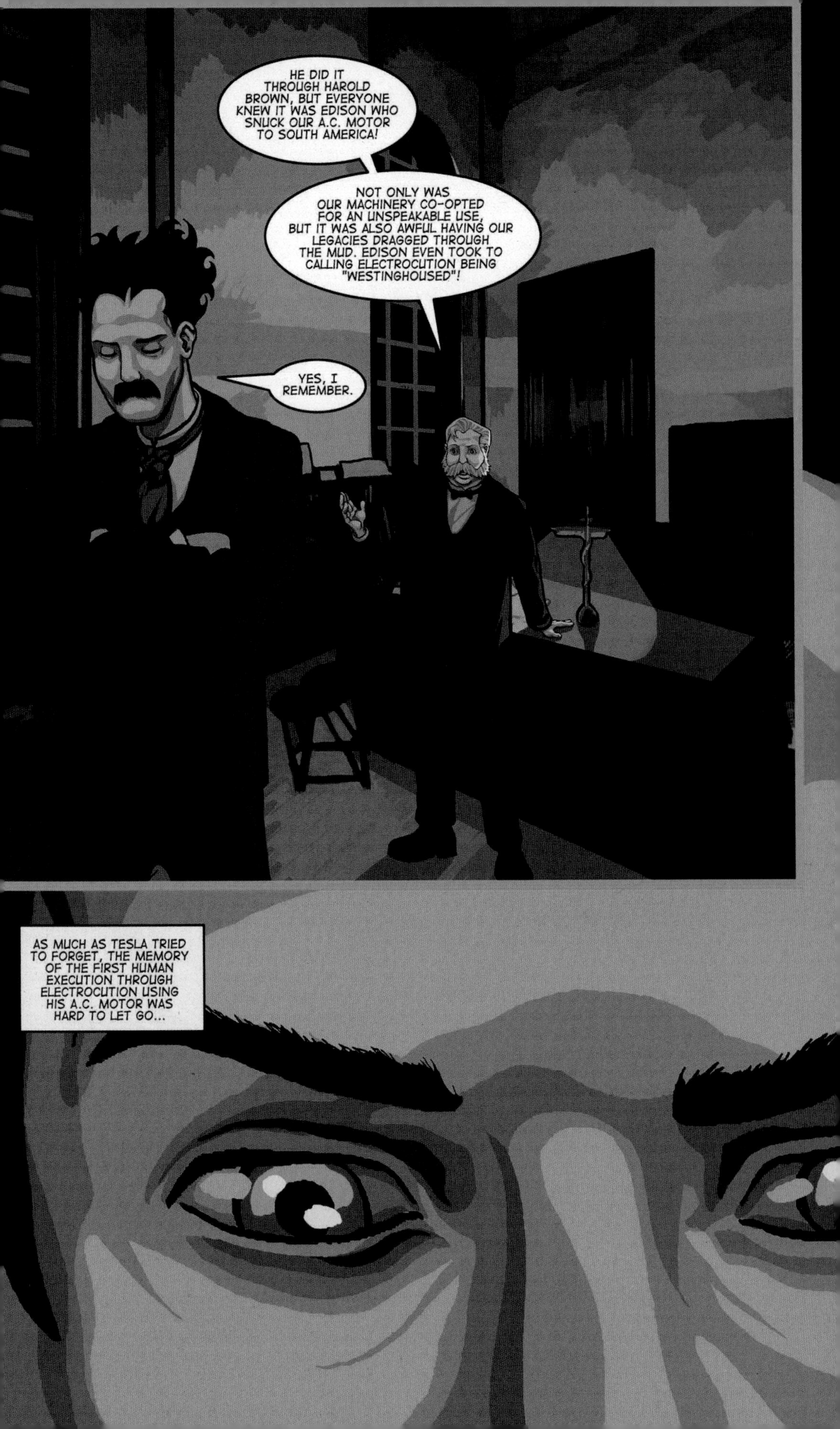
HE DID IT THROUGH HAROLD BROWN, BUT EVERYONE KNEW IT WAS EDISON WHO SNUCK OUR A.C. MOTOR TO SOUTH AMERICA!
NOT ONLY WAS OUR MACHINERY CO-OPTED FOR AN UNSPEAKABLE USE, BUT IT WAS ALSO AWFUL HAVING OUR LEGACIES DRAGGED THROUGH THE MUD. EDISON EVEN TOOK TO CALLING ELECTROCUTION BEING "WESTINGHOUSED"!
YES, I REMEMBER.
AS MUCH AS TESLA TRIED TO FORGET, THE MEMORY OF THE FIRST HUMAN EXECUTION THROUGH ELECTROCUTION USING HIS A.C. MOTOR WAS HARD TO LET GO...

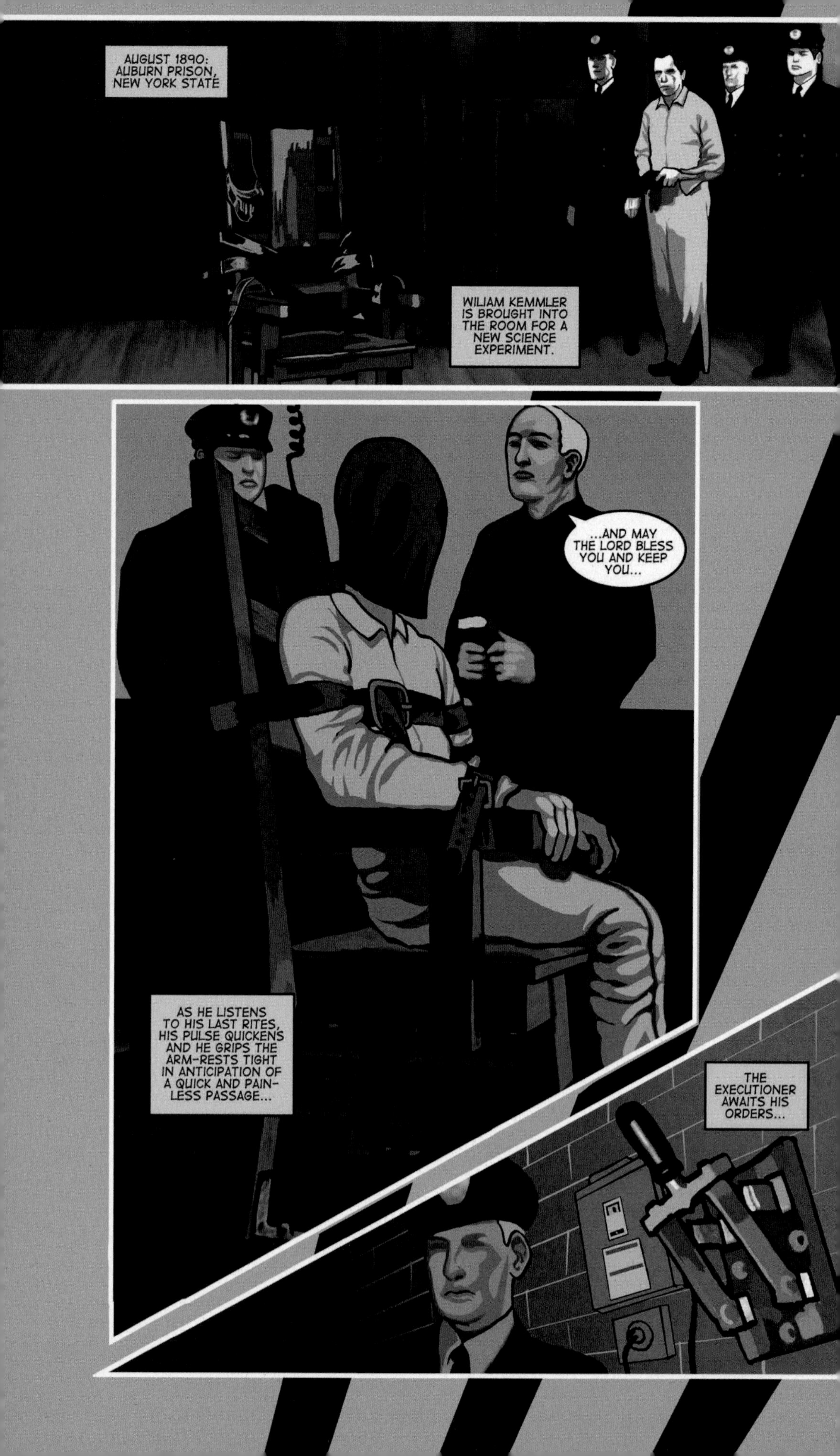
AUGUST 1890: AUBURN PRISON, NEW YORK STATE
WILIAM KEMMLER IS BROUGHT INTO THE ROOM FOR A NEW SCIENCE EXPERIMENT.
...AND MAY THE LORD BLESS YOU AND KEEP YOU...
AS HE LISTENS TO HIS LAST RITES, HIS PULSE QUICKENS AND HE GRIPS THE ARM-RESTS TIGHT IN ANTICIPATION OF A QUICK AND PAIN-LESS PASSAGE...
THE EXECUTIONER AWAITS HIS ORDERS...

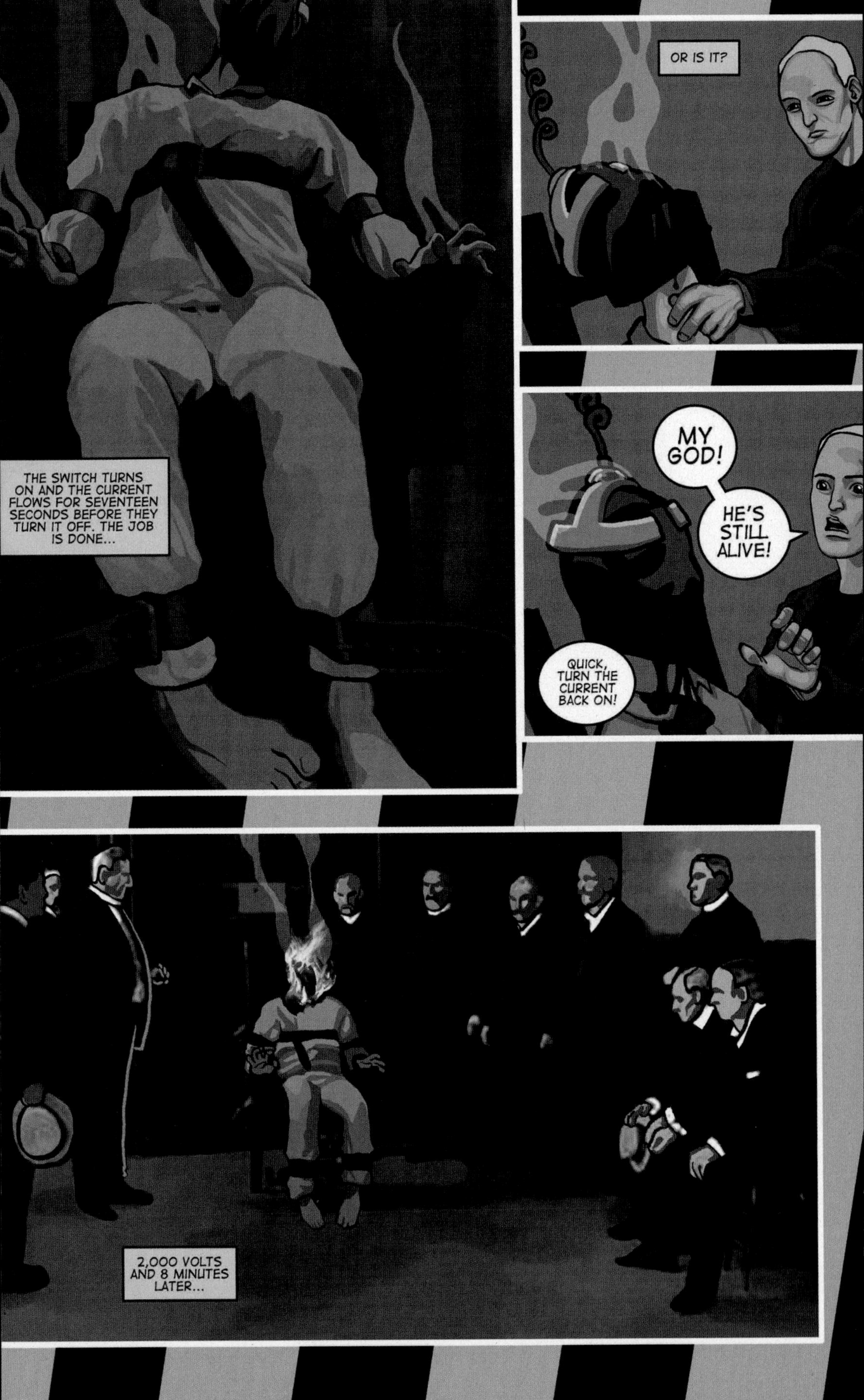
THE SWITCH TURNS ON AND THE CURRENT FLOWS FOR SEVENTEEN SECONDS BEFORE THEY TURN IT OFF. THE JOB IS DONE...
OR IS IT?
MY GOD!
HE'S STILL ALIVE!
QUICK, TURN THE CURRENT BACK ON!
2,000 VOLTS AND 8 MINUTES LATER...

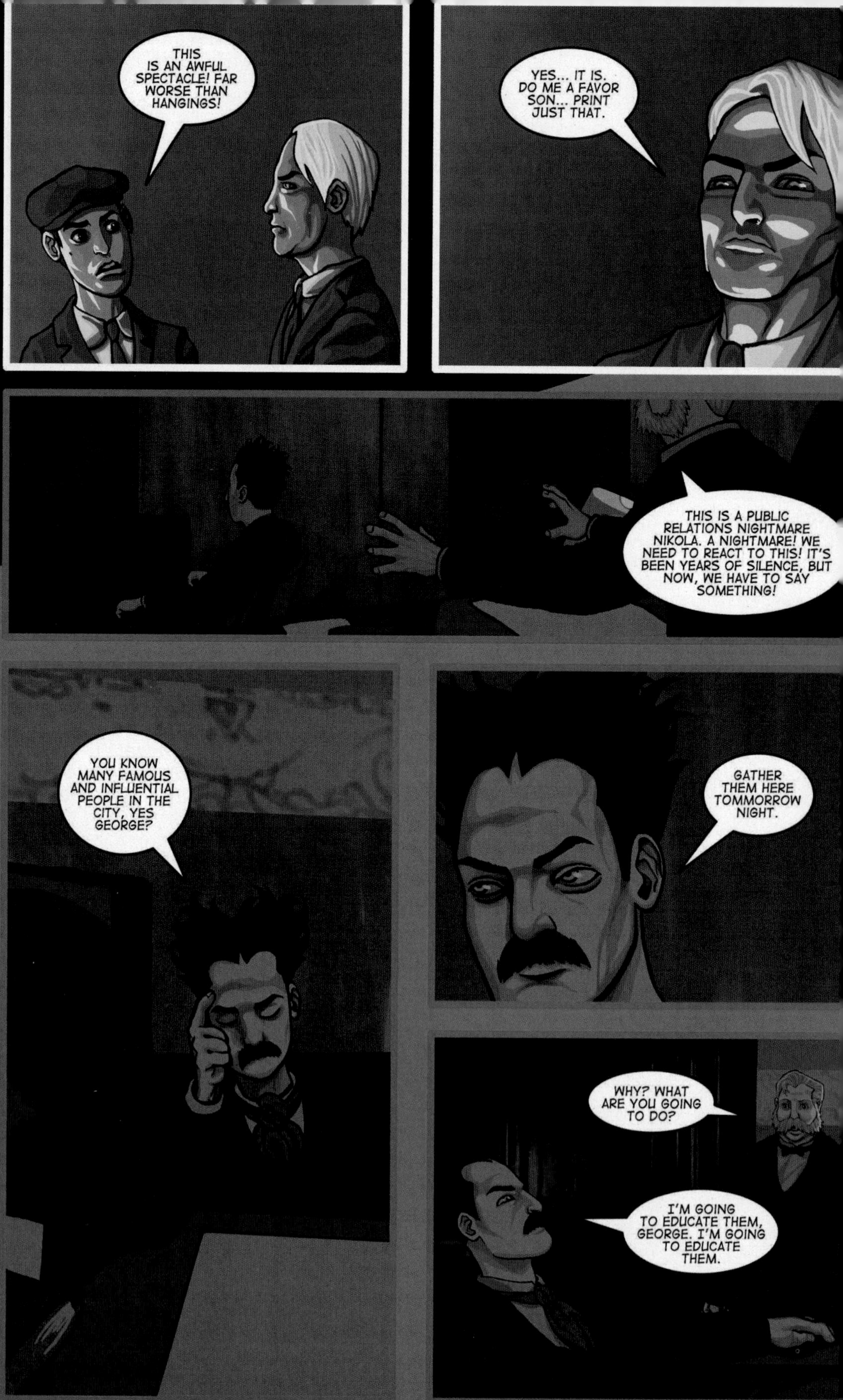
THIS IS AN AWFUL SPECTACLE! FAR WORSE THAN HANGINGS!
YES... IT IS. DO ME A FAVOR SON... PRINT JUST THAT.
THIS IS A PUBLIC RELATIONS NIGHTMARE NIKOLA. A NIGHTMARE! WE NEED TO REACT TO THIS! IT'S BEEN YEARS OF SILENCE, BUT NOW, WE HAVE TO SAY SOMETHING!
YOU KNOW MANY FAMOUS AND INFLUENTIAL PEOPLE IN THE CITY, YES GEORGE?
GATHER THEM HERE TOMMORROW NIGHT.
WHY? WHAT ARE YOU GOING TO DO?
I'M GOING TO EDUCATE THEM, GEORGE. I'M GOING TO EDUCATE THEM.

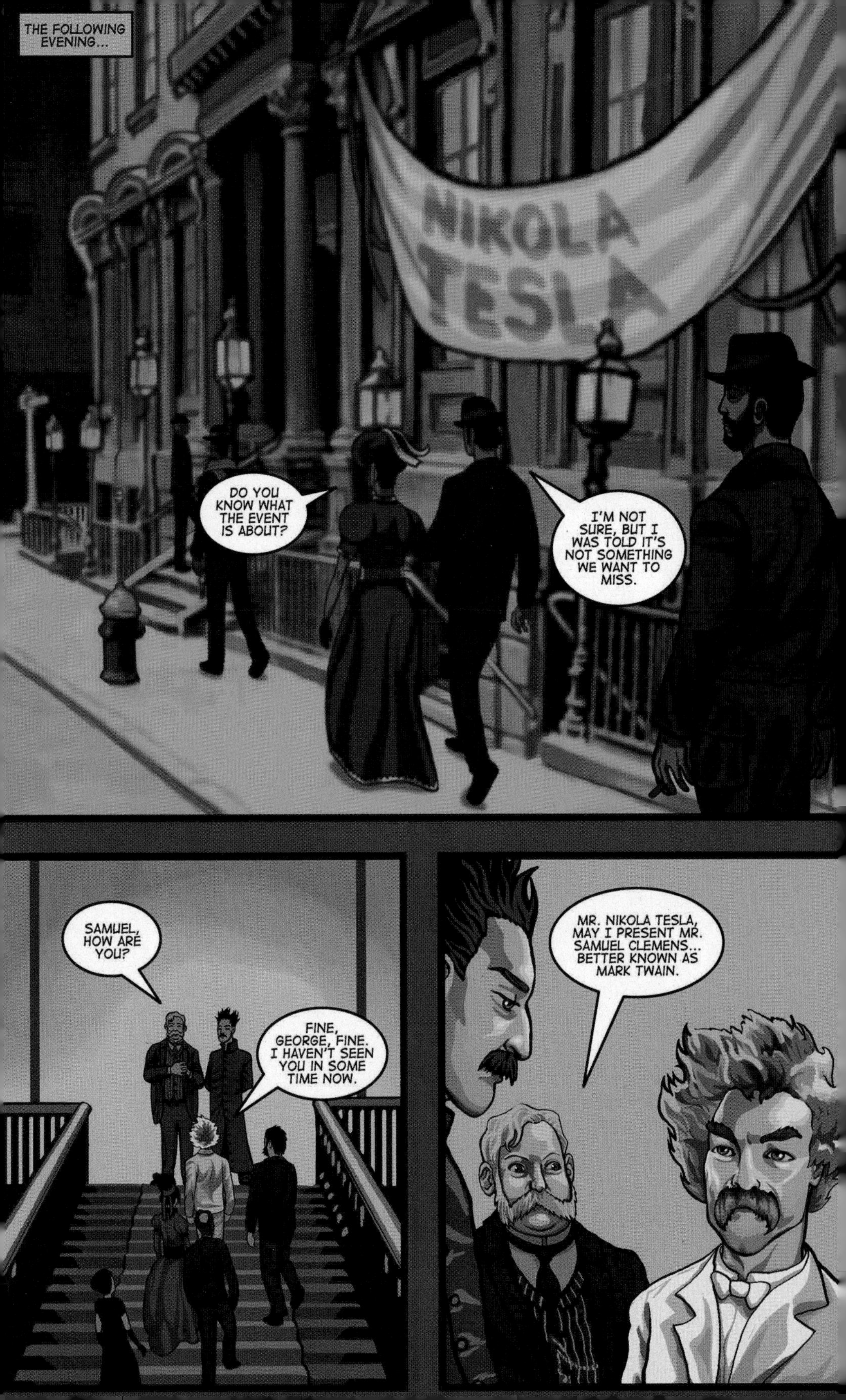
THE FOLLOWING EVENING...
NIKOLA TESLA
DO YOU KNOW WHAT THE EVENT IS ABOUT?
I'M NOT SURE, BUT I WAS TOLD IT'S NOT SOMETHING WE WANT TO MISS.
SAMUEL, HOW ARE YOU?
FINE, GEORGE, FINE. I HAVEN'T SEEN YOU IN SOME TIME NOW.
MR. NIKOLA TESLA, MAY I PRESENT MR. SAMUEL CLEMENS... BETTER KNOWN AS MARK TWAIN.

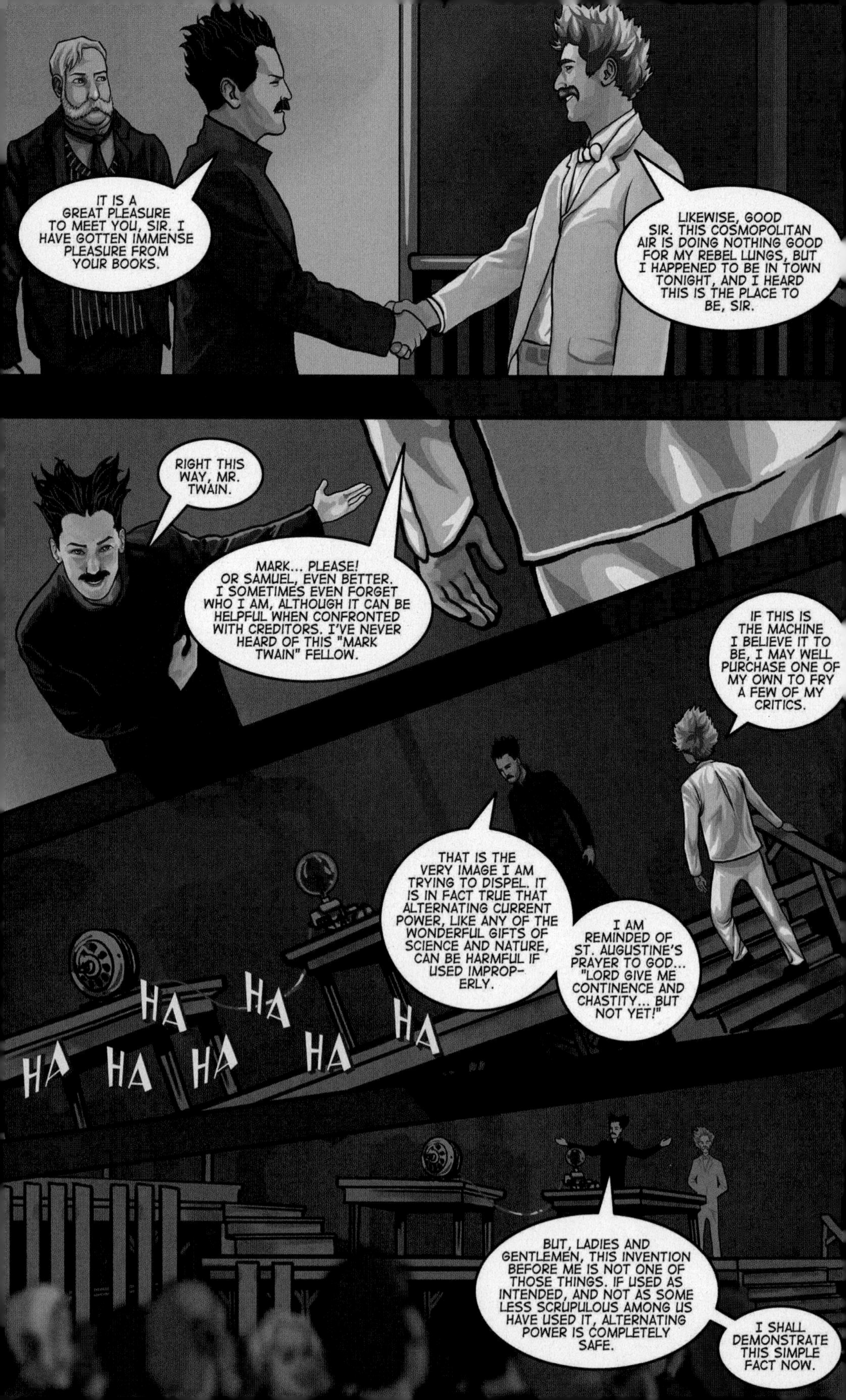
IT IS A GREAT PLEASURE TO MEET YOU, SIR. I HAVE GOTTEN IMMENSE PLEASURE FROM YOUR BOOKS.
LIKEWISE, GOOD SIR. THIS COSMOPOLITAN AIR IS DOING NOTHING GOOD FOR MY REBEL LUNGS, BUT I HAPPENED TO BE IN TOWN TONIGHT, AND I HEARD THIS IS THE PLACE TO BE, SIR.
RIGHT THIS WAY, MR. TWAIN.
MARK... PLEASE! OR SAMUEL, EVEN BETTER. I SOMETIMES EVEN FORGET WHO I AM, ALTHOUGH IT CAN BE HELPFUL WHEN CONFRONTED WITH CREDITORS. I'VE NEVER HEARD OF THIS "MARK TWAIN" FELLOW.
IF THIS IS THE MACHINE I BELIEVE IT TO BE, I MAY WELL PURCHASE ONE OF MY OWN TO FRY A FEW OF MY CRITICS.
THAT IS THE VERY IMAGE I AM TRYING TO DISPEL. IT IS IN FACT TRUE THAT ALTERNATING CURRENT POWER, LIKE ANY OF THE WONDERFUL GIFTS OF SCIENCE AND NATURE, CAN BE HARMFUL IF USED IMPROP-ERLY.
I AM REMINDED OF ST. AUGUSTINE'S PRAYER TO GOD... "LORD GIVE ME CONTINENCE AND CHASTITY... BUT NOT YET!"
HA HA HA HA HA HA HA HA
BUT, LADIES AND GENTLEMEN, THIS INVENTION BEFORE ME IS NOT ONE OF THOSE THINGS. IF USED AS INTENDED, AND NOT AS SOME LESS SCRUPULOUS AMONG US HAVE USED IT, ALTERNATING POWER IS COMPLETELY SAFE.
I SHALL DEMONSTRATE THIS SIMPLE FACT NOW.

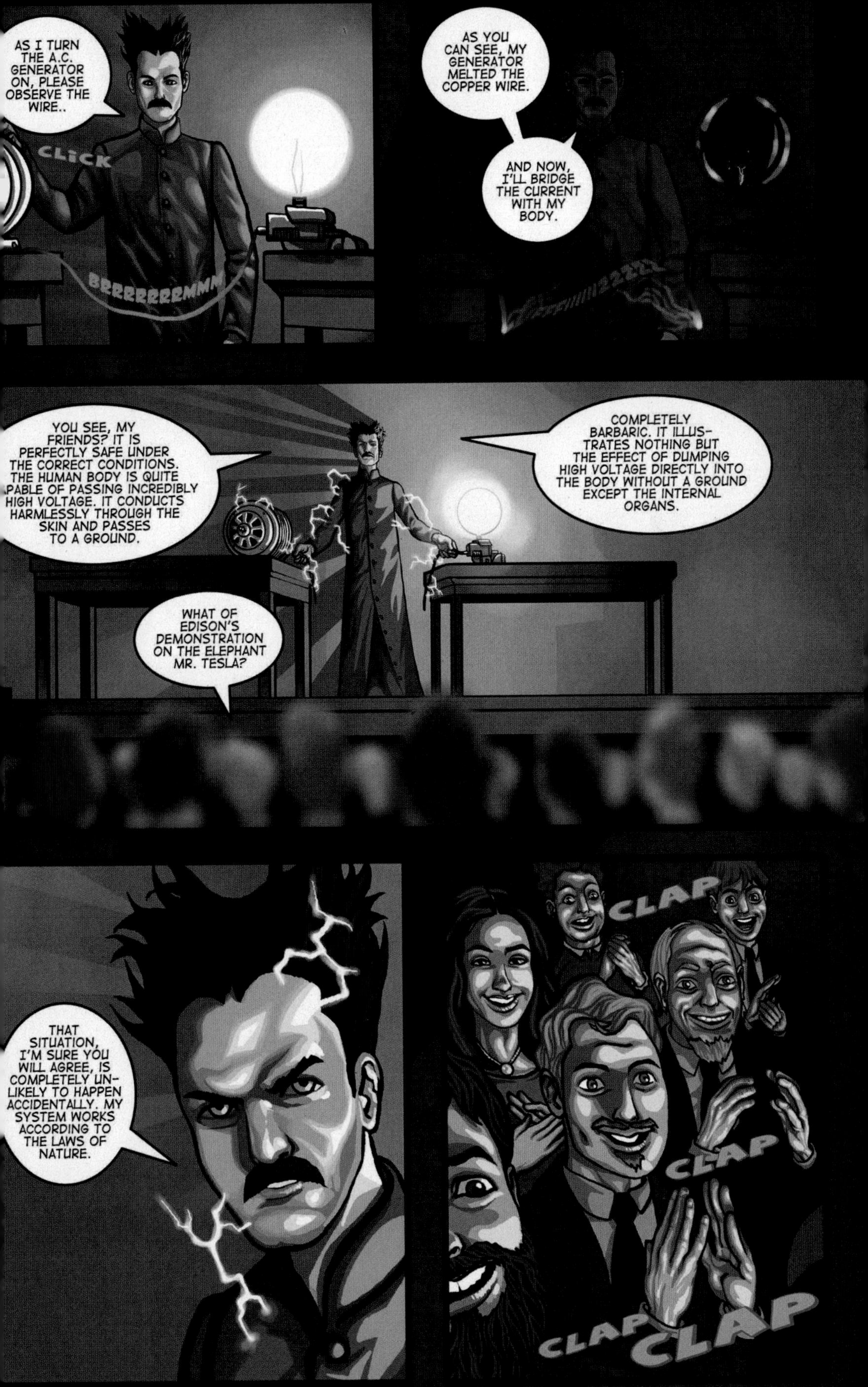
AS I TURN THE A.C. GENERATOR ON, PLEASE OBSERVE THE WIRE..
CLICK
AS YOU CAN SEE, MY GENERATOR MELTED THE COPPER WIRE.
AND NOW, I'LL BRIDGE THE CURRENT WITH MY BODY.
YOU SEE, MY FRIENDS? IT IS PERFECTLY SAFE UNDER THE CORRECT CONDITIONS. THE HUMAN BODY IS QUITE APABLE OF PASSING INCREDIBLY HIGH VOLTAGE. IT CONDUCTS HARMLESSLY THROUGH THE SKIN AND PASSES TO A GROUND.
WHAT OF EDISON'S DEMONSTRATION ON THE ELEPHANT MR. TESLA?
COMPLETELY BARBARIC. IT ILLUSTRATES NOTHING BUT THE EFFECT OF DUMPING HIGH VOLTAGE DIRECTLY INTO THE BODY WITHOUT A GROUND EXCEPT THE INTERNAL ORGANS.
THAT SITUATION, I'M SURE YOU WILL AGREE, IS COMPLETELY UNLIKELY TO HAPPEN ACCIDENTALLY. MY SYSTEM WORKS ACCORDING TO THE LAWS OF NATURE.
CLAP
CLAP
CLAP
CLAP

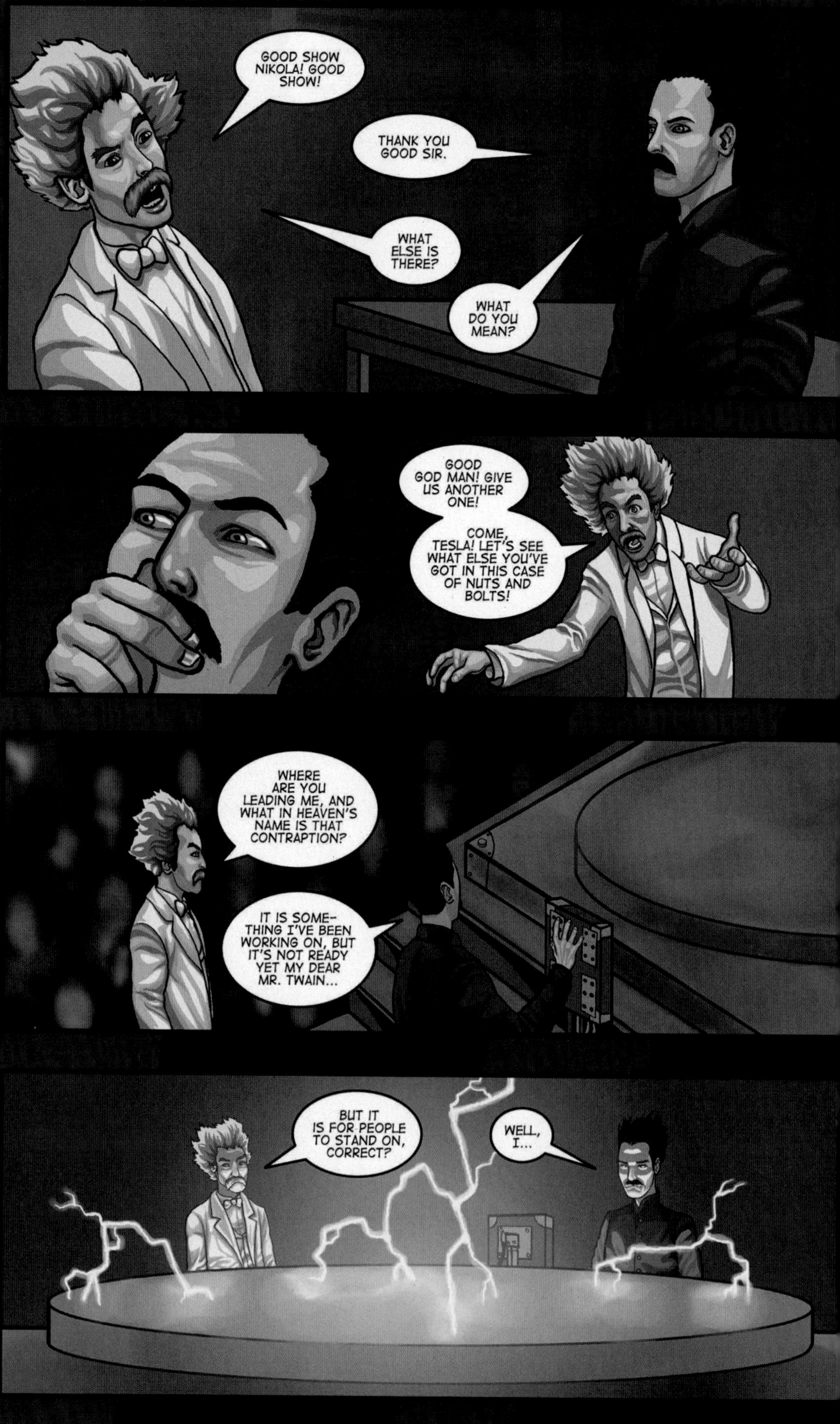
GOOD SHOW NIKOLA! GOOD SHOW!
THANK YOU GOOD SIR.
WHAT ELSE IS THERE?
WHAT DO YOU MEAN?
GOOD GOD MAN! GIVE US ANOTHER ONE!
COME, TESLA! LET'S SEE WHAT ELSE YOU'VE GOT IN THIS CASE OF NUTS AND BOLTS!
WHERE ARE YOU LEADING ME, AND WHAT IN HEAVEN'S NAME IS THAT CONTRAPTION?
IT IS SOME-THING I'VE BEEN WORKING ON, BUT IT'S NOT READY YET MY DEAR MR. TWAIN...
BUT IT IS FOR PEOPLE TO STAND ON, CORRECT?
WELL, I...

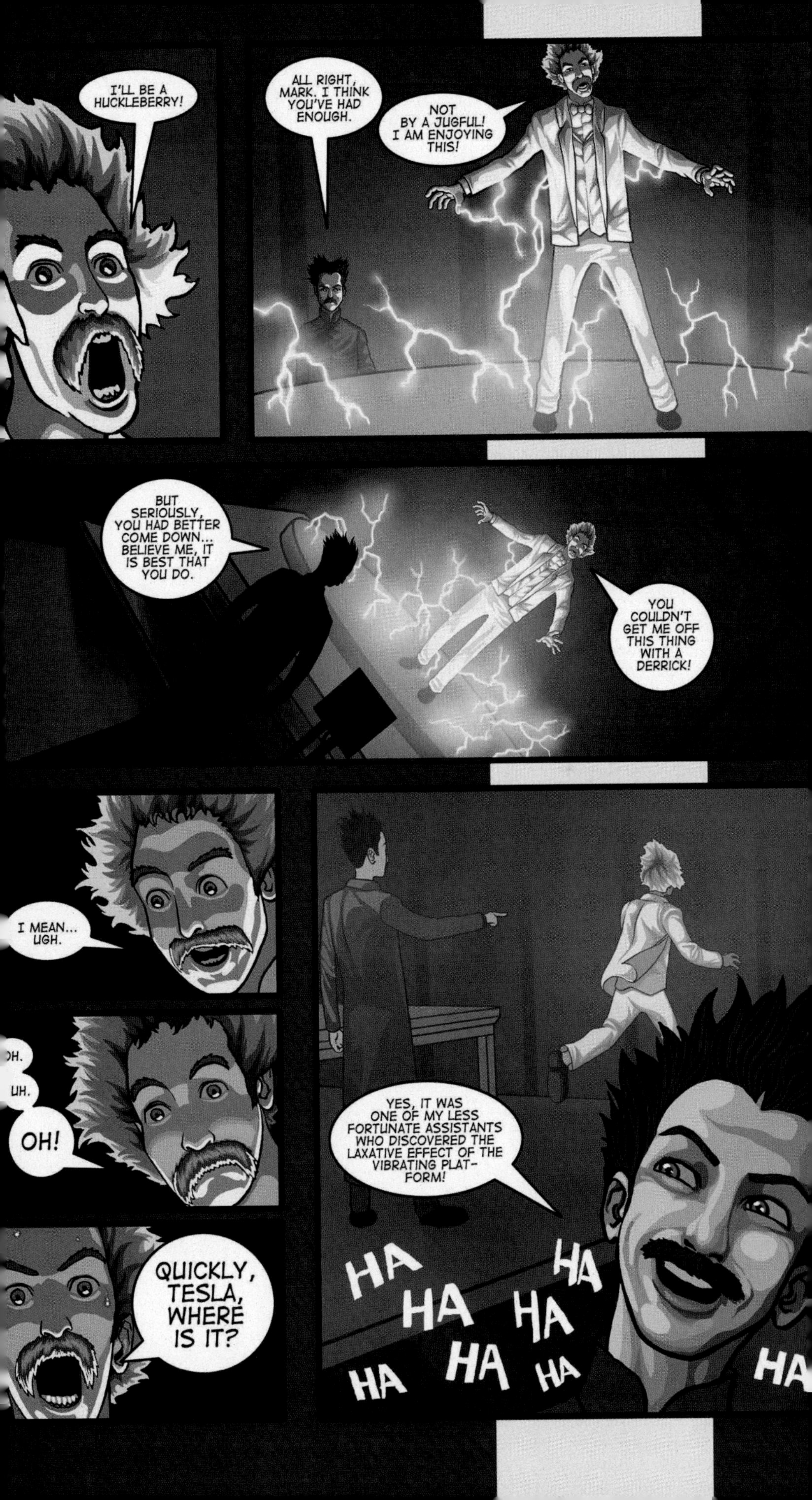
I'LL BE A HUCKLEBERRY!
ALL RIGHT, MARK. I THINK YOU'VE HAD ENOUGH.
NOT BY A JUGFUL! I AM ENJOYING THIS!
BUT SERIOUSLY, YOU HAD BETTER COME DOWN... BELIEVE ME, IT IS BEST THAT YOU DO.
YOU COULDN'T GET ME OFF THIS THING WITH A DERRICK!
I MEAN... UGH.
OH.
UH.
OH!
QUICKLY, TESLA, WHERE IS IT?
YES, IT WAS ONE OF MY LESS FORTUNATE ASSISTANTS WHO DISCOVERED THE LAXATIVE EFFECT OF THE VIBRATING PLAT-FORM!
HA HA HA HA HA HA HA HA

"THE DAY WHEN WE SHALL KNOW EXACTLY WHAT "ELECTRICITY" IS, WILL CHRONICLE AN EVENT PROBABLY GREATER, MORE IMPORTANT THAN ANY OTHER RECORDED IN THE HISTORY OF THE HUMAN RACE. THE TIME WILL COME WHEN THE COMFORT, THE VERY EXISTENCE, PER-HAPS, OF MAN WILL DEPEND UPON THAT WONDERFUL AGENT."

- NIKOLA TESLA (1856-1943)

Chapter 4
POWER SWITCH

THE STAKES ARE RISING AND THE WAR BETWEEN THE WIZARD AND THE INVENTOR WAGES ON. WHEN ALL SEEMS LOST, TESLA CASTS HIS FINAL SPELL AND TURNS NIGHT INTO DAY AND REVEALS THE SCIENCE BEHIND HIS MAGIC. AS THE WORLD CATCHES A GLIMPSE OF THE FUTURE, EDISON'S KINGDOM BEGINS TO CRUMBLE AROUND HIM AND TESLA SEIZES HIS DESTINY SO HE MAY FULFILL HIS CHILDHOOD FANTASY - THE SPINNING WATER WHEEL.

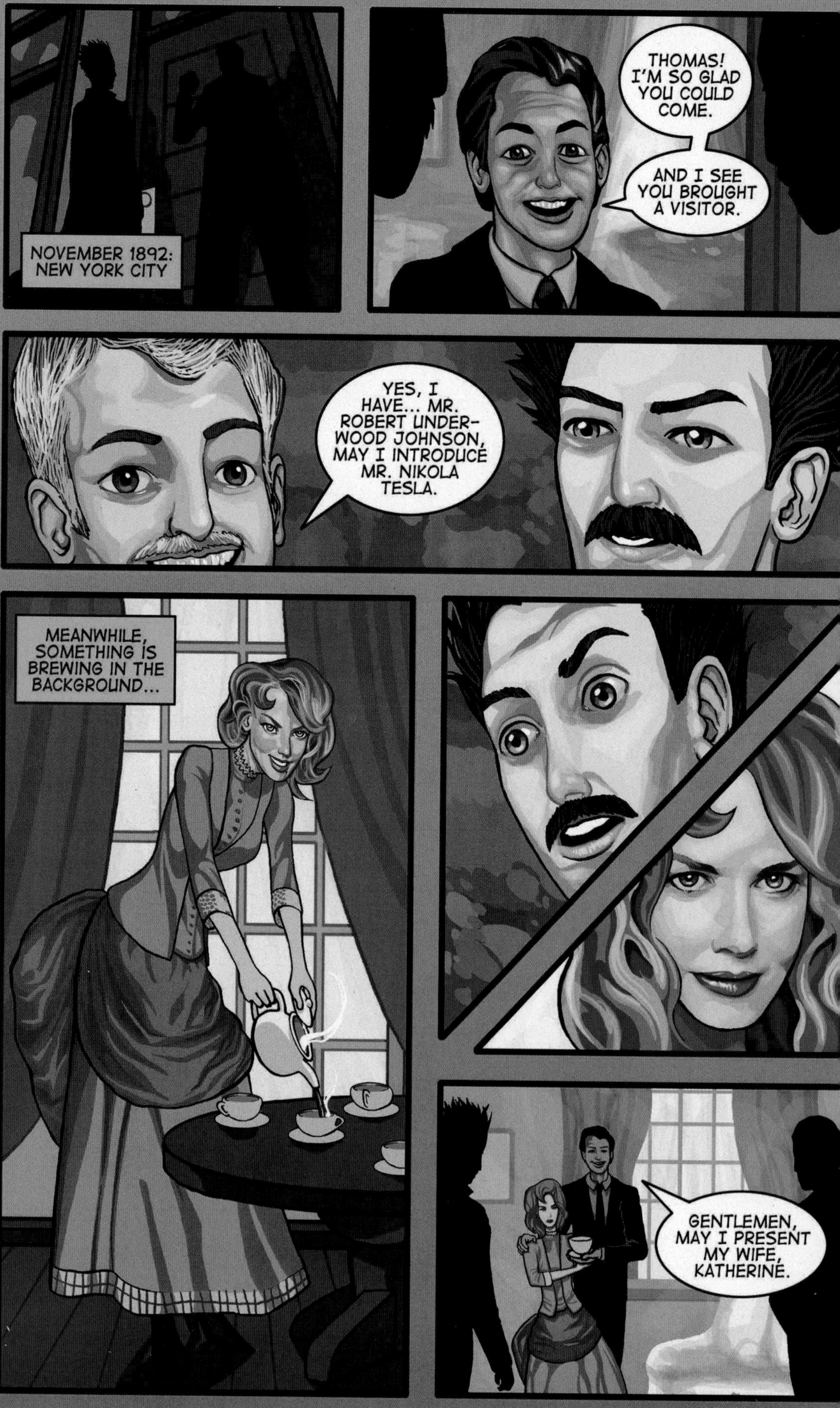
NOVEMBER 1892: NEW YORK CITY
THOMAS! I'M SO GLAD YOU COULD COME.
AND I SEE YOU BROUGHT A VISITOR.
YES, I HAVE... MR. ROBERT UNDER-WOOD JOHNSON, MAY I INTRODUCE MR. NIKOLA TESLA.
MEANWHILE, SOMETHING IS BREWING IN THE BACKGROUND...
GENTLEMEN, MAY I PRESENT MY WIFE, KATHERINE.

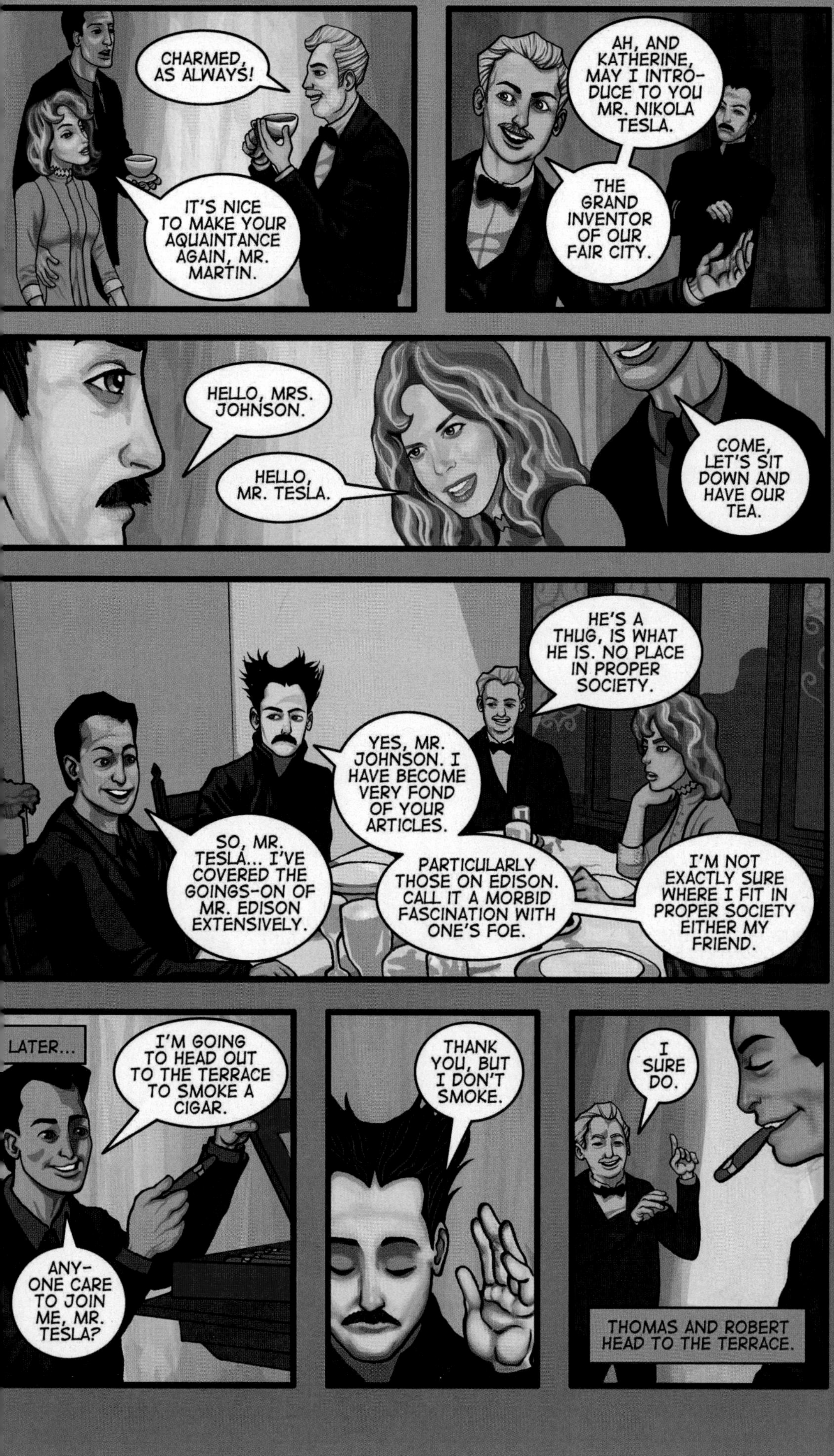
CHARMED, AS ALWAYS!
IT'S NICE TO MAKE YOUR AQUAINTANCE AGAIN, MR. MARTIN.
AH, AND KATHERINE, MAY I INTRO-DUCE TO YOU MR. NIKOLA TESLA.
THE GRAND INVENTOR OF OUR FAIR CITY.
HELLO, MRS. JOHNSON.
HELLO, MR. TESLA.
COME, LET'S SIT DOWN AND HAVE OUR TEA.
SO, MR. TESLA... I'VE COVERED THE GOINGS-ON OF MR. EDISON EXTENSIVELY.
YES, MR. JOHNSON. I HAVE BECOME VERY FOND OF YOUR ARTICLES.
PARTICULARLY THOSE ON EDISON. CALL IT A MORBID FASCINATION WITH ONE'S FOE.
HE'S A THUG, IS WHAT HE IS. NO PLACE IN PROPER SOCIETY.
I'M NOT EXACTLY SURE WHERE I FIT IN PROPER SOCIETY EITHER MY FRIEND.
LATER...
I'M GOING TO HEAD OUT TO THE TERRACE TO SMOKE A CIGAR.
ANY-ONE CARE TO JOIN ME, MR. TESLA?
THANK YOU, BUT I DON'T SMOKE.
I SURE DO.
THOMAS AND ROBERT HEAD TO THE TERRACE.

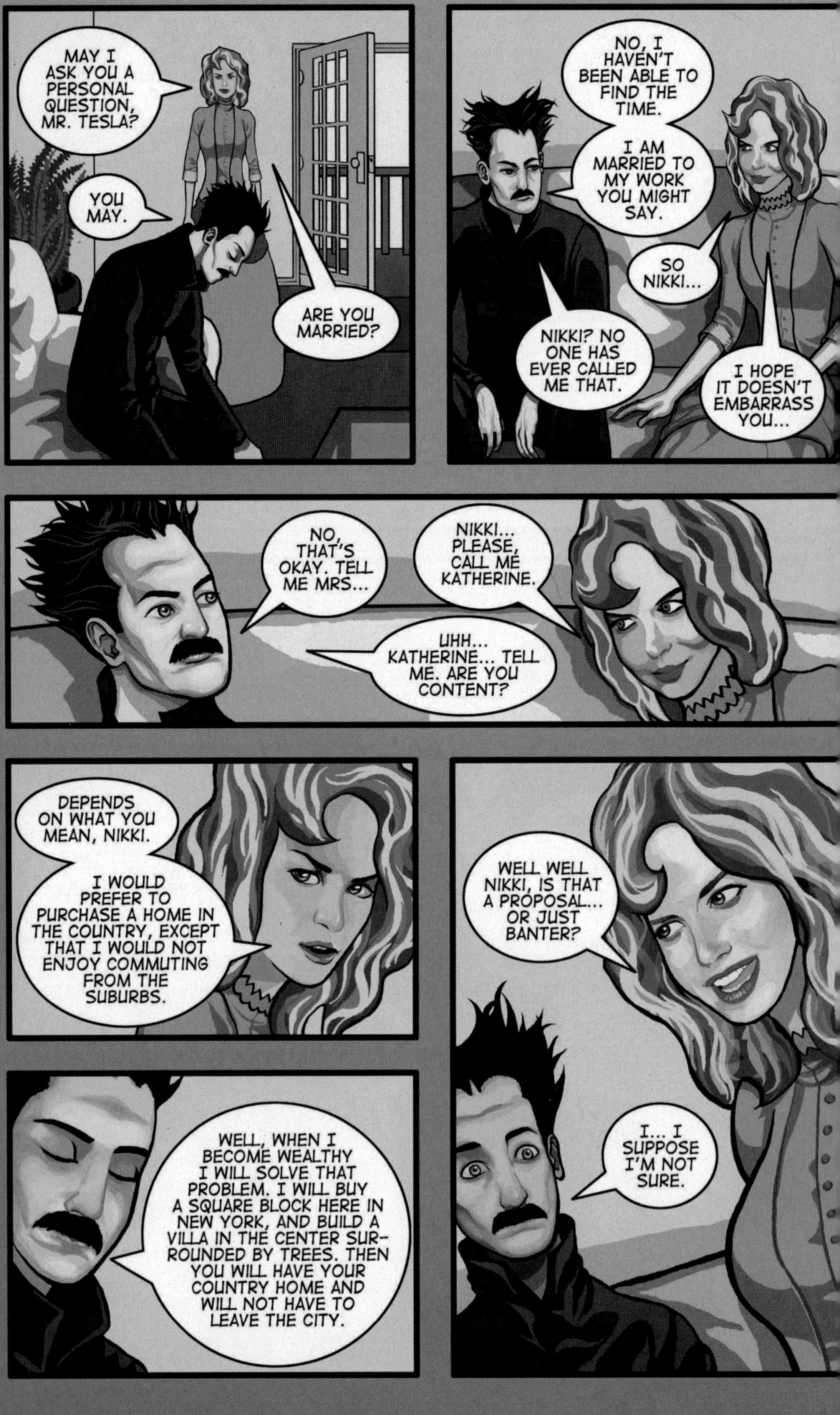
MAY I ASK YOU A PERSONAL QUESTION, MR. TESLA?
YOU MAY.
ARE YOU MARRIED?
NO, I HAVEN'T BEEN ABLE TO FIND THE TIME.
I AM MARRIED TO MY WORK YOU MIGHT SAY.
SO NIKKI...
NIKKI? NO ONE HAS EVER CALLED ME THAT.
I HOPE IT DOESN'T EMBARRASS YOU...
NO, THAT'S OKAY. TELL ME MRS...
NIKKI... PLEASE, CALL ME KATHERINE.
UHH... KATHERINE... TELL ME. ARE YOU CONTENT?
DEPENDS ON WHAT YOU MEAN, NIKKI.
I WOULD PREFER TO PURCHASE A HOME IN THE COUNTRY, EXCEPT THAT I WOULD NOT ENJOY COMMUTING FROM THE SUBURBS.
WELL, WHEN I BECOME WEALTHY I WILL SOLVE THAT PROBLEM. I WILL BUY A SQUARE BLOCK HERE IN NEW YORK, AND BUILD A VILLA IN THE CENTER SURROUNDED BY TREES. THEN YOU WILL HAVE YOUR COUNTRY HOME AND WILL NOT HAVE TO LEAVE THE CITY.
WELL WELL NIKKI, IS THAT A PROPOSAL... OR JUST BANTER?
I... I SUPPOSE I'M NOT SURE.

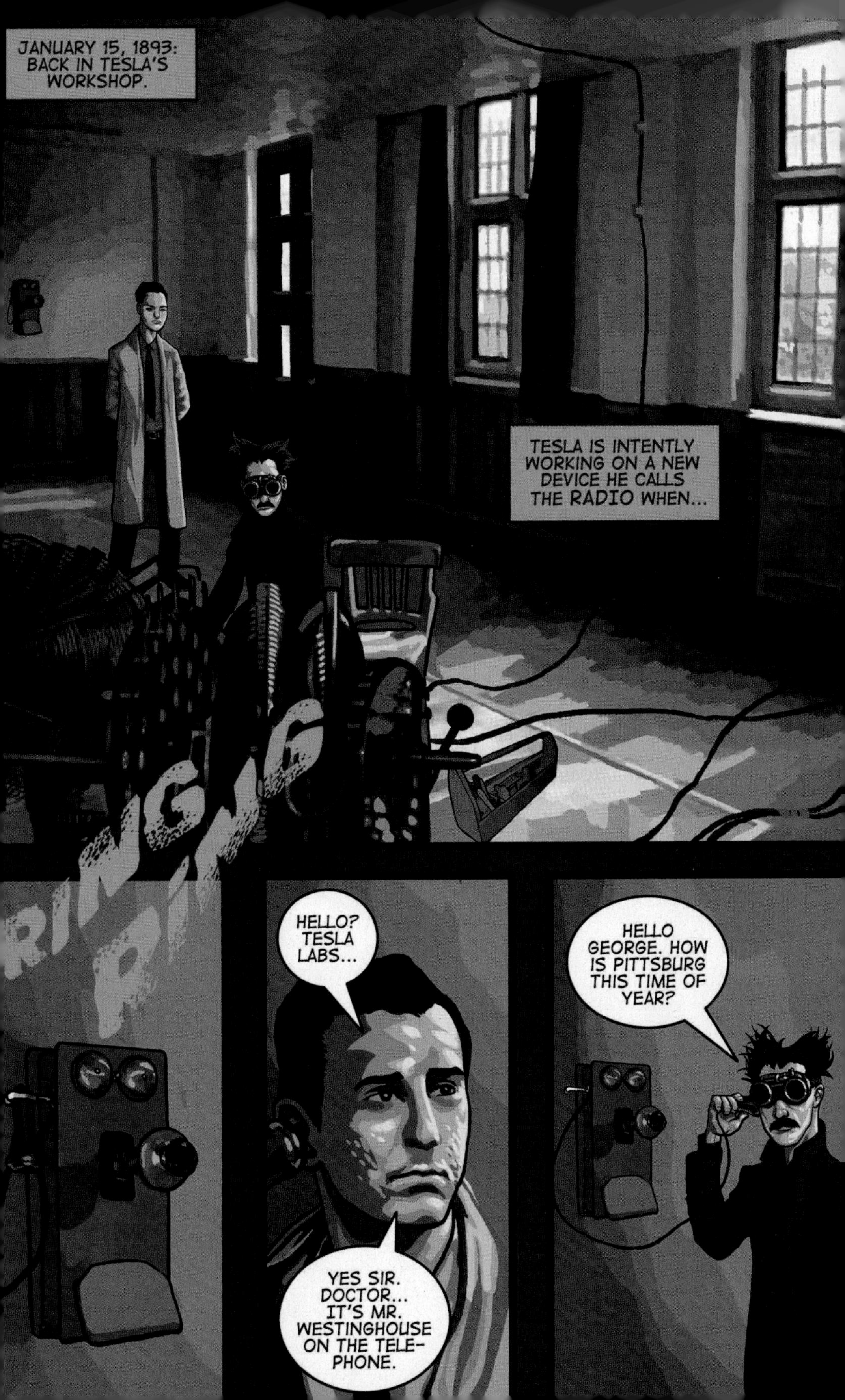
JANUARY 15, 1893: BACK IN TESLA'S WORKSHOP.
TESLA IS INTENTLY WORKING ON A NEW DEVICE HE CALLS THE RADIO WHEN...
RING RING
HELLO? TESLA LABS...
YES SIR. DOCTOR... IT'S MR. WESTINGHOUSE ON THE TELE-PHONE.
HELLO GEORGE. HOW IS PITTSBURG THIS TIME OF YEAR?

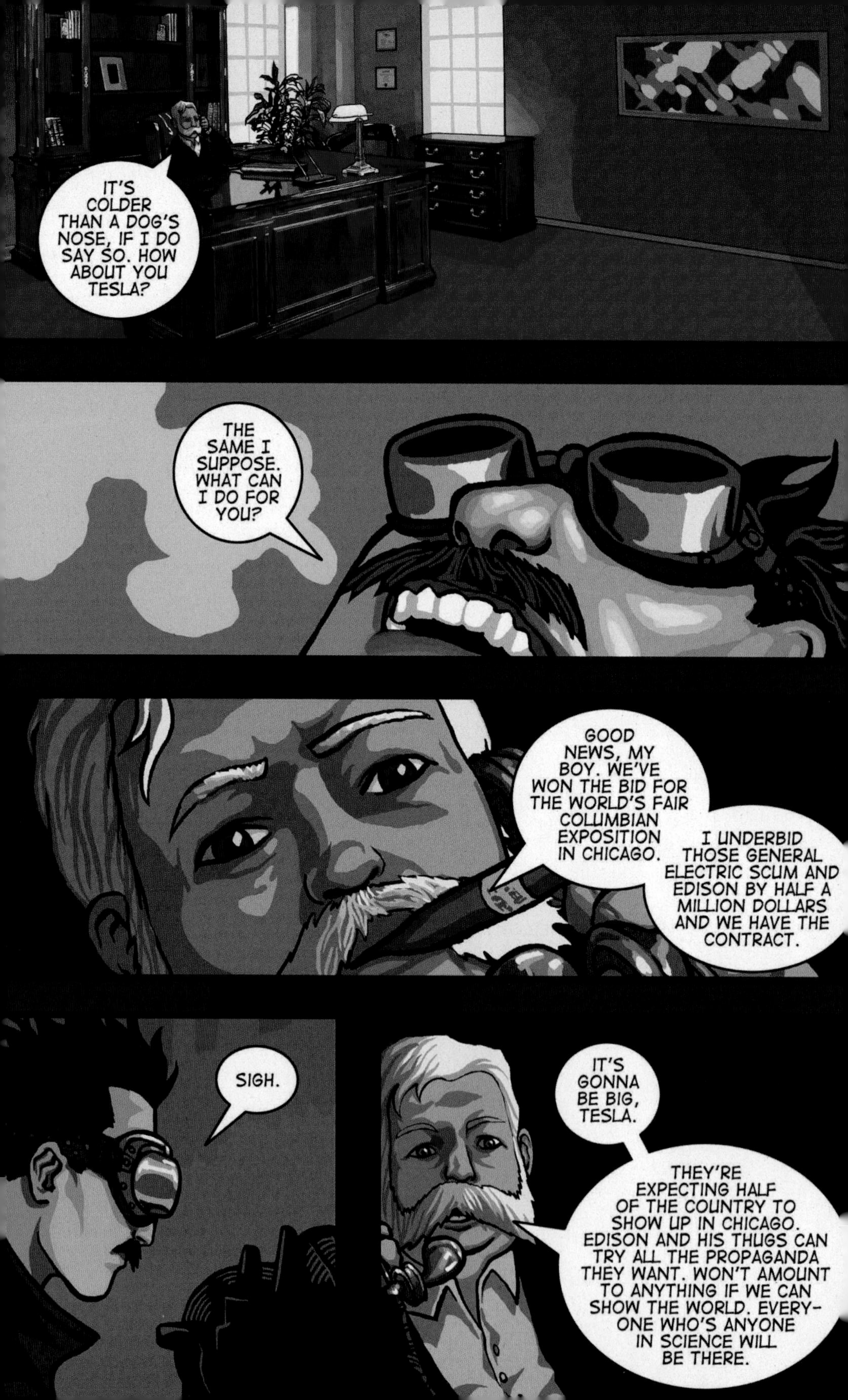
IT'S COLDER THAN A DOG'S NOSE, IF I DO SAY SO. HOW ABOUT YOU TESLA?
THE SAME I SUPPOSE. WHAT CAN I DO FOR YOU?
GOOD NEWS, MY BOY. WE'VE WON THE BID FOR THE WORLD'S FAIR COLUMBIAN EXPOSITION IN CHICAGO.
I UNDERBID THOSE GENERAL ELECTRIC SCUM AND EDISON BY HALF A MILLION DOLLARS AND WE HAVE THE CONTRACT.
SIGH.
IT'S GONNA BE BIG, TESLA.
THEY'RE EXPECTING HALF OF THE COUNTRY TO SHOW UP IN CHICAGO. EDISON AND HIS THUGS CAN TRY ALL THE PROPAGANDA THEY WANT. WON'T AMOUNT TO ANYTHING IF WE CAN SHOW THE WORLD. EVERY-ONE WHO'S ANYONE IN SCIENCE WILL BE THERE.

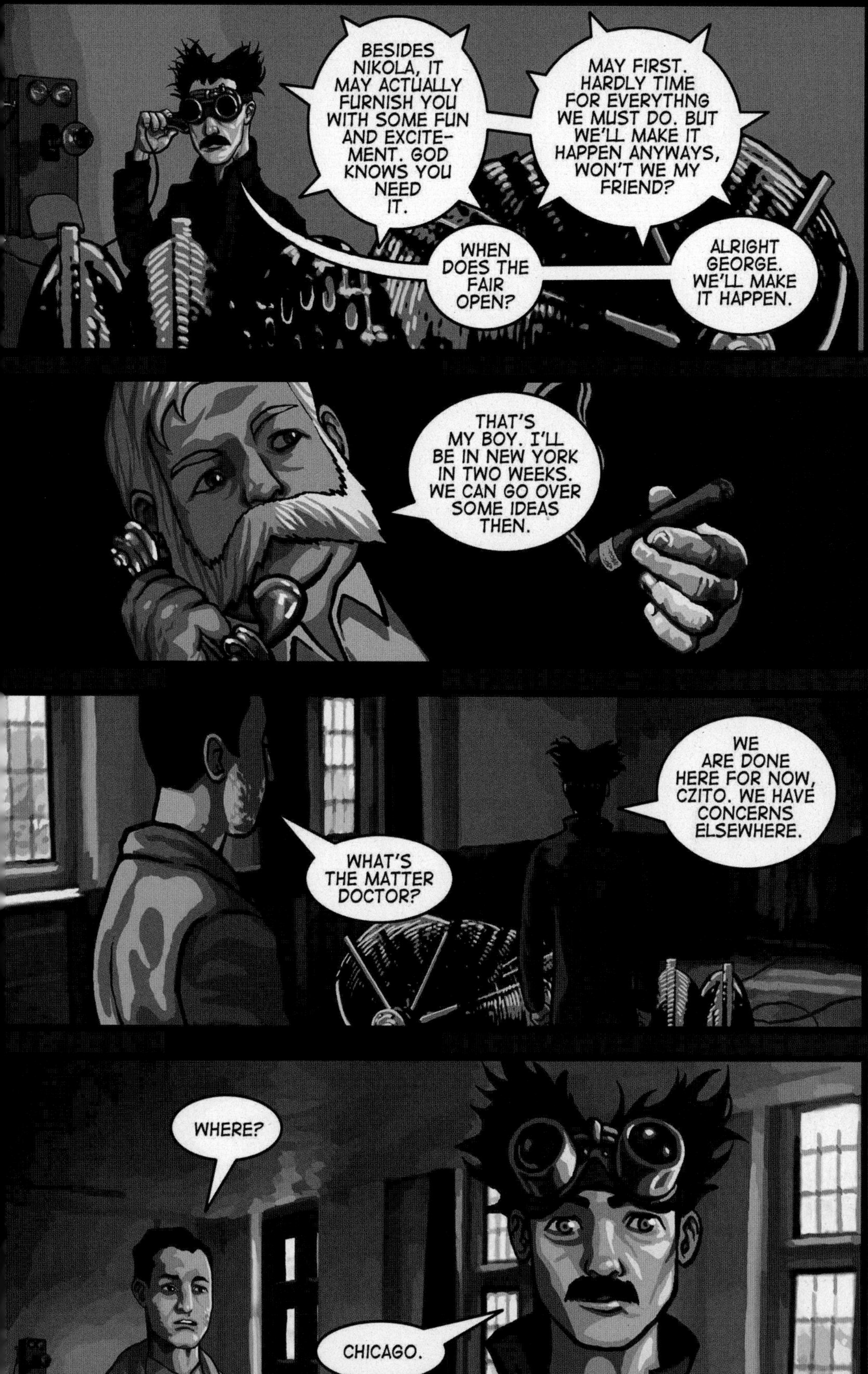

BESIDES NIKOLA, IT MAY ACTUALLY FURNISH YOU WITH SOME FUN AND EXCITE-MENT. GOD KNOWS YOU NEED IT.
WHEN DOES THE FAIR OPEN?
MAY FIRST. HARDLY TIME FOR EVERYTHNG WE MUST DO. BUT WE'LL MAKE IT HAPPEN ANYWAYS, WON'T WE MY FRIEND?
ALRIGHT GEORGE. WE'LL MAKE IT HAPPEN.
THAT'S MY BOY. I'LL BE IN NEW YORK IN TWO WEEKS. WE CAN GO OVER SOME IDEAS THEN.
WE ARE DONE HERE FOR NOW, CZITO. WE HAVE CONCERNS ELSEWHERE.
WHAT'S THE MATTER DOCTOR?
WHERE?
CHICAGO.

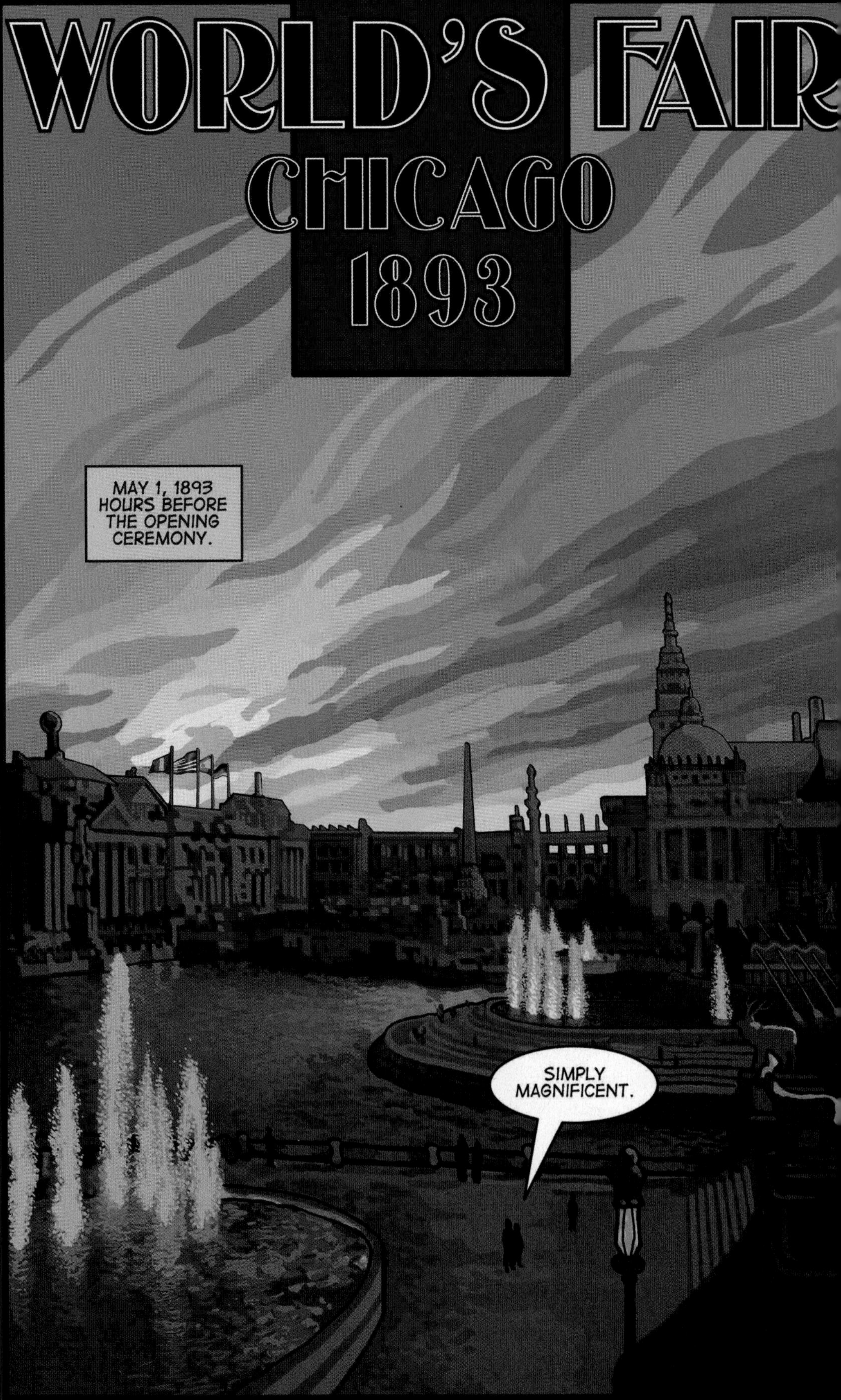
WORLD'S FAIR
CHICAGO
1893
MAY 1, 1893
HOURS BEFORE
THE OPENING
CEREMONY.
SIMPLY
MAGNIFICENT.

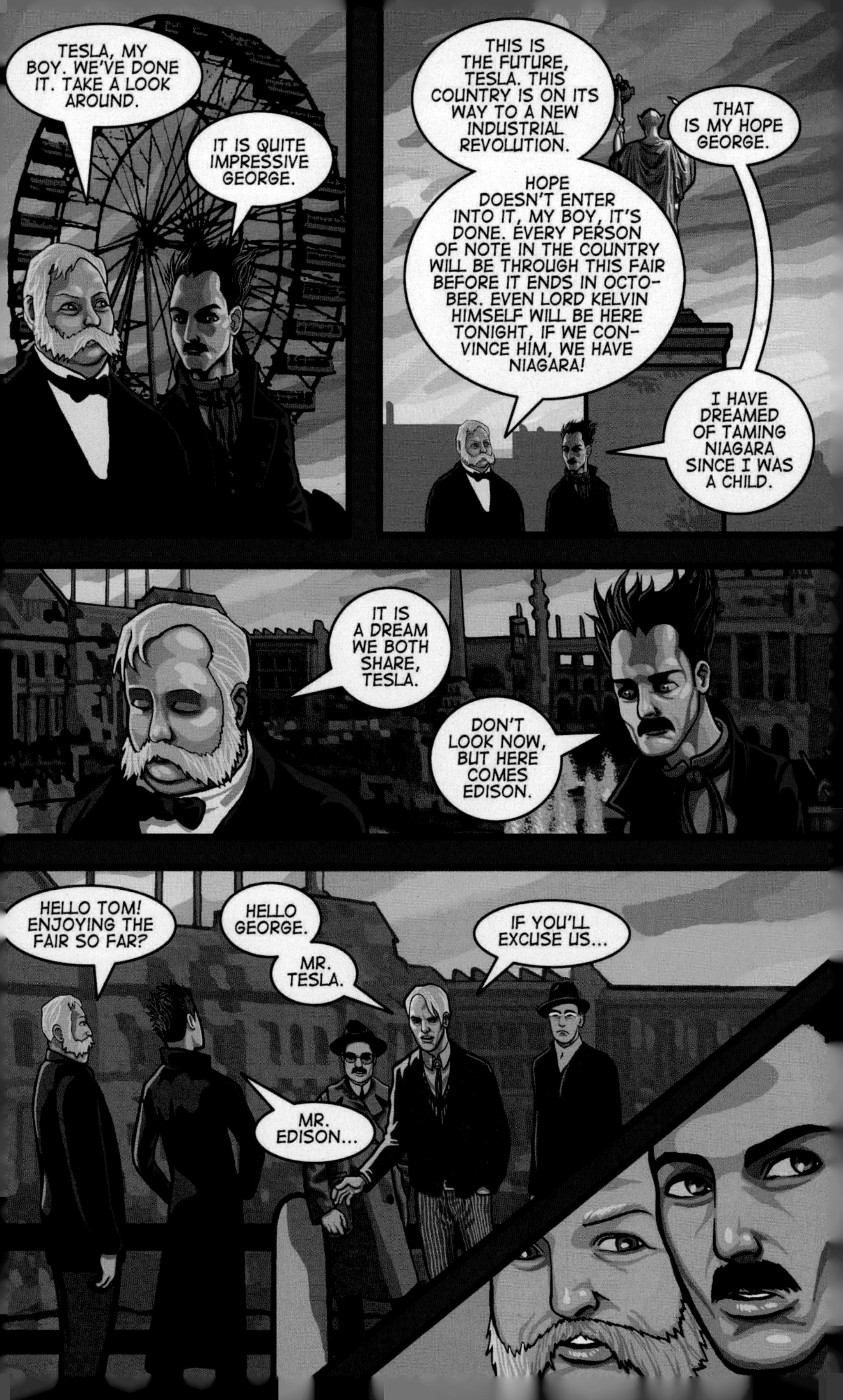
TESLA, MY BOY. WE'VE DONE IT. TAKE A LOOK AROUND.
IT IS QUITE IMPRESSIVE GEORGE.
THIS IS THE FUTURE, TESLA. THIS COUNTRY IS ON ITS WAY TO A NEW INDUSTRIAL REVOLUTION.
THAT IS MY HOPE GEORGE.
HOPE DOESN'T ENTER INTO IT, MY BOY, IT'S DONE. EVERY PERSON OF NOTE IN THE COUNTRY WILL BE THROUGH THIS FAIR BEFORE IT ENDS IN OCTO-BER. EVEN LORD KELVIN HIMSELF WILL BE HERE TONIGHT, IF WE CON-VINCE HIM, WE HAVE NIAGARA!
I HAVE DREAMED OF TAMING NIAGARA SINCE I WAS A CHILD.
IT IS A DREAM WE BOTH SHARE, TESLA.
DON'T LOOK NOW, BUT HERE COMES EDISON.
HELLO TOM! ENJOYING THE FAIR SO FAR?
HELLO GEORGE.
MR. TESLA.
MR. EDISON...
IF YOU'LL EXCUSE US...

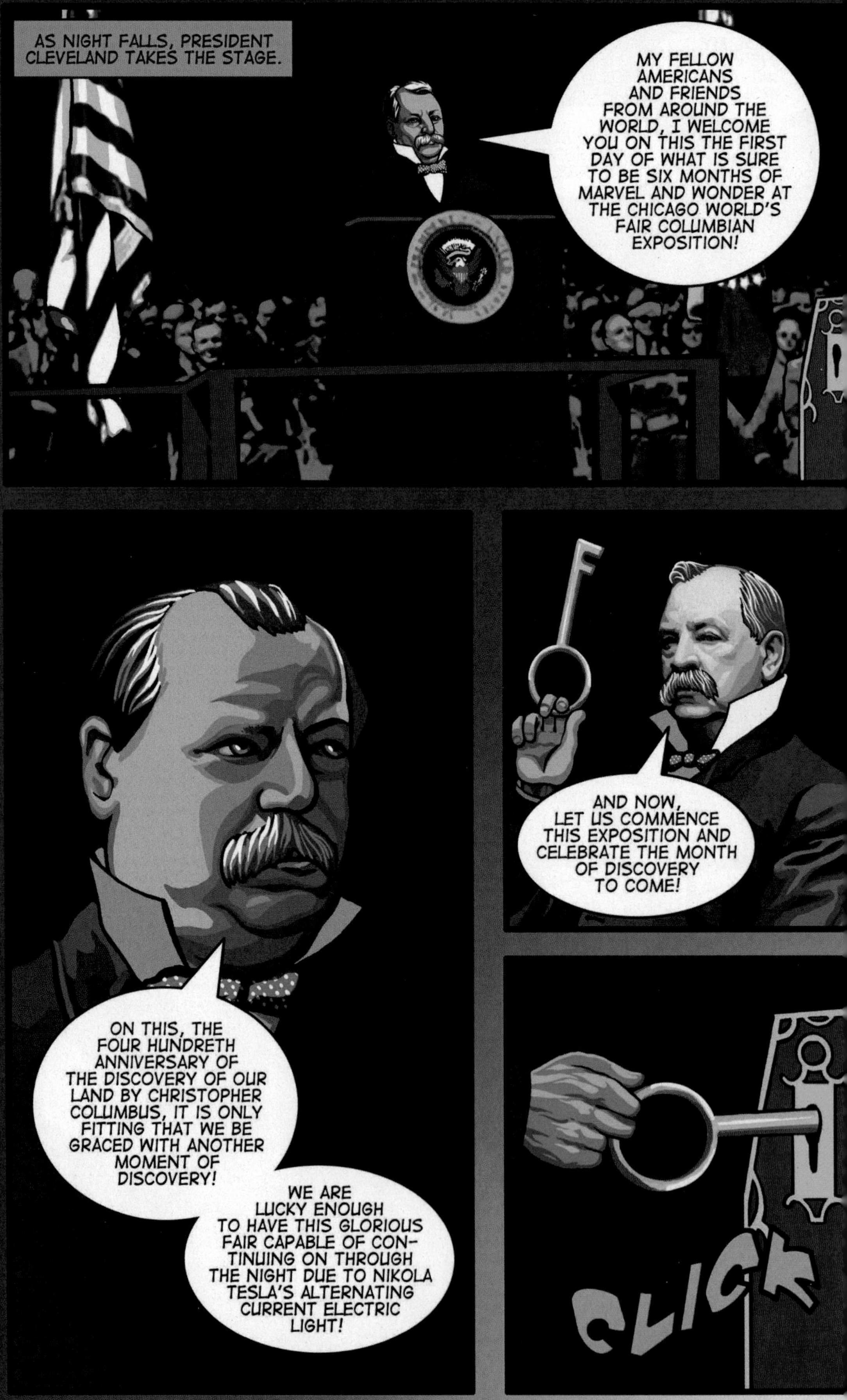
AS NIGHT FALLS, PRESIDENT CLEVELAND TAKES THE STAGE.
MY FELLOW AMERICANS AND FRIENDS FROM AROUND THE WORLD, I WELCOME YOU ON THIS THE FIRST DAY OF WHAT IS SURE TO BE SIX MONTHS OF MARVEL AND WONDER AT THE CHICAGO WORLD'S FAIR COLUMBIAN EXPOSITION!
ON THIS, THE FOUR HUNDRETH ANNIVERSARY OF THE DISCOVERY OF OUR LAND BY CHRISTOPHER COLUMBUS, IT IS ONLY FITTING THAT WE BE GRACED WITH ANOTHER MOMENT OF DISCOVERY!
WE ARE LUCKY ENOUGH TO HAVE THIS GLORIOUS FAIR CAPABLE OF CON-TINUING ON THROUGH THE NIGHT DUE TO NIKOLA TESLA'S ALTERNATING CURRENT ELECTRIC LIGHT!
AND NOW, LET US COMMENCE THIS EXPOSITION AND CELEBRATE THE MONTH OF DISCOVERY TO COME!
CLICK

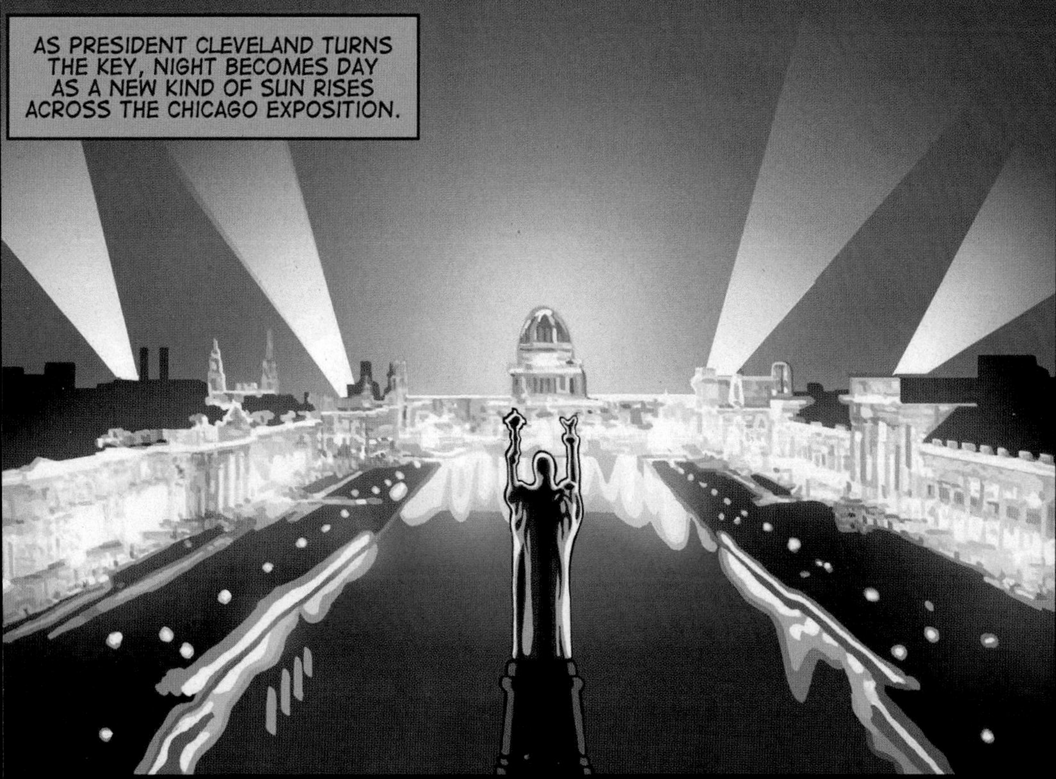
AS PRESIDENT CLEVELAND TURNS THE KEY, NIGHT BECOMES DAY AS A NEW KIND OF SUN RISES ACROSS THE CHICAGO EXPOSITION.

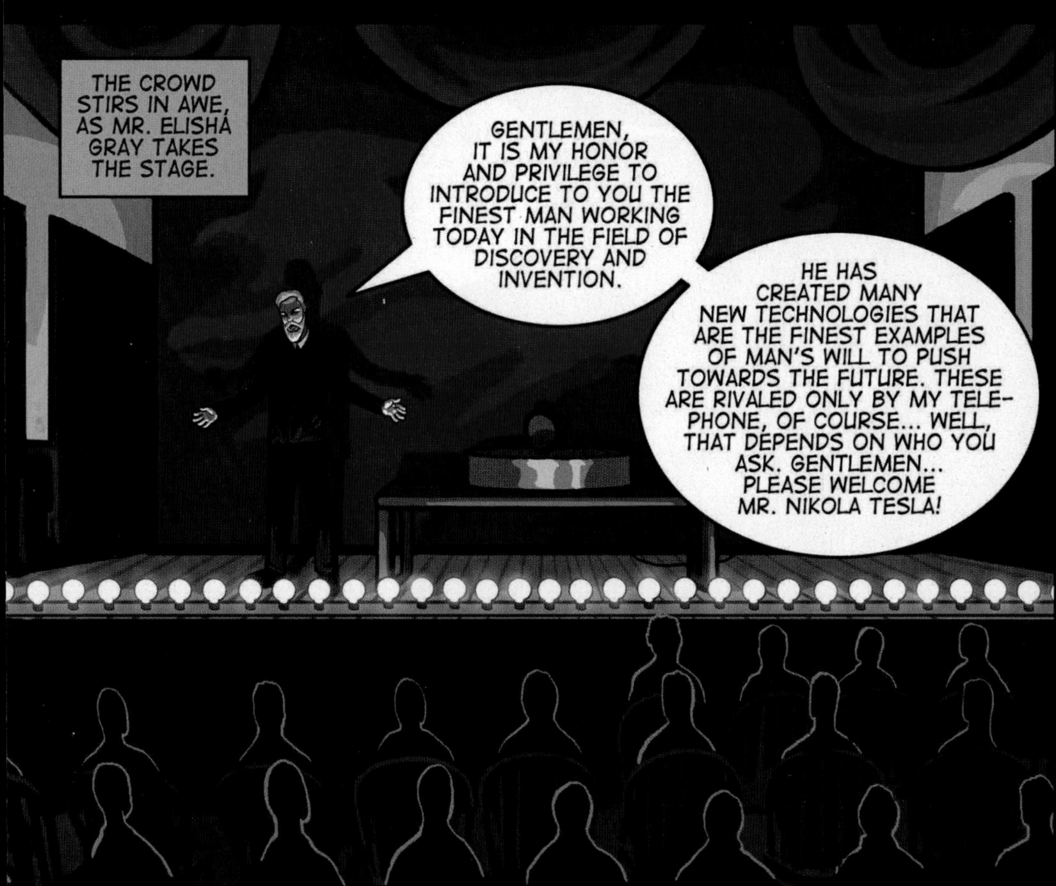
THE CROWD STIRS IN AWE, AS MR. ELISHA GRAY TAKES THE STAGE.
GENTLEMEN, IT IS MY HONOR AND PRIVILEGE TO INTRODUCE TO YOU THE FINEST MAN WORKING TODAY IN THE FIELD OF DISCOVERY AND INVENTION.
HE HAS CREATED MANY NEW TECHNOLOGIES THAT ARE THE FINEST EXAMPLES OF MAN'S WILL TO PUSH TOWARDS THE FUTURE. THESE ARE RIVALED ONLY BY MY TELE-PHONE, OF COURSE... WELL, THAT DEPENDS ON WHO YOU ASK. GENTLEMEN... PLEASE WELCOME MR. NIKOLA TESLA!

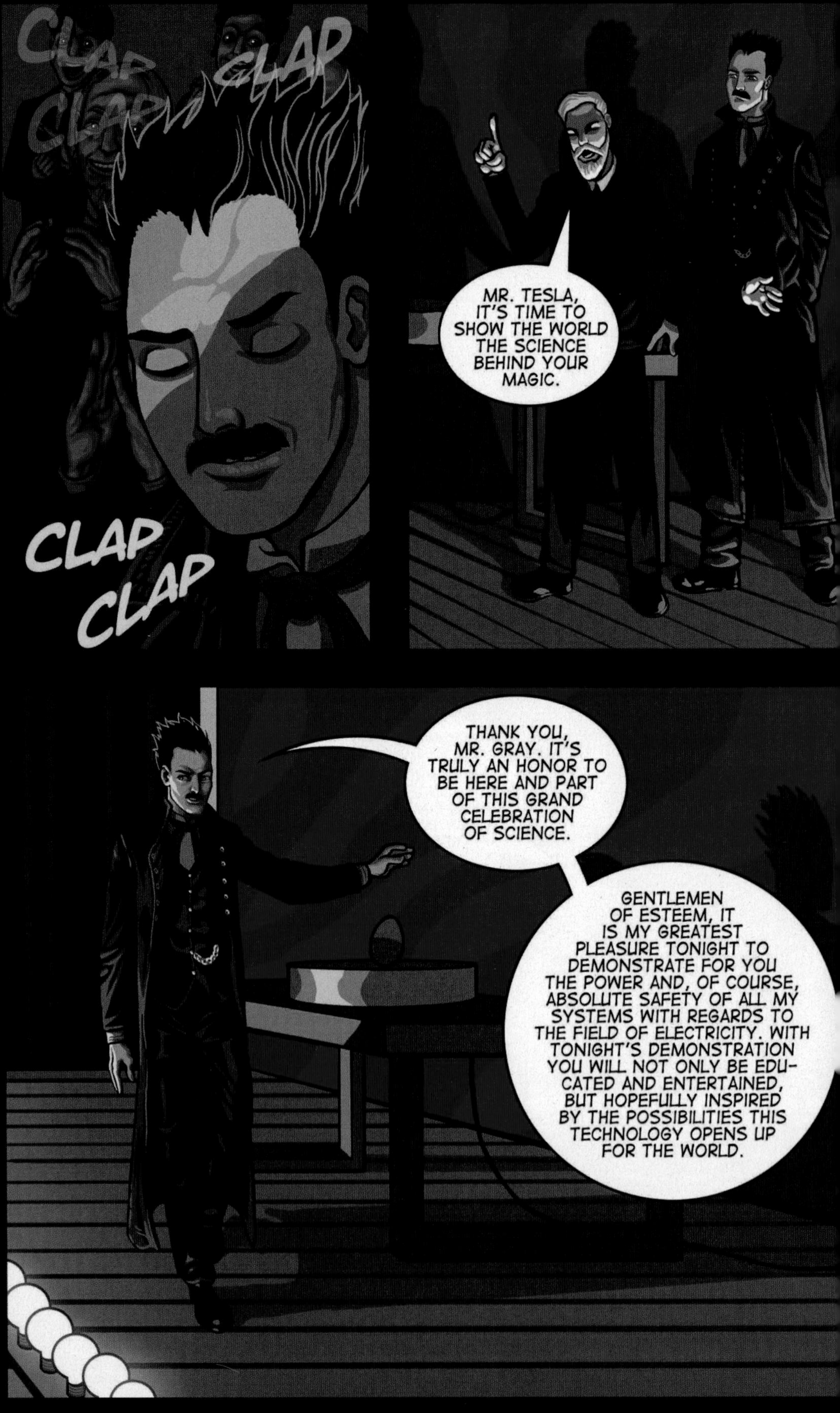
CLAP CLAP CLAP
CLAP CLAP
MR. TESLA, IT'S TIME TO SHOW THE WORLD THE SCIENCE BEHIND YOUR MAGIC.
THANK YOU, MR. GRAY. IT'S TRULY AN HONOR TO BE HERE AND PART OF THIS GRAND CELEBRATION OF SCIENCE.
GENTLEMEN OF ESTEEM, IT IS MY GREATEST PLEASURE TONIGHT TO DEMONSTRATE FOR YOU THE POWER AND, OF COURSE, ABSOLUTE SAFETY OF ALL MY SYSTEMS WITH REGARDS TO THE FIELD OF ELECTRICITY. WITH TONIGHT'S DEMONSTRATION YOU WILL NOT ONLY BE EDU-CATED AND ENTERTAINED, BUT HOPEFULLY INSPIRED BY THE POSSIBILITIES THIS TECHNOLOGY OPENS UP FOR THE WORLD.

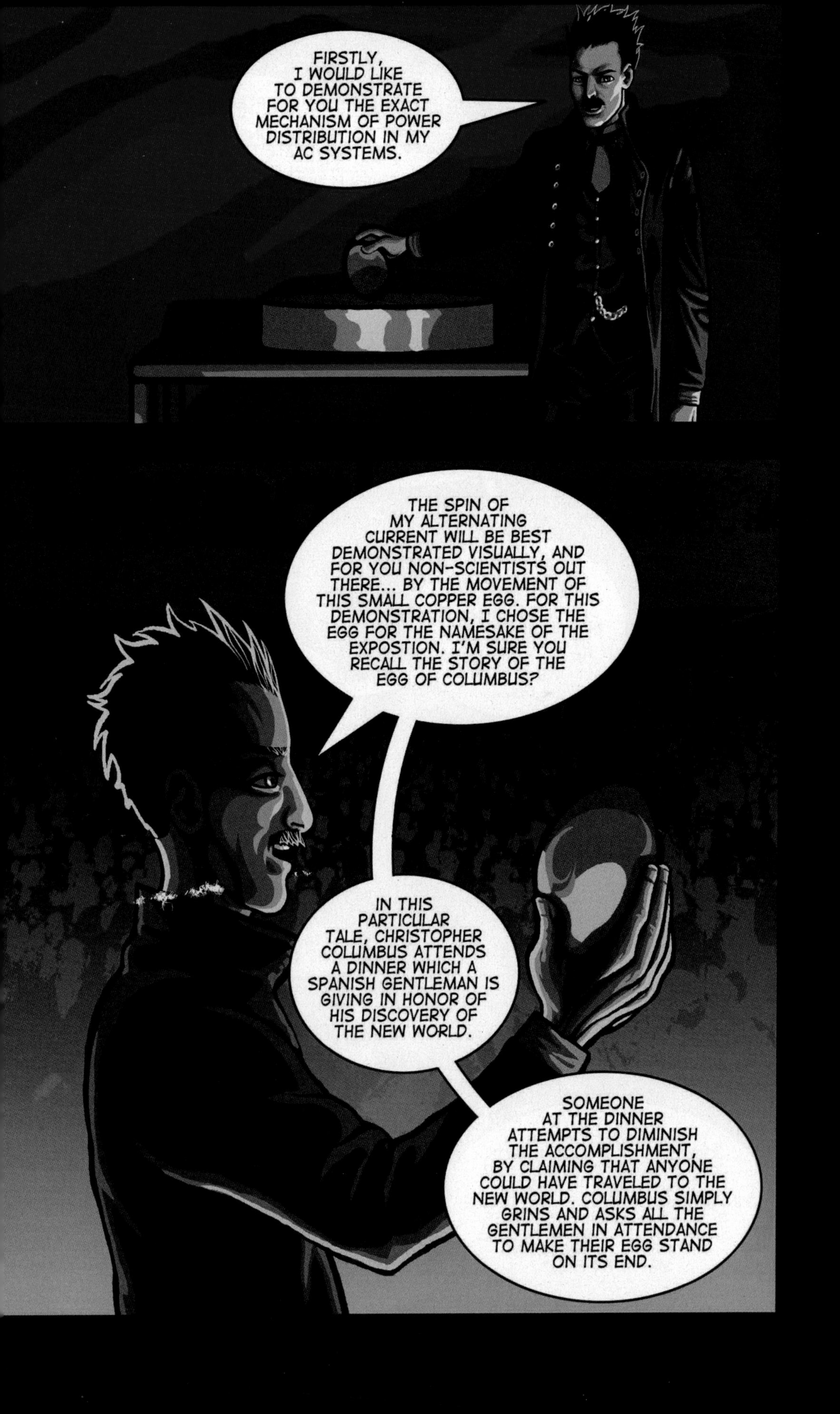
FIRSTLY, I WOULD LIKE TO DEMONSTRATE FOR YOU THE EXACT MECHANISM OF POWER DISTRIBUTION IN MY AC SYSTEMS.
THE SPIN OF MY ALTERNATING CURRENT WILL BE BEST DEMONSTRATED VISUALLY, AND FOR YOU NON-SCIENTISTS OUT THERE... BY THE MOVEMENT OF THIS SMALL COPPER EGG. FOR THIS DEMONSTRATION, I CHOSE THE EGG FOR THE NAMESAKE OF THE EXPOSTION. I'M SURE YOU RECALL THE STORY OF THE EGG OF COLUMBUS?
IN THIS PARTICULAR TALE, CHRISTOPHER COLUMBUS ATTENDS A DINNER WHICH A SPANISH GENTLEMAN IS GIVING IN HONOR OF HIS DISCOVERY OF THE NEW WORLD.
SOMEONE AT THE DINNER ATTEMPTS TO DIMINISH THE ACCOMPLISHMENT, BY CLAIMING THAT ANYONE COULD HAVE TRAVELED TO THE NEW WORLD. COLUMBUS SIMPLY GRINS AND ASKS ALL THE GENTLEMEN IN ATTENDANCE TO MAKE THEIR EGG STAND ON ITS END.

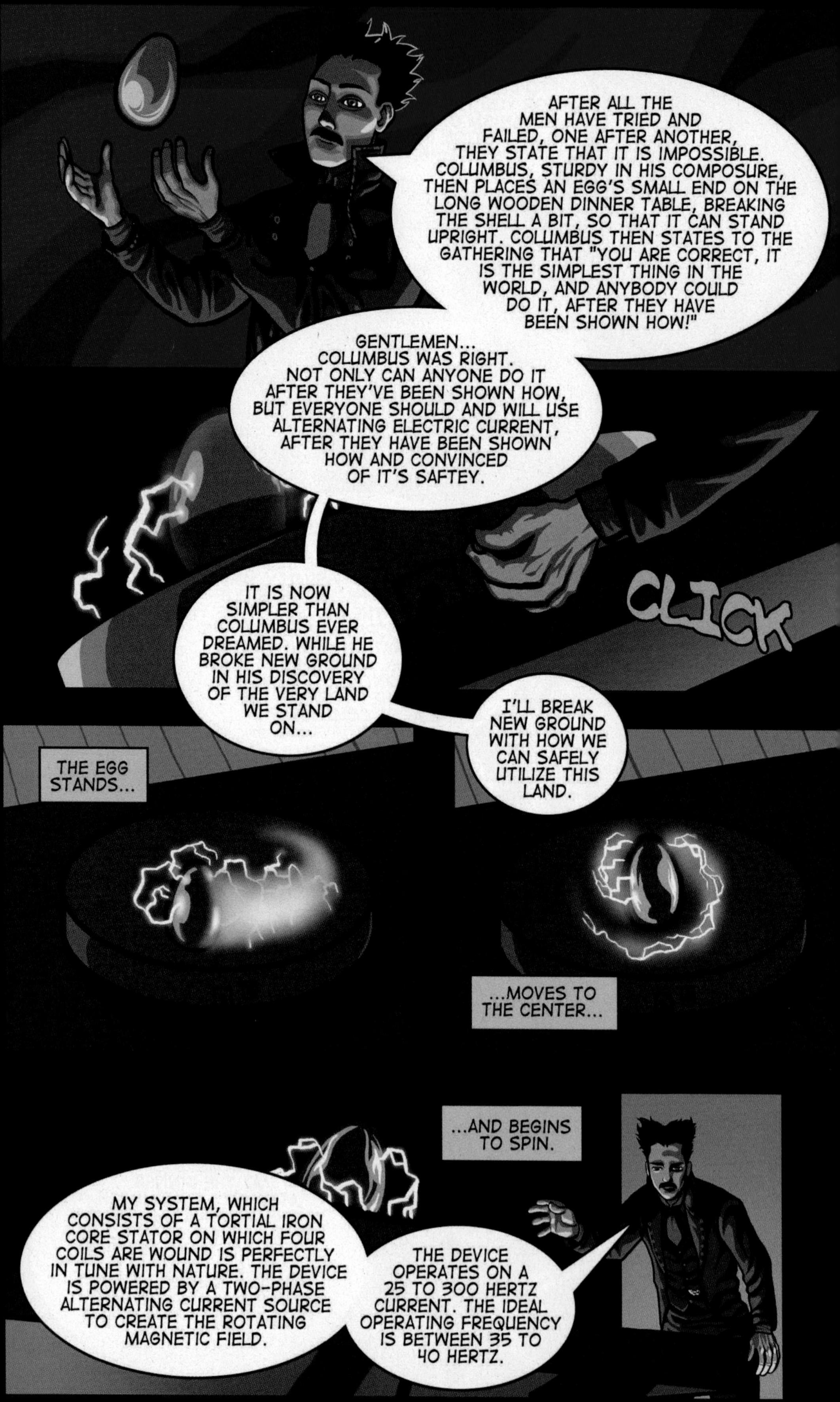
AFTER ALL THE MEN HAVE TRIED AND FAILED, ONE AFTER ANOTHER, THEY STATE THAT IT IS IMPOSSIBLE. COLUMBUS, STURDY IN HIS COMPOSURE, THEN PLACES AN EGG'S SMALL END ON THE LONG WOODEN DINNER TABLE, BREAKING THE SHELL A BIT, SO THAT IT CAN STAND UPRIGHT. COLUMBUS THEN STATES TO THE GATHERING THAT "YOU ARE CORRECT, IT IS THE SIMPLEST THING IN THE WORLD, AND ANYBODY COULD DO IT, AFTER THEY HAVE BEEN SHOWN HOW!"
GENTLEMEN... COLUMBUS WAS RIGHT. NOT ONLY CAN ANYONE DO IT AFTER THEY'VE BEEN SHOWN HOW, BUT EVERYONE SHOULD AND WILL USE ALTERNATING ELECTRIC CURRENT, AFTER THEY HAVE BEEN SHOWN HOW AND CONVINCED OF IT'S SAFTEY.
IT IS NOW SIMPLER THAN COLUMBUS EVER DREAMED. WHILE HE BROKE NEW GROUND IN HIS DISCOVERY OF THE VERY LAND WE STAND ON...
CLICK
I'LL BREAK NEW GROUND WITH HOW WE CAN SAFELY UTILIZE THIS LAND.
THE EGG STANDS...
...MOVES TO THE CENTER...
...AND BEGINS TO SPIN.
MY SYSTEM, WHICH CONSISTS OF A TORTIAL IRON CORE STATOR ON WHICH FOUR COILS ARE WOUND IS PERFECTLY IN TUNE WITH NATURE. THE DEVICE IS POWERED BY A TWO-PHASE ALTERNATING CURRENT SOURCE TO CREATE THE ROTATING MAGNETIC FIELD.
THE DEVICE OPERATES ON A 25 TO 300 HERTZ CURRENT. THE IDEAL OPERATING FREQUENCY IS BETWEEN 35 TO 40 HERTZ.

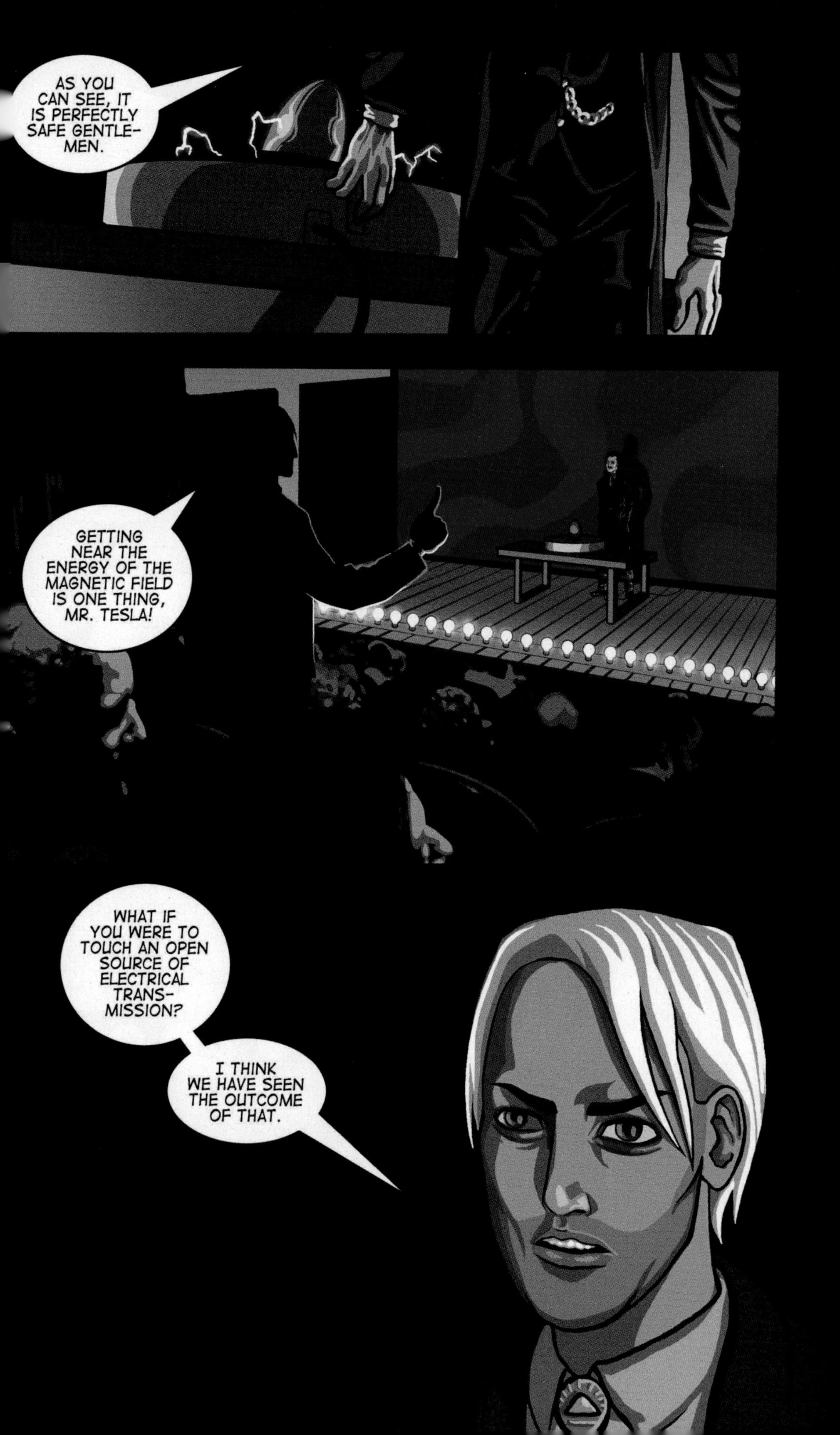
AS YOU CAN SEE, IT IS PERFECTLY SAFE GENTLE-MEN.
GETTING NEAR THE ENERGY OF THE MAGNETIC FIELD IS ONE THING, MR. TESLA!
WHAT IF YOU WERE TO TOUCH AN OPEN SOURCE OF ELECTRICAL TRANS-MISSION?
I THINK WE HAVE SEEN THE OUTCOME OF THAT.

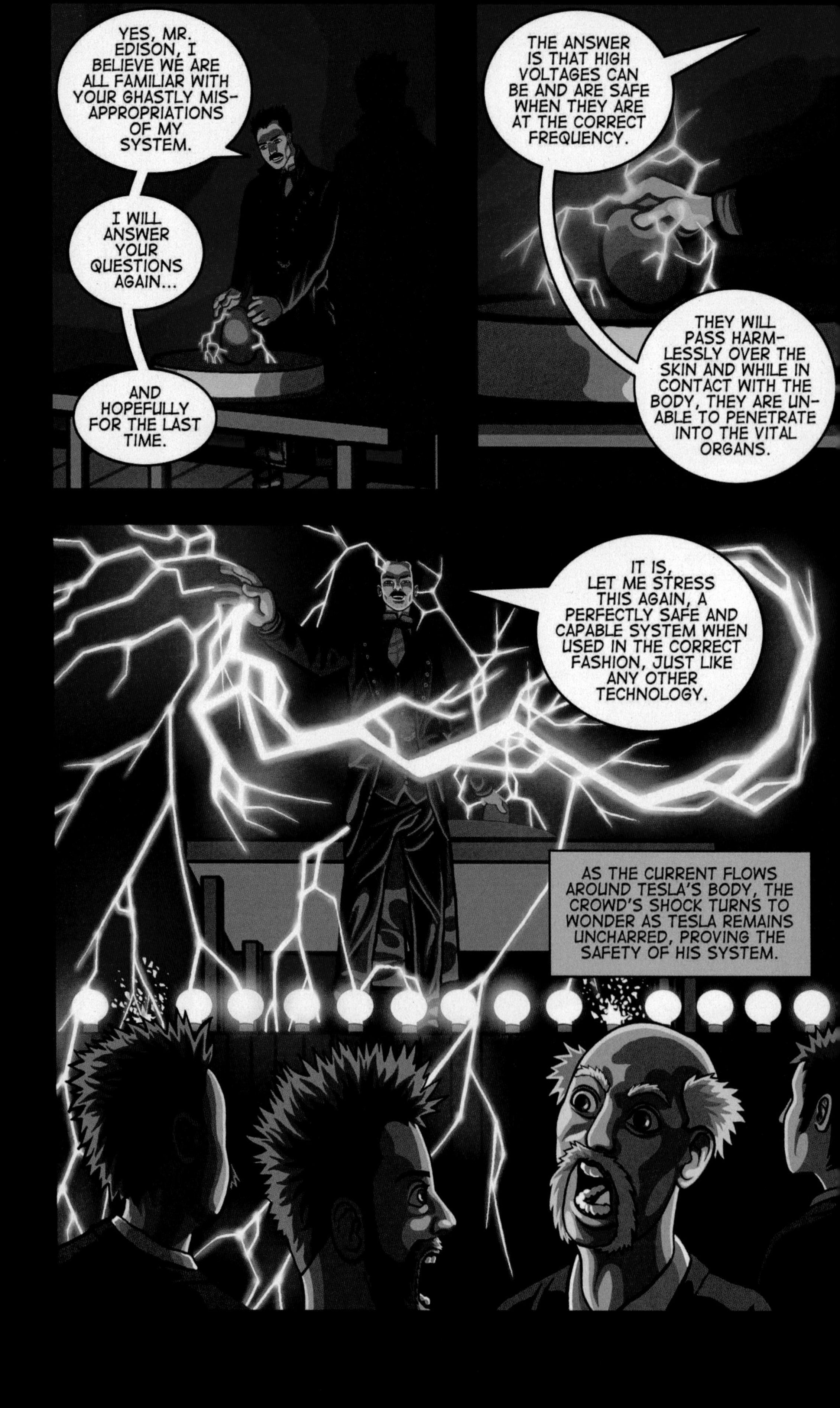

YES, MR. EDISON, I BELIEVE WE ARE ALL FAMILIAR WITH YOUR GHASTLY MIS-APPROPRIATIONS OF MY SYSTEM.
I WILL ANSWER YOUR QUESTIONS AGAIN...
AND HOPEFULLY FOR THE LAST TIME.
THE ANSWER IS THAT HIGH VOLTAGES CAN BE AND ARE SAFE WHEN THEY ARE AT THE CORRECT FREQUENCY.
THEY WILL PASS HARM-LESSLY OVER THE SKIN AND WHILE IN CONTACT WITH THE BODY, THEY ARE UN-ABLE TO PENETRATE INTO THE VITAL ORGANS.
IT IS, LET ME STRESS THIS AGAIN, A PERFECTLY SAFE AND CAPABLE SYSTEM WHEN USED IN THE CORRECT FASHION, JUST LIKE ANY OTHER TECHNOLOGY.
AS THE CURRENT FLOWS AROUND TESLA'S BODY, THE CROWD'S SHOCK TURNS TO WONDER AS TESLA REMAINS UNCHARRED, PROVING THE SAFETY OF HIS SYSTEM.

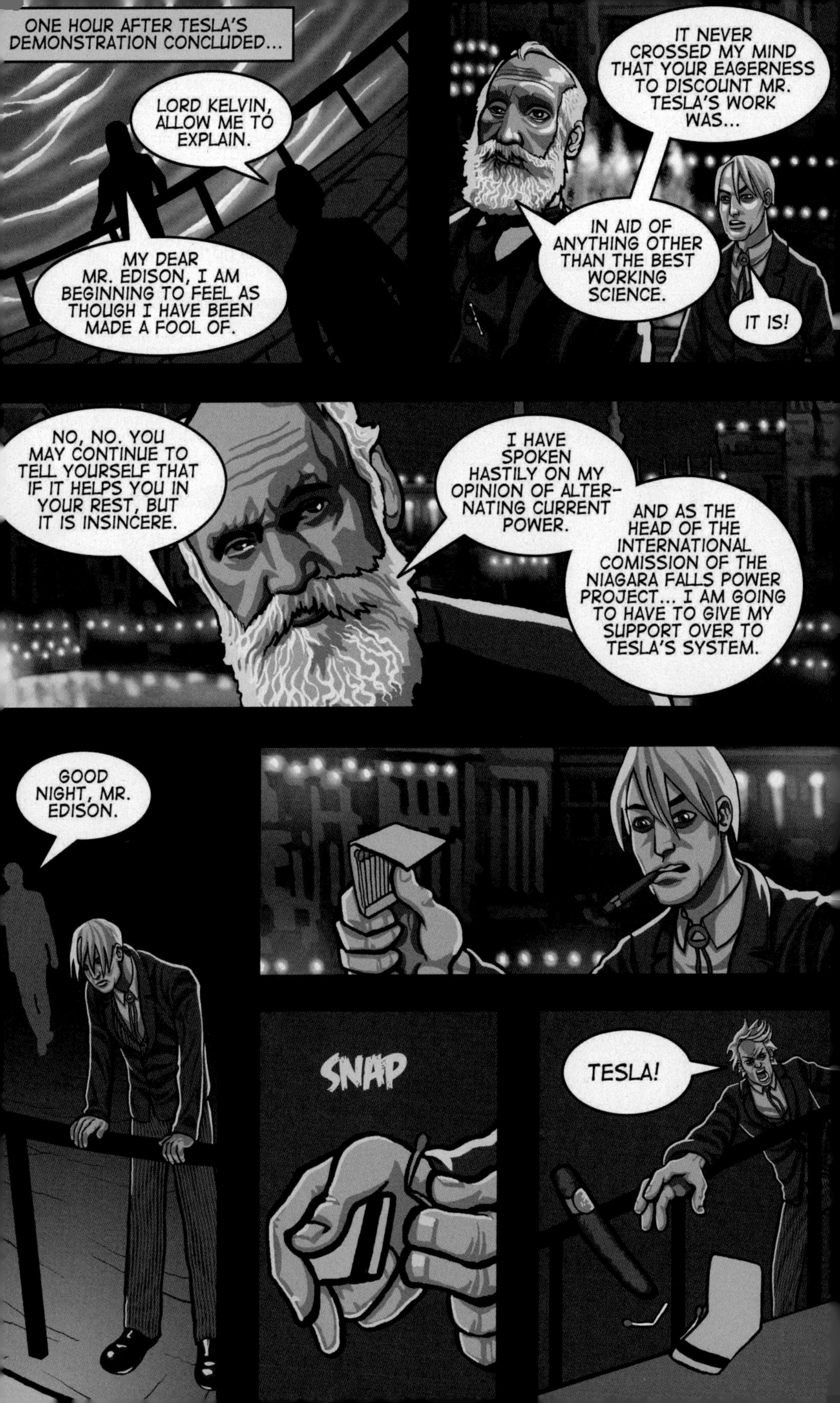
ONE HOUR AFTER TESLA'S DEMONSTRATION CONCLUDED...
LORD KELVIN, ALLOW ME TO EXPLAIN.
MY DEAR MR. EDISON, I AM BEGINNING TO FEEL AS THOUGH I HAVE BEEN MADE A FOOL OF.
IT NEVER CROSSED MY MIND THAT YOUR EAGERNESS TO DISCOUNT MR. TESLA'S WORK WAS...
IN AID OF ANYTHING OTHER THAN THE BEST WORKING SCIENCE.
IT IS!
NO, NO. YOU MAY CONTINUE TO TELL YOURSELF THAT IF IT HELPS YOU IN YOUR REST, BUT IT IS INSINCERE.
I HAVE SPOKEN HASTILY ON MY OPINION OF ALTERNATING CURRENT POWER.
AND AS THE HEAD OF THE INTERNATIONAL COMISSION OF THE NIAGARA FALLS POWER PROJECT... I AM GOING TO HAVE TO GIVE MY SUPPORT OVER TO TESLA'S SYSTEM.
GOOD NIGHT, MR. EDISON.
SNAP
TESLA!

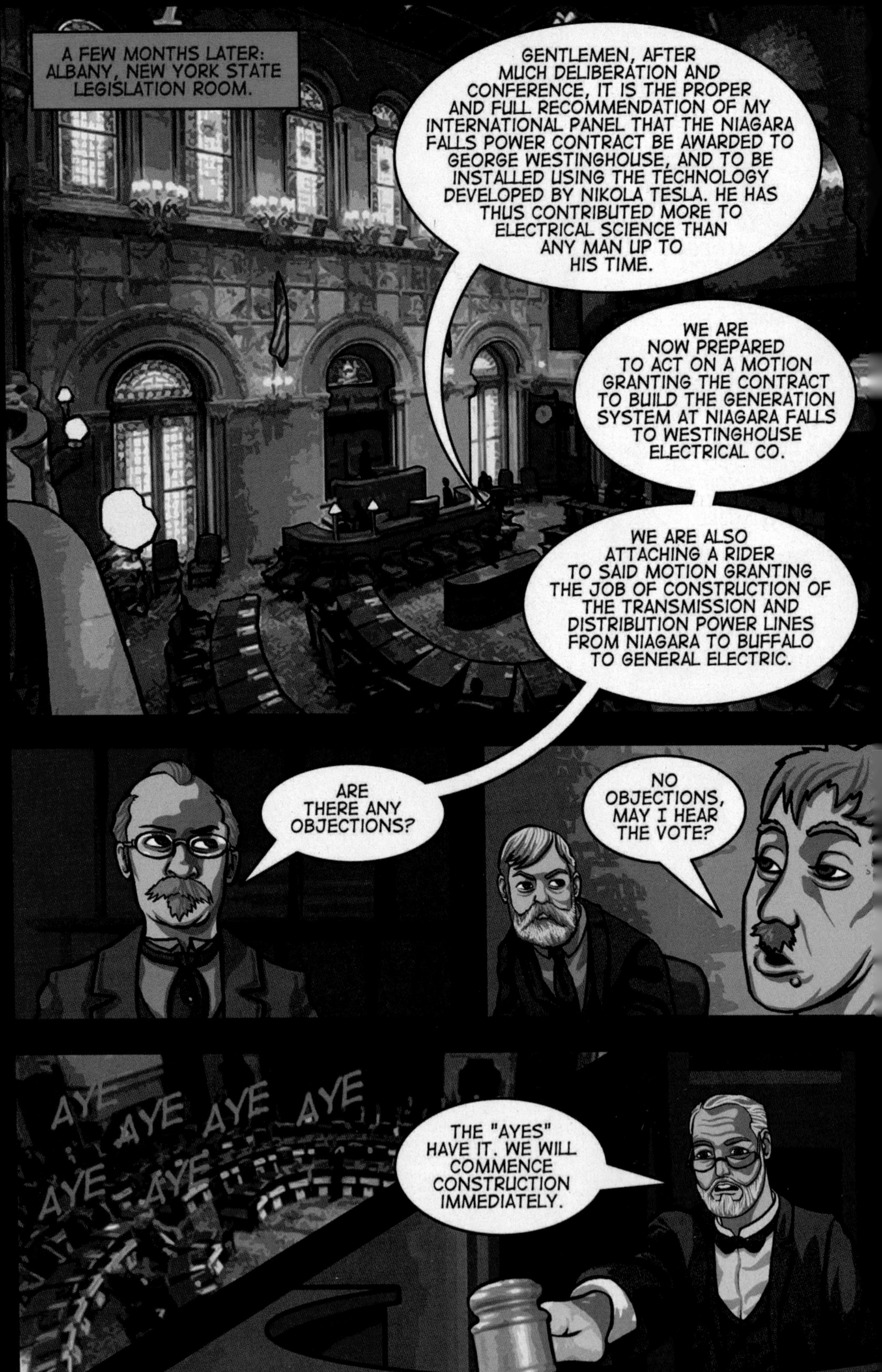
A FEW MONTHS LATER: ALBANY, NEW YORK STATE LEGISLATION ROOM.
GENTLEMEN, AFTER MUCH DELIBERATION AND CONFERENCE, IT IS THE PROPER AND FULL RECOMMENDATION OF MY INTERNATIONAL PANEL THAT THE NIAGARA FALLS POWER CONTRACT BE AWARDED TO GEORGE WESTINGHOUSE, AND TO BE INSTALLED USING THE TECHNOLOGY DEVELOPED BY NIKOLA TESLA. HE HAS THUS CONTRIBUTED MORE TO ELECTRICAL SCIENCE THAN ANY MAN UP TO HIS TIME.
WE ARE NOW PREPARED TO ACT ON A MOTION GRANTING THE CONTRACT TO BUILD THE GENERATION SYSTEM AT NIAGARA FALLS TO WESTINGHOUSE ELECTRICAL CO.
WE ARE ALSO ATTACHING A RIDER TO SAID MOTION GRANTING THE JOB OF CONSTRUCTION OF THE TRANSMISSION AND DISTRIBUTION POWER LINES FROM NIAGARA TO BUFFALO TO GENERAL ELECTRIC.
ARE THERE ANY OBJECTIONS?
NO OBJECTIONS, MAY I HEAR THE VOTE?
AYE AYE AYE AYE
AYE AYE
THE "AYES" HAVE IT. WE WILL COMMENCE CONSTRUCTION IMMEDIATELY.

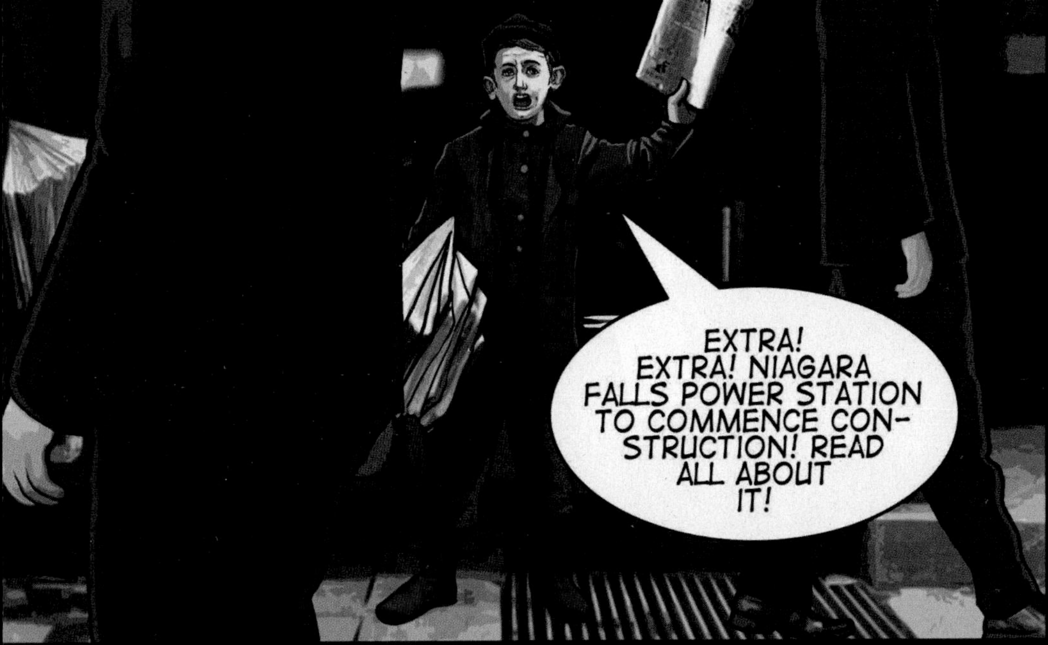
EXTRA! EXTRA! NIAGARA FALLS POWER STATION TO COMMENCE CONSTRUCTION! READ ALL ABOUT IT!

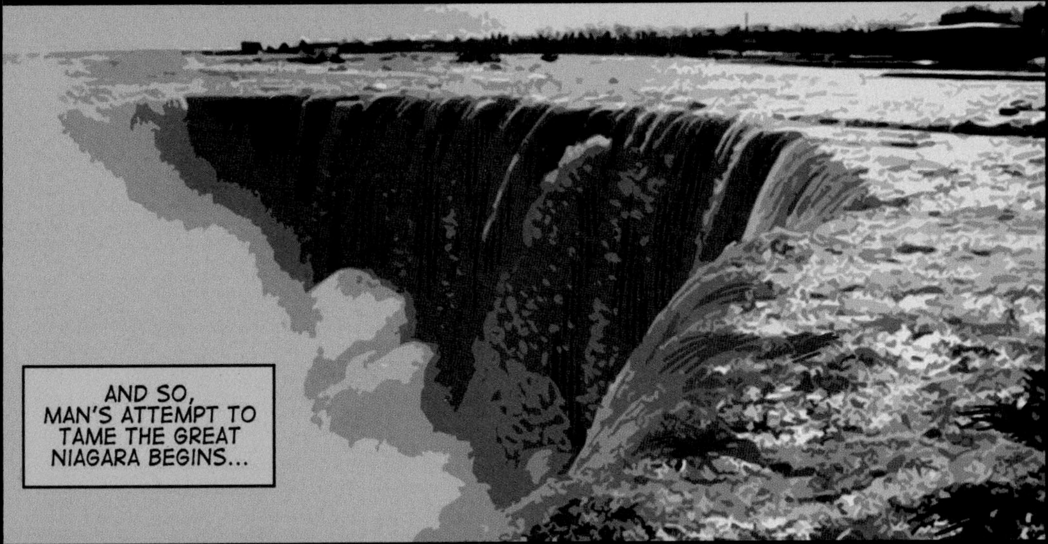
AND SO, MAN'S ATTEMPT TO TAME THE GREAT NIAGARA BEGINS...

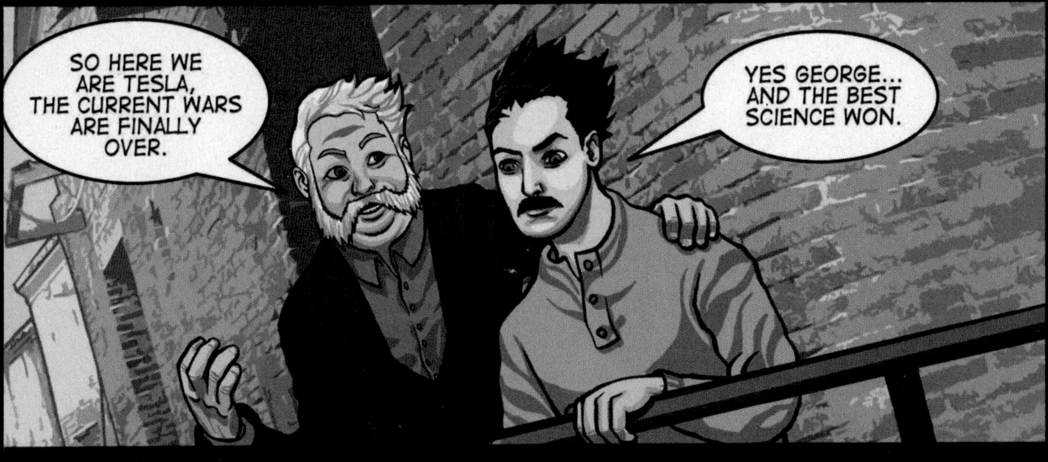
SO HERE WE ARE TESLA, THE CURRENT WARS ARE FINALLY OVER.
YES GEORGE... AND THE BEST SCIENCE WON.

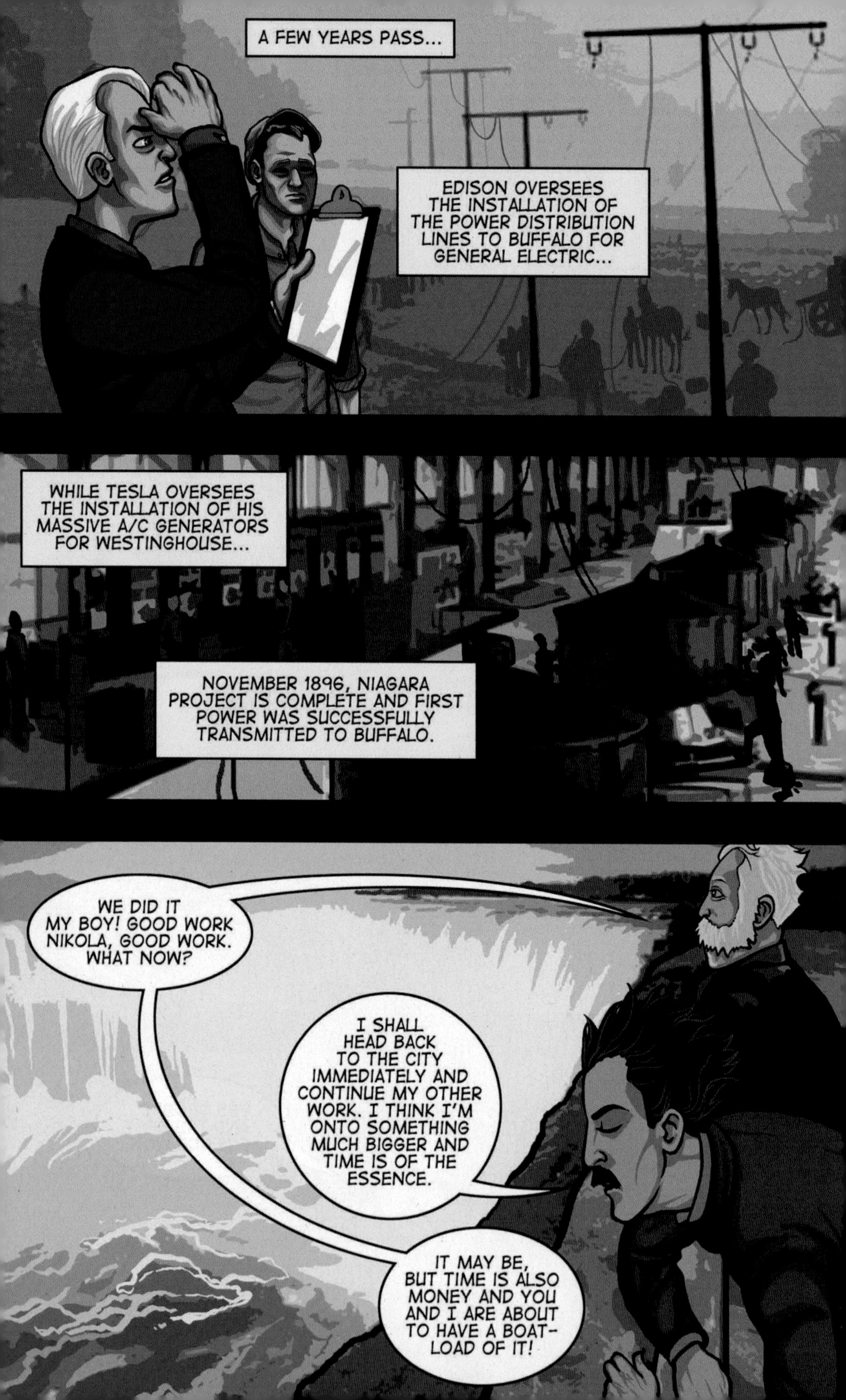
A FEW YEARS PASS...
EDISON OVERSEES THE INSTALLATION OF THE POWER DISTRIBUTION LINES TO BUFFALO FOR GENERAL ELECTRIC...
WHILE TESLA OVERSEES THE INSTALLATION OF HIS MASSIVE A/C GENERATORS FOR WESTINGHOUSE...
NOVEMBER 1896, NIAGARA PROJECT IS COMPLETE AND FIRST POWER WAS SUCCESSFULLY TRANSMITTED TO BUFFALO.
WE DID IT MY BOY! GOOD WORK NIKOLA, GOOD WORK. WHAT NOW?
I SHALL HEAD BACK TO THE CITY IMMEDIATELY AND CONTINUE MY OTHER WORK. I THINK I'M ONTO SOMETHING MUCH BIGGER AND TIME IS OF THE ESSENCE.
IT MAY BE, BUT TIME IS ALSO MONEY AND YOU AND I ARE ABOUT TO HAVE A BOAT-LOAD OF IT!

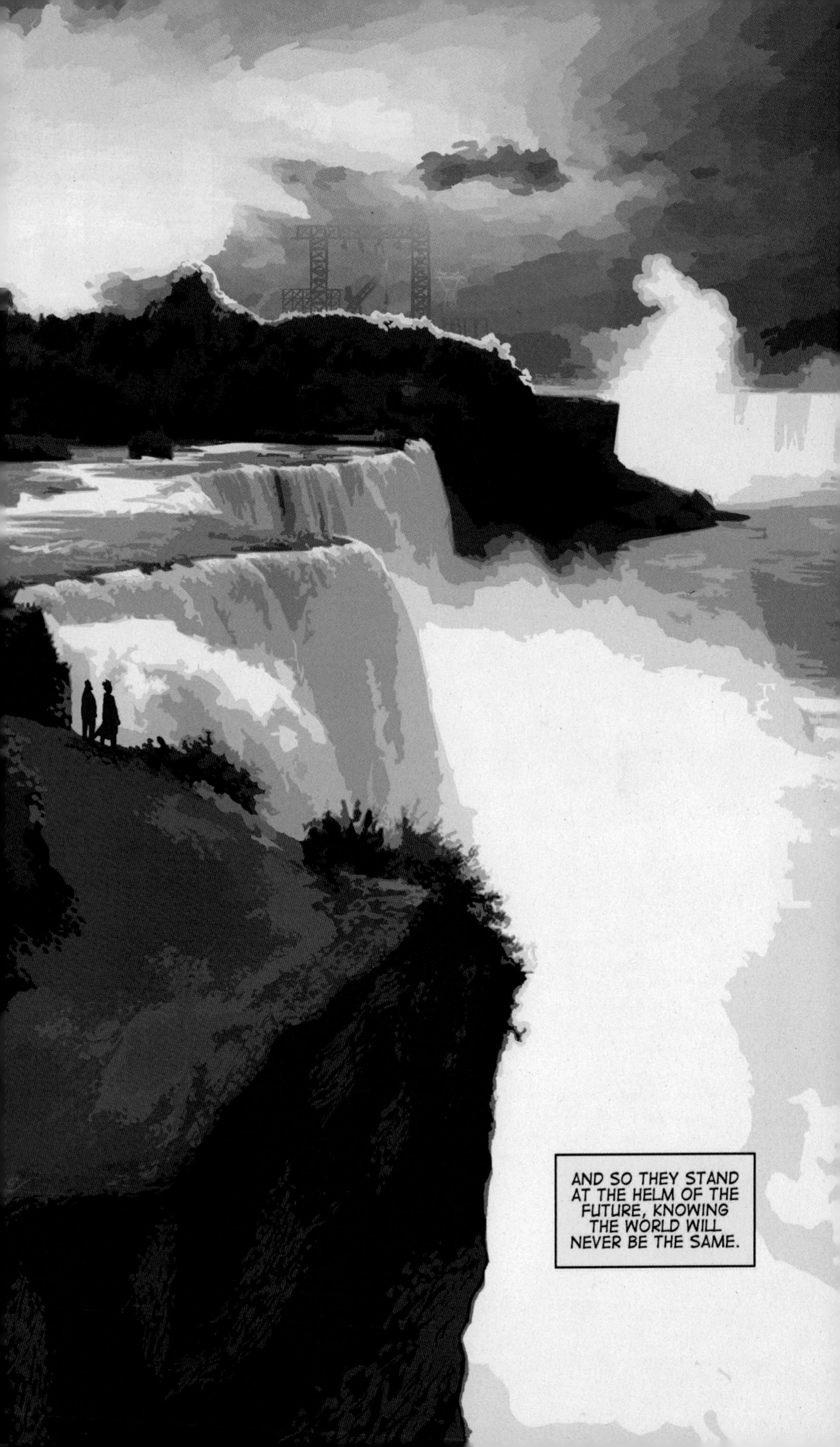
AND SO THEY STAND AT THE HELM OF THE FUTURE, KNOWING THE WORLD WILL NEVER BE THE SAME.

KNOCK KNOCK

THANK YOU.

A LETTER HAS COME FOR YOU DOCTOR.

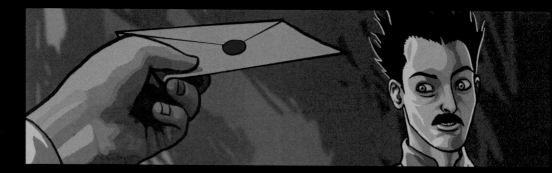

Nikki,

What are you so wrapped up in these stormy days? Niagara should be almost complete. Both Robert and I eagerly long for your company, sitting here, a twosome in front of a roaring fire.

We... are wondering if anybody is coming this evening to cheer us up, say about, 9, or at 7 for dinner. We are very dull. Please come if you can.

Katherine

WHO WAS THAT FROM, DOCTOR?

NO ONE...

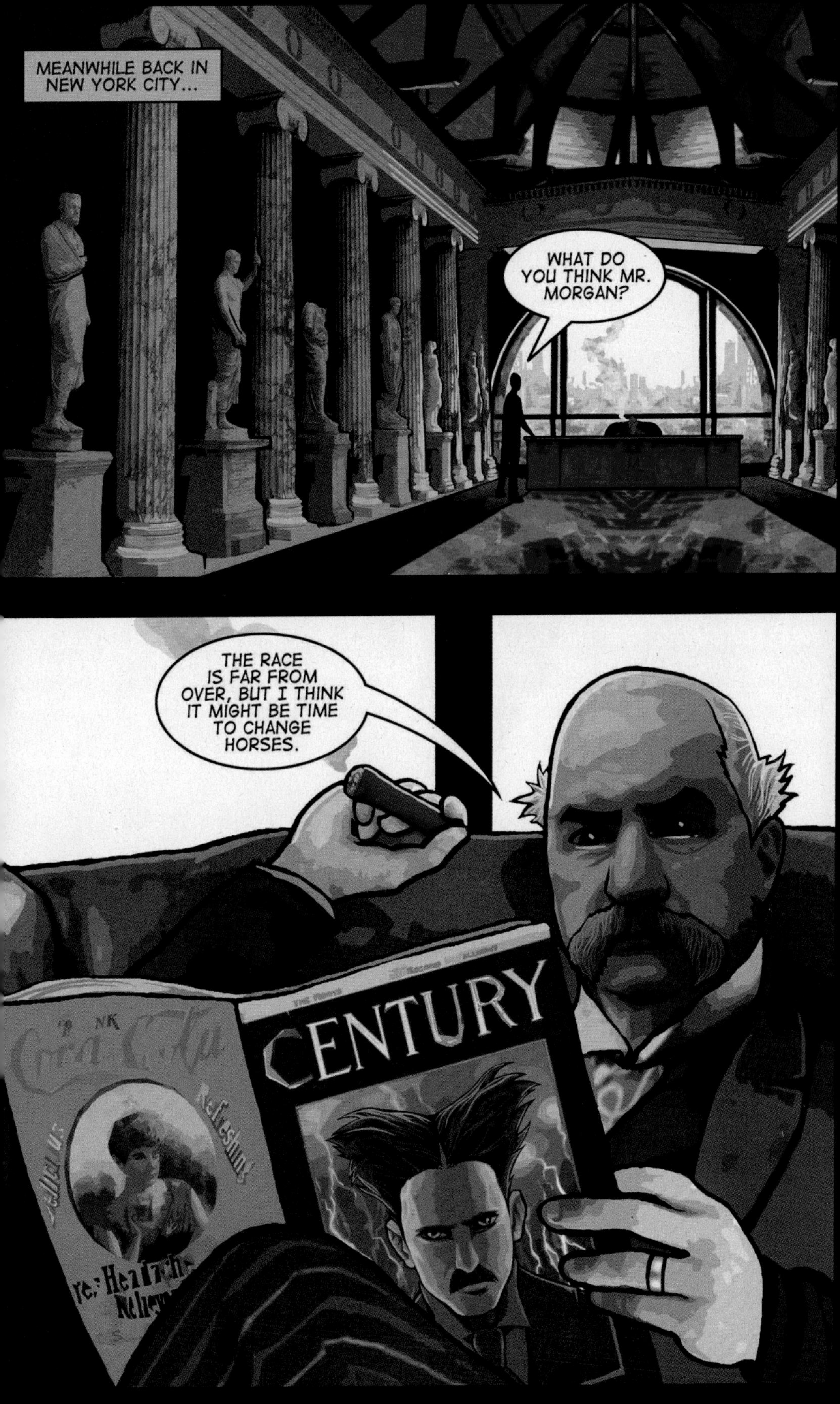
MEANWHILE BACK IN NEW YORK CITY...
WHAT DO YOU THINK MR. MORGAN?
THE RACE IS FAR FROM OVER, BUT I THINK IT MIGHT BE TIME TO CHANGE HORSES.
CENTURY

"WHEN THE GREAT TRUTH ACCIDENTALLY REVEALED AND EXPERIMENTALLY CONFIRMED IS FULLY RECOGNIZED, THAT THIS PLANET, WITH ALL ITS APPALLING IMMENSITY, IS TO ELECTRIC CURRENTS VIRTUALLY NO MORE THAN A SMALL METAL BALL AND THAT BY THIS FACT MANY POSSIBILITIES, EACH BAFFLING IMAGINATION AND OF INCALCULABLE CONSEQUENCE, ARE RENDERED ABSOLUTELY SURE OF ACCOMPLISHMENT."

- NIKOLA TESLA (1856-1943)

CHAPTER 5

VIBRATO

THE CURRENT WARS ARE OVER AND THE ELECTRICAL ERA IS BORN AS 'ALTERNATING CURRENT' BECOMES THE NEW FORM OF POWER TRANSMISSION ACROSS THE GLOBE. MEANWHILE, TESLA RETURNS TO HIS LAB IN NEW YORK AND BEGINS EXPERIMENTING WITH THE 'OSCILLATING CURRENT', WHICH HE DISCOVERS IS VASTLY MORE POWERFUL AND MORE DIFFICULT TO CONTROL. IT IS SAID HE COULD SPLIT THE EARTH IN TWO UNDER THE RIGHT CONDITIONS.

ALL THE WHILE TESLA'S DREAMS ARE BECOMING MORE AND MORE VIVID AS HE COMES CLOSER TO UNLOCKING THE SECRET TO THESE VIBRATIONAL FREQUENCIES AND UNDERSTANDING THE FUNDAMENTAL PRINCIPLE OF THE UNIVERSE...RESONANCE.

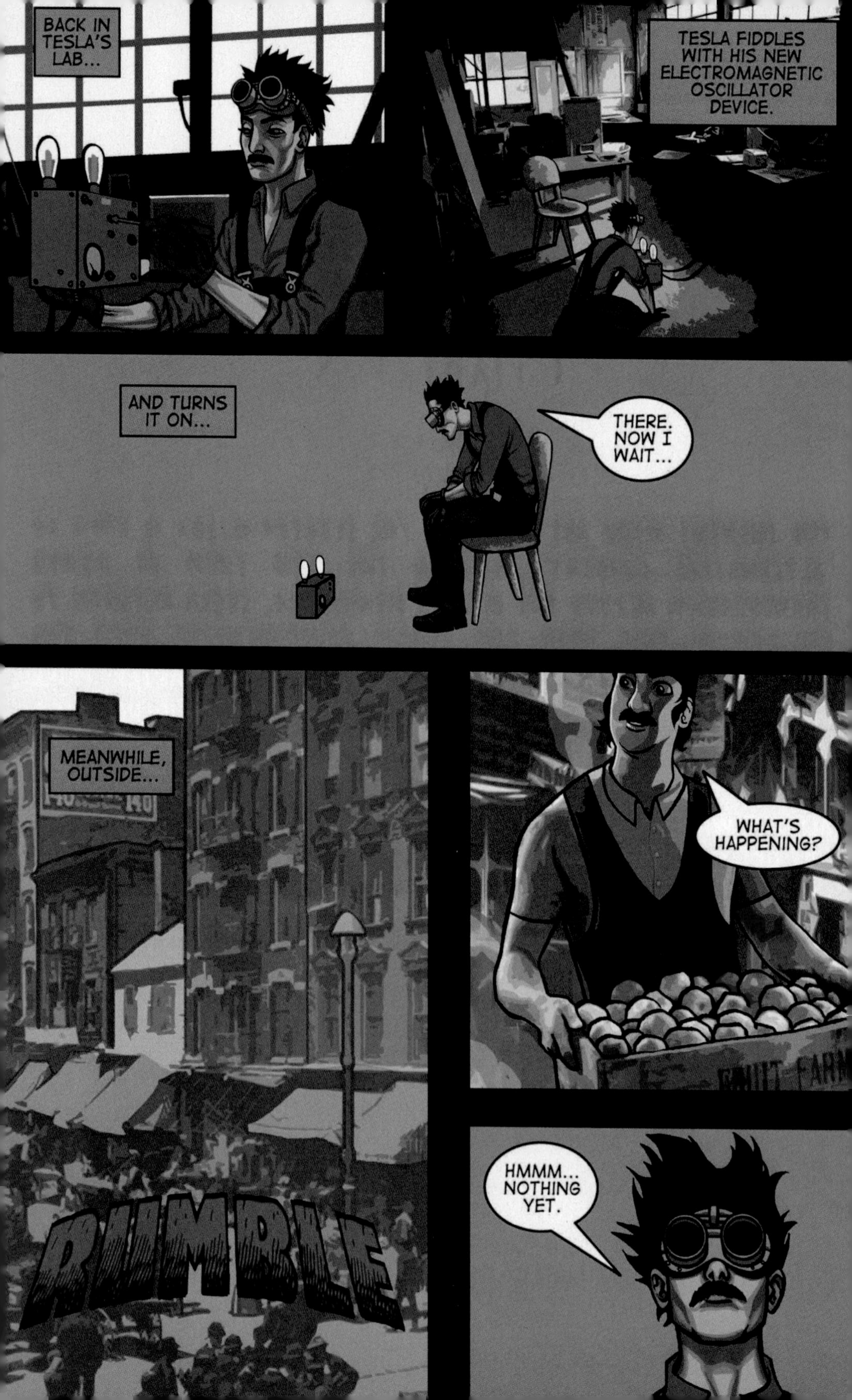
BACK IN TESLA'S LAB...
TESLA FIDDLES WITH HIS NEW ELECTROMAGNETIC OSCILLATOR DEVICE.
AND TURNS IT ON...
THERE. NOW I WAIT...
MEANWHILE, OUTSIDE...
RUMBLE
WHAT'S HAPPENING?
HMMM... NOTHING YET.

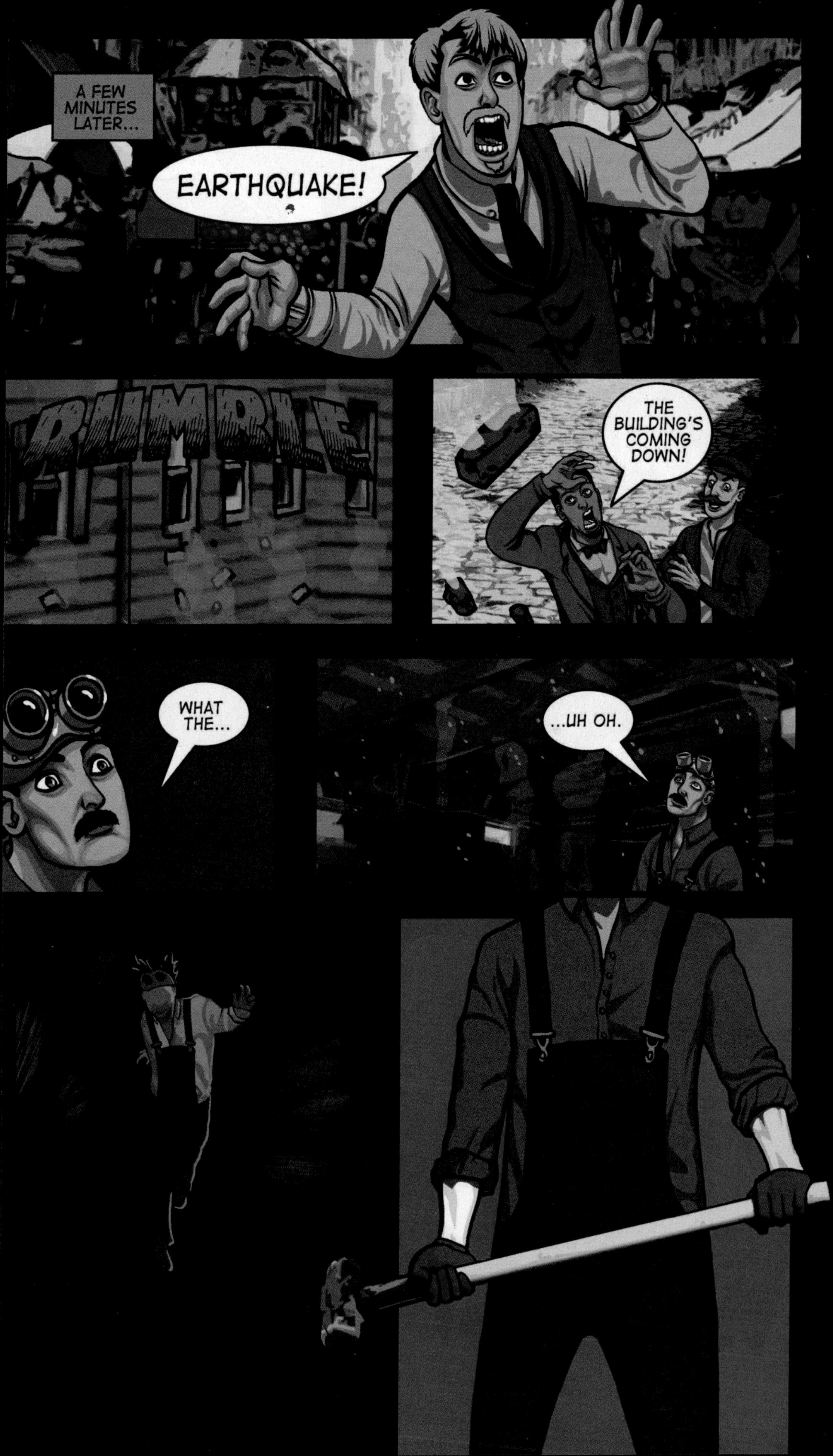
A FEW MINUTES LATER...
EARTHQUAKE!
RUMBLE!
THE BUILDING'S COMING DOWN!
WHAT THE...
...UH OH.

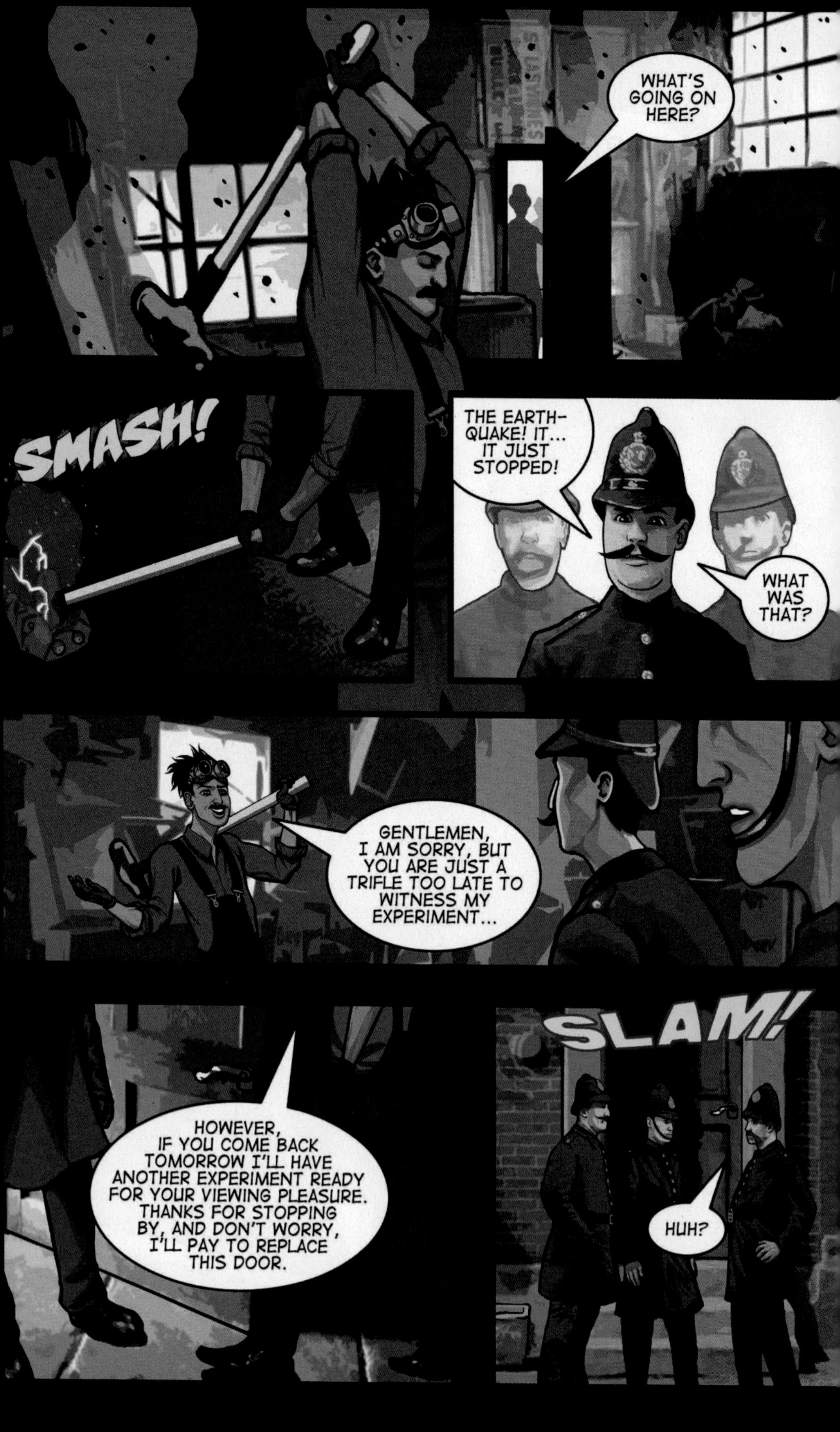
WHAT'S GOING ON HERE?
SMASH!
THE EARTH-QUAKE! IT... IT JUST STOPPED!
WHAT WAS THAT?
GENTLEMEN, I AM SORRY, BUT YOU ARE JUST A TRIFLE TOO LATE TO WITNESS MY EXPERIMENT...
HOWEVER, IF YOU COME BACK TOMORROW I'LL HAVE ANOTHER EXPERIMENT READY FOR YOUR VIEWING PLEASURE. THANKS FOR STOPPING BY, AND DON'T WORRY, I'LL PAY TO REPLACE THIS DOOR.
SLAM!
HUH?

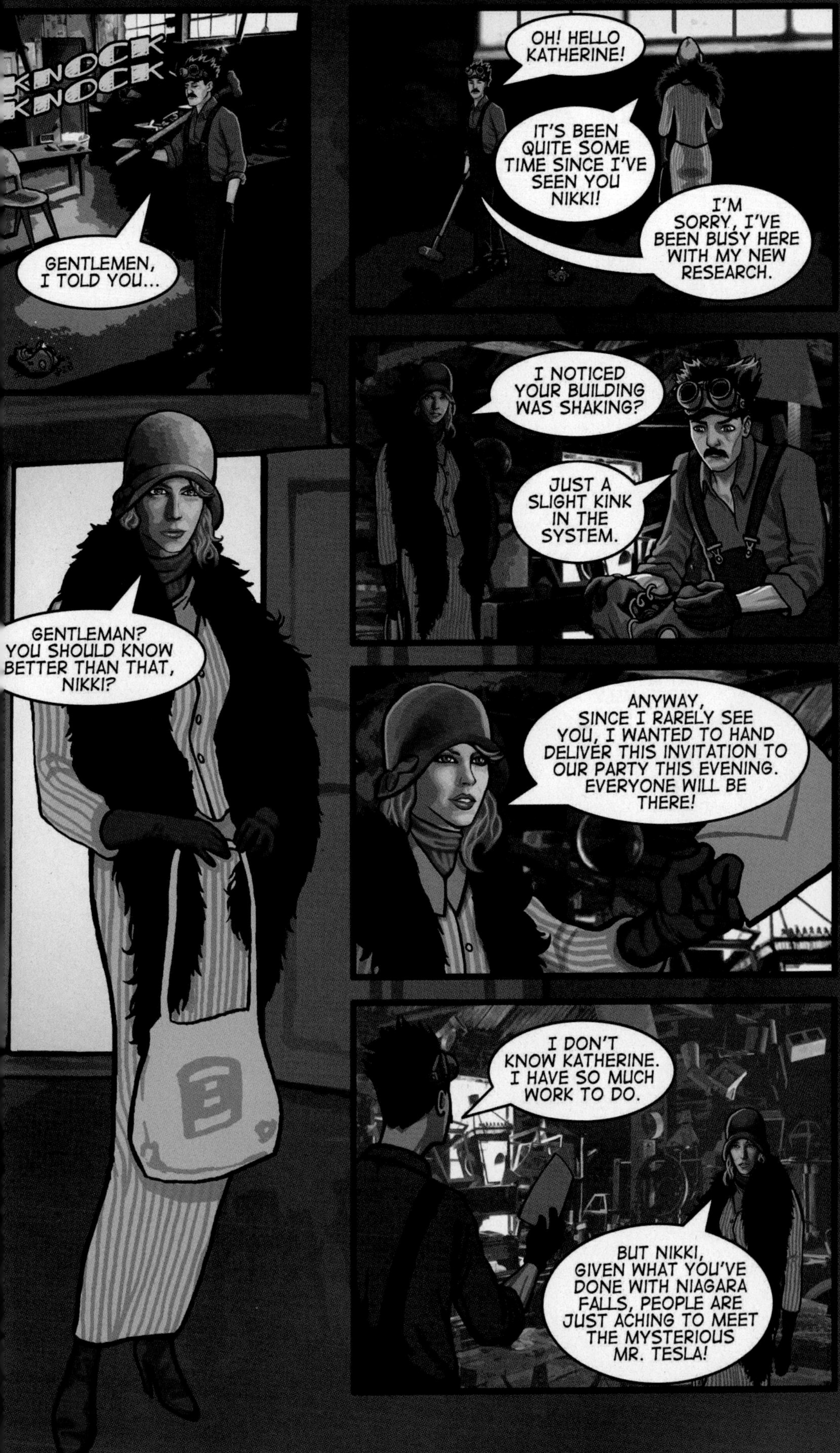
KNOCK
KNOCK
GENTLEMEN, I TOLD YOU...
OH! HELLO KATHERINE!
IT'S BEEN QUITE SOME TIME SINCE I'VE SEEN YOU NIKKI!
I'M SORRY, I'VE BEEN BUSY HERE WITH MY NEW RESEARCH.
GENTLEMAN? YOU SHOULD KNOW BETTER THAN THAT, NIKKI?
I NOTICED YOUR BUILDING WAS SHAKING?
JUST A SLIGHT KINK IN THE SYSTEM.
ANYWAY, SINCE I RARELY SEE YOU, I WANTED TO HAND DELIVER THIS INVITATION TO OUR PARTY THIS EVENING. EVERYONE WILL BE THERE!
I DON'T KNOW KATHERINE. I HAVE SO MUCH WORK TO DO.
BUT NIKKI, GIVEN WHAT YOU'VE DONE WITH NIAGARA FALLS, PEOPLE ARE JUST ACHING TO MEET THE MYSTERIOUS MR. TESLA!

LATER THAT EVENING...

LOOK! IT'S TESLA!

THAT'S MR. TESLA, THE INVENTOR.

AT KATHERINE'S REQUEST, TESLA MAKES A RARE PUBLIC APPEARANCE.

MR. TESLA, WHAT AN HONOR TO FINALLY MEET YOU!

HE CHARMS THE WEALTHY AND INFLUENTIAL OF NEW YORK IN HOPES OF FURTHERING HIS OWN GOALS.

PLEASURE TO MEET YOU, MR. TESLA. YOU'RE MUCH MORE HANDSOME IN PERSON.

AND AFTER A FEW HOURS OF MINGLING WITH THE NEW YORK CITY ELITE...

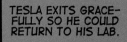

TESLA EXITS GRACE-FULLY SO HE COULD RETURN TO HIS LAB.

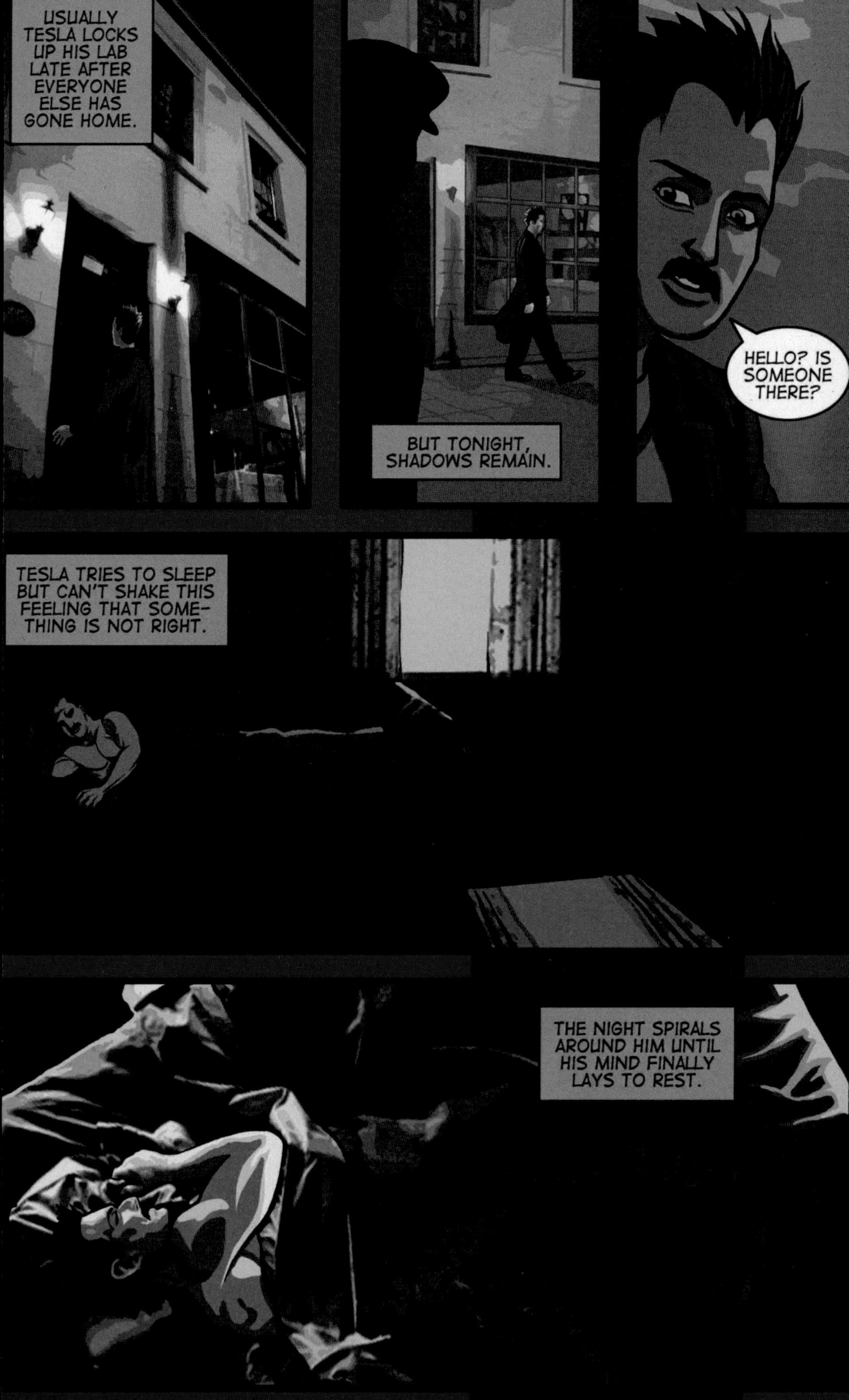
USUALLY TESLA LOCKS UP HIS LAB LATE AFTER EVERYONE ELSE HAS GONE HOME.
BUT TONIGHT, SHADOWS REMAIN.
HELLO? IS SOMEONE THERE?
TESLA TRIES TO SLEEP BUT CAN'T SHAKE THIS FEELING THAT SOME-THING IS NOT RIGHT.
THE NIGHT SPIRALS AROUND HIM UNTIL HIS MIND FINALLY LAYS TO REST.

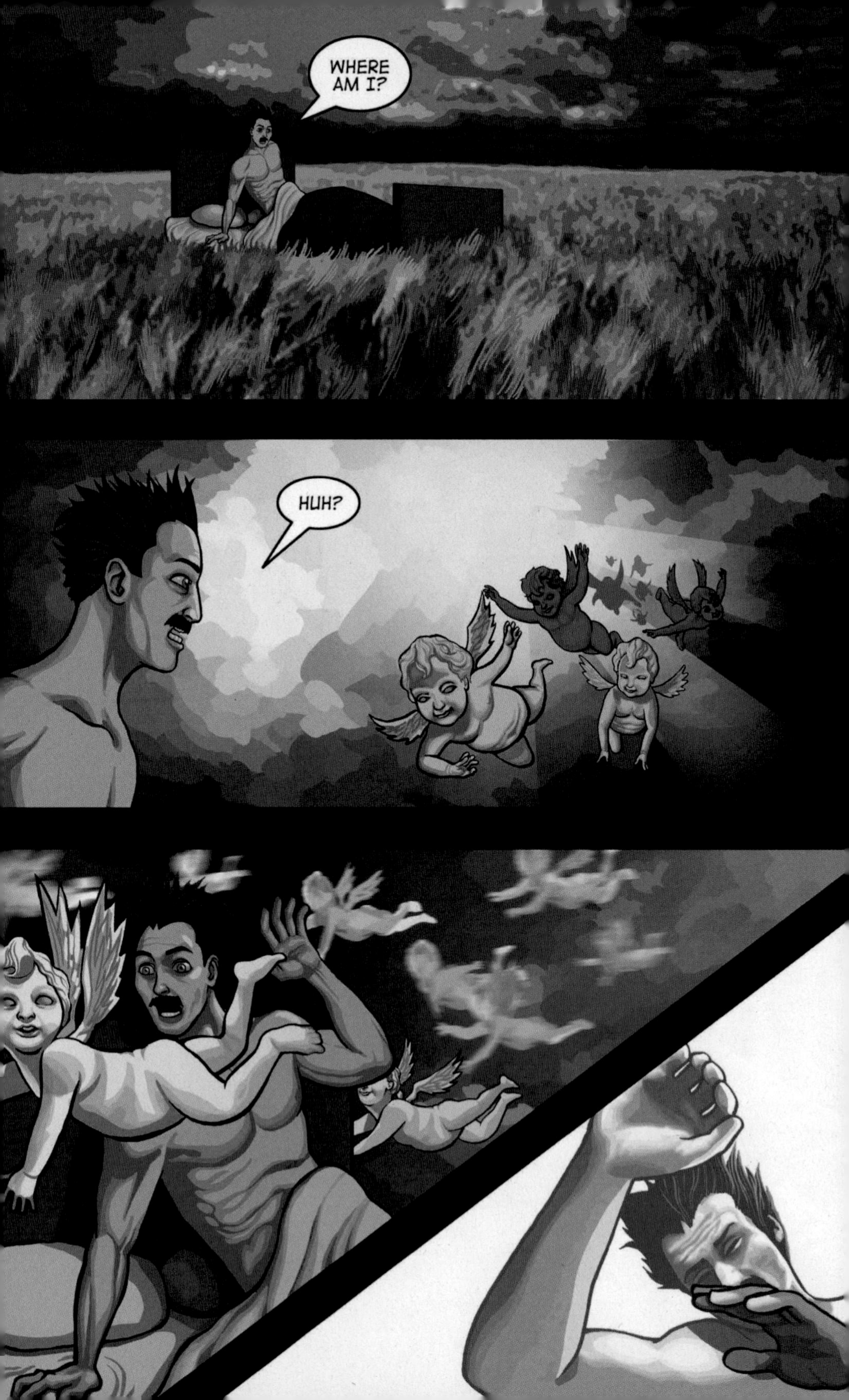
WHERE AM I?
HUH?

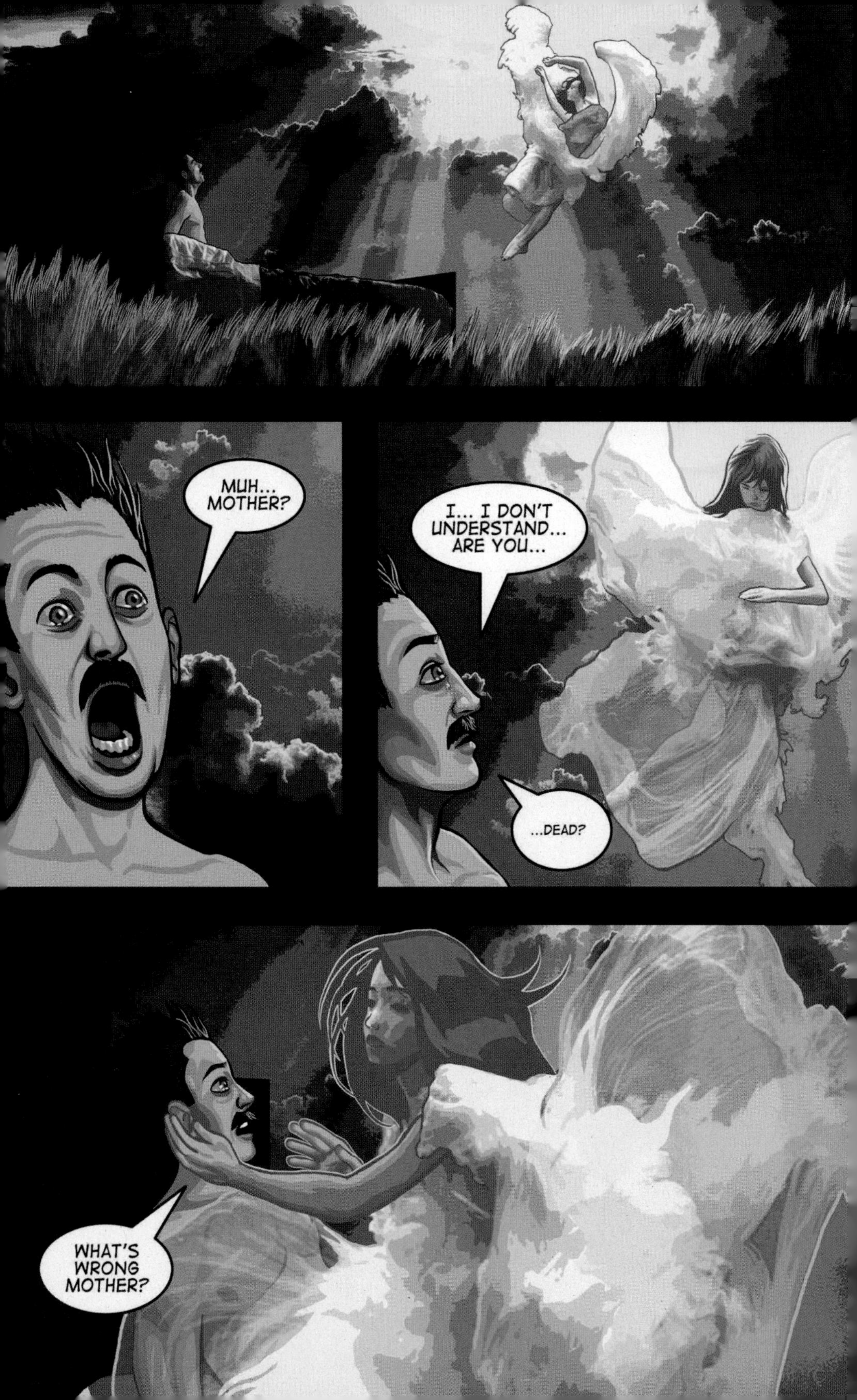
MUH... MOTHER?
I... I DON'T UNDERSTAND... ARE YOU...
...DEAD?
WHAT'S WRONG MOTHER?

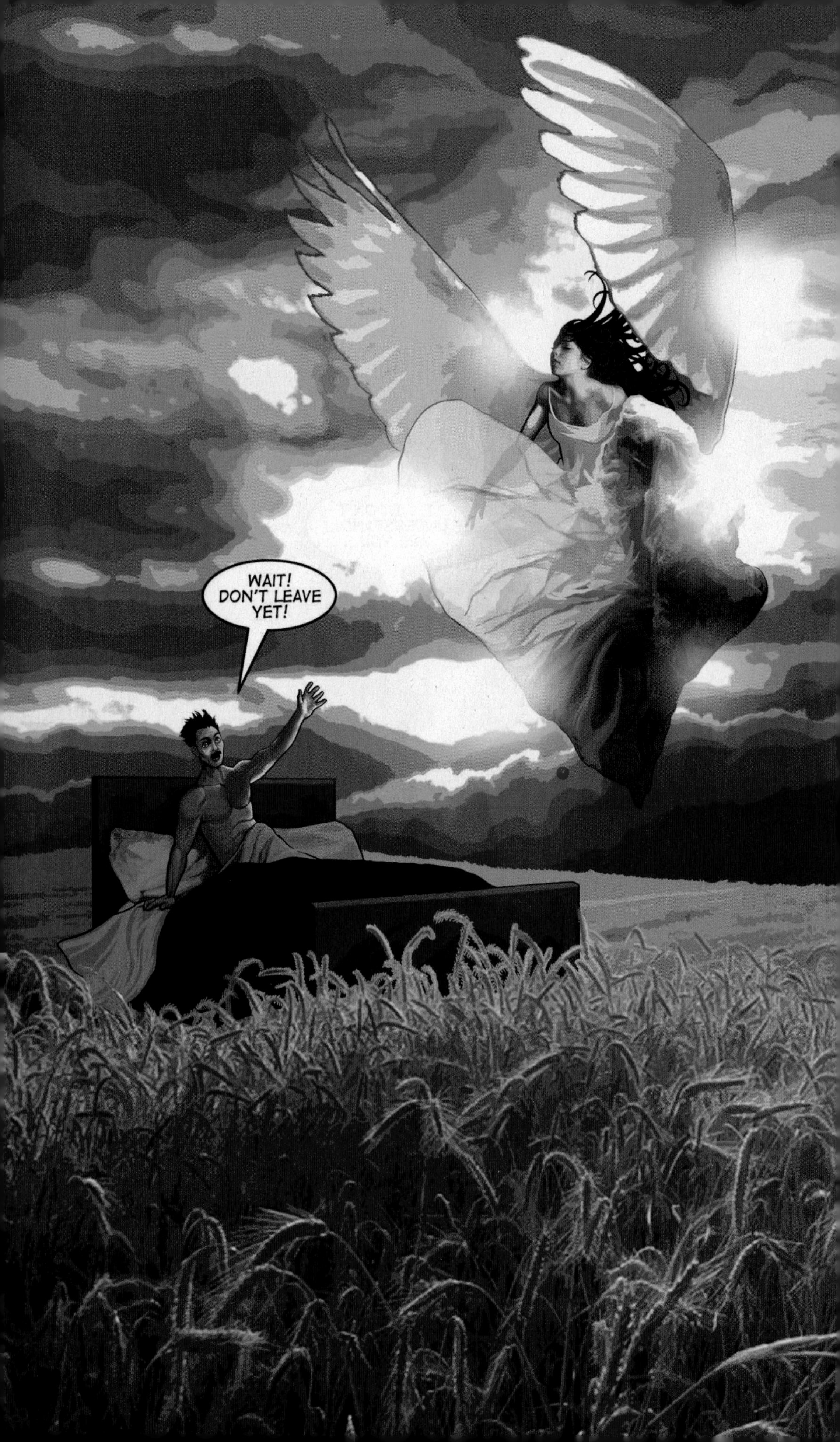
WAIT! DON'T LEAVE YET!

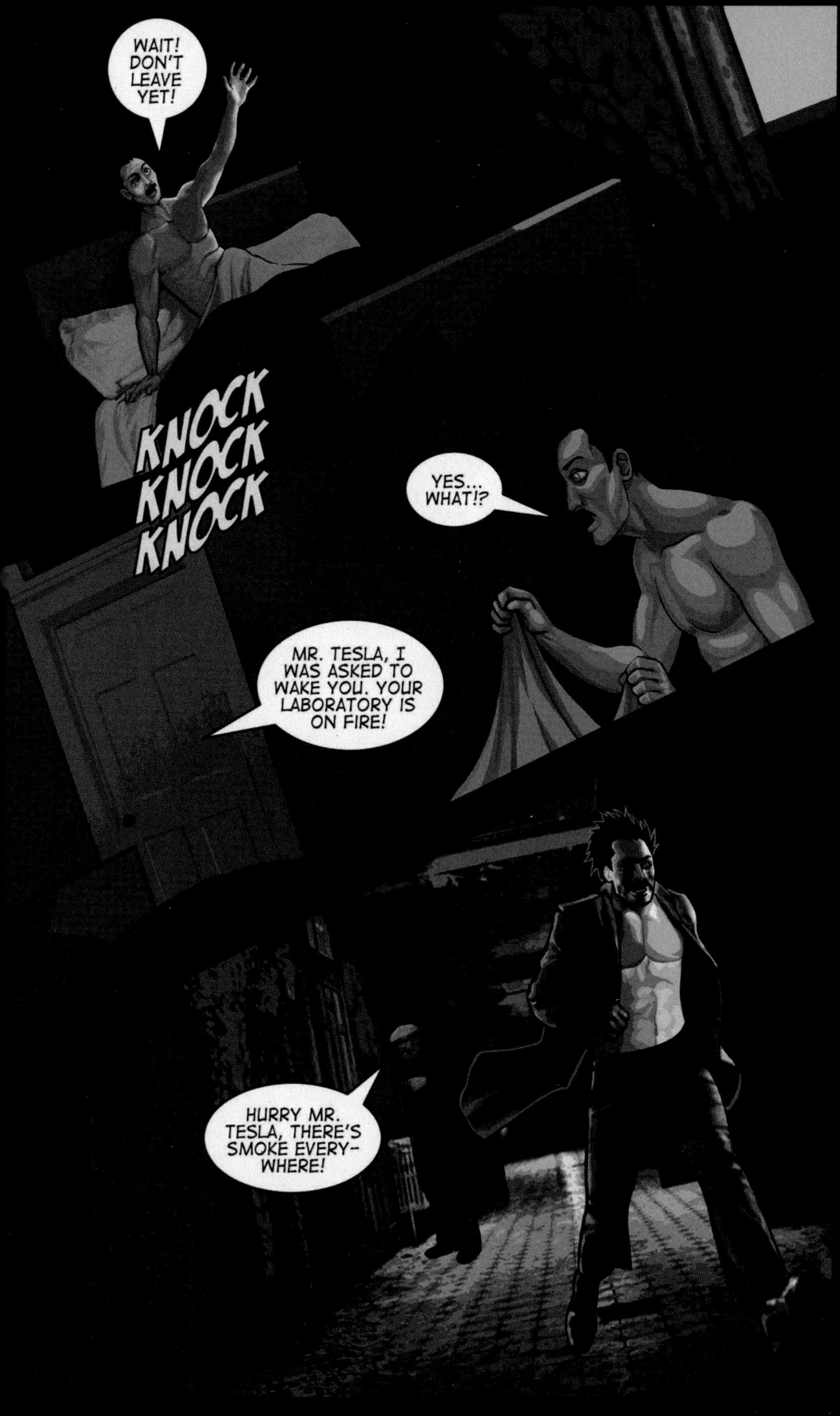
WAIT! DON'T LEAVE YET!
KNOCK KNOCK KNOCK
YES... WHAT!?
MR. TESLA, I WAS ASKED TO WAKE YOU. YOUR LABORATORY IS ON FIRE!
HURRY MR. TESLA, THERE'S SMOKE EVERY-WHERE!

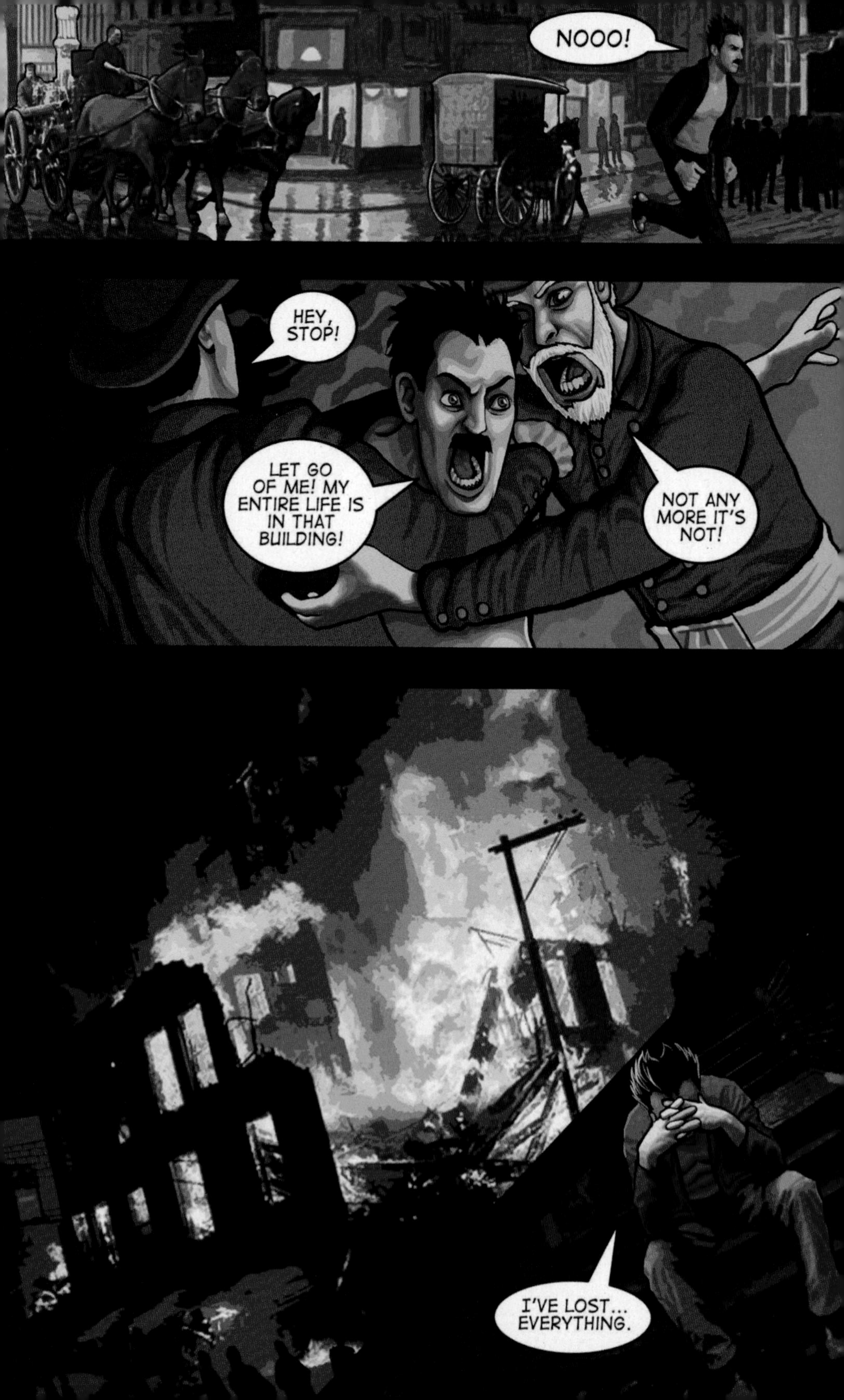
NOOO!
HEY, STOP!
LET GO OF ME! MY ENTIRE LIFE IS IN THAT BUILDING!
NOT ANY MORE IT'S NOT!
I'VE LOST... EVERYTHING.

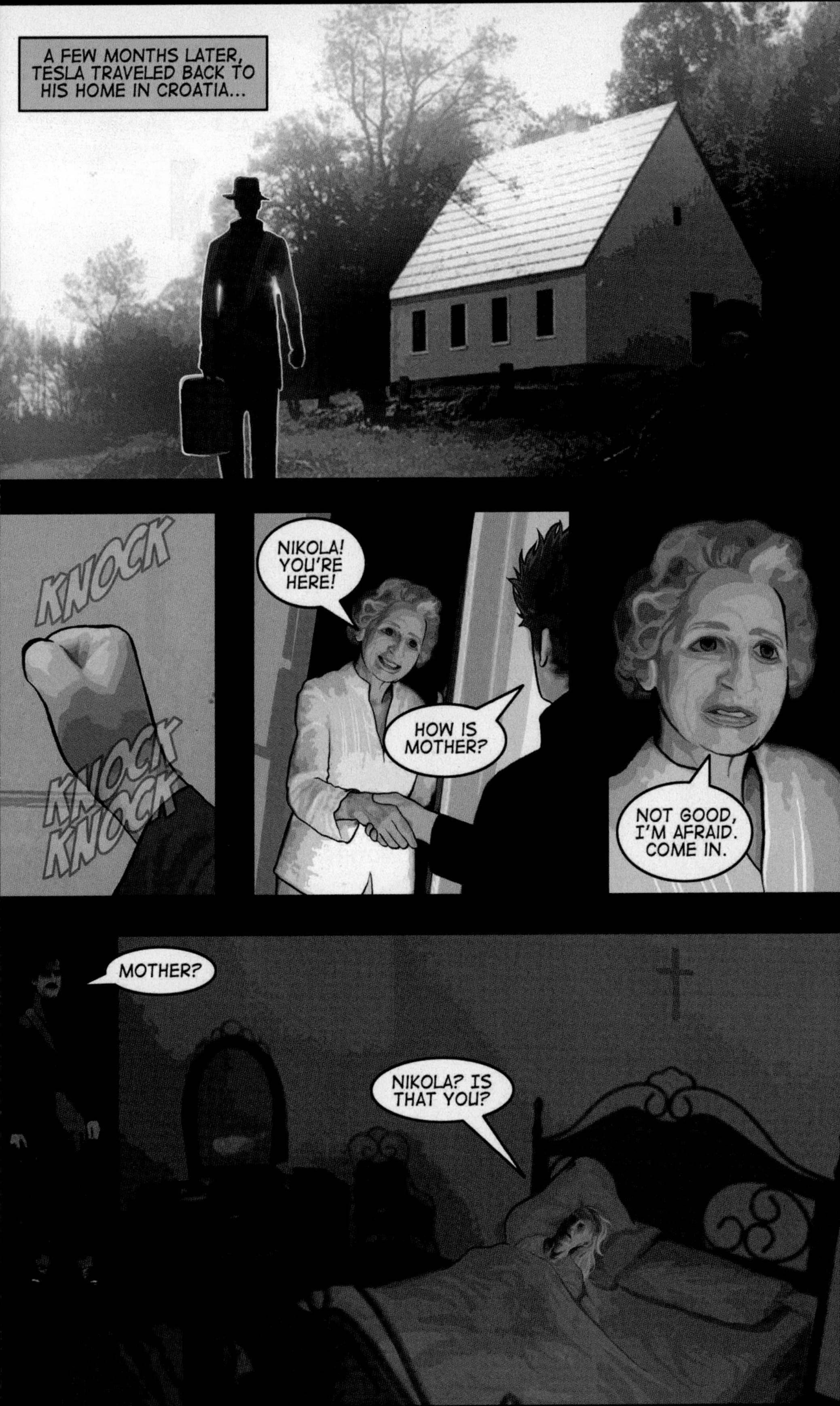

A FEW MONTHS LATER, TESLA TRAVELED BACK TO HIS HOME IN CROATIA...
KNOCK
KNOCK KNOCK
NIKOLA! YOU'RE HERE!
HOW IS MOTHER?
NOT GOOD, I'M AFRAID. COME IN.
MOTHER?
NIKOLA? IS THAT YOU?

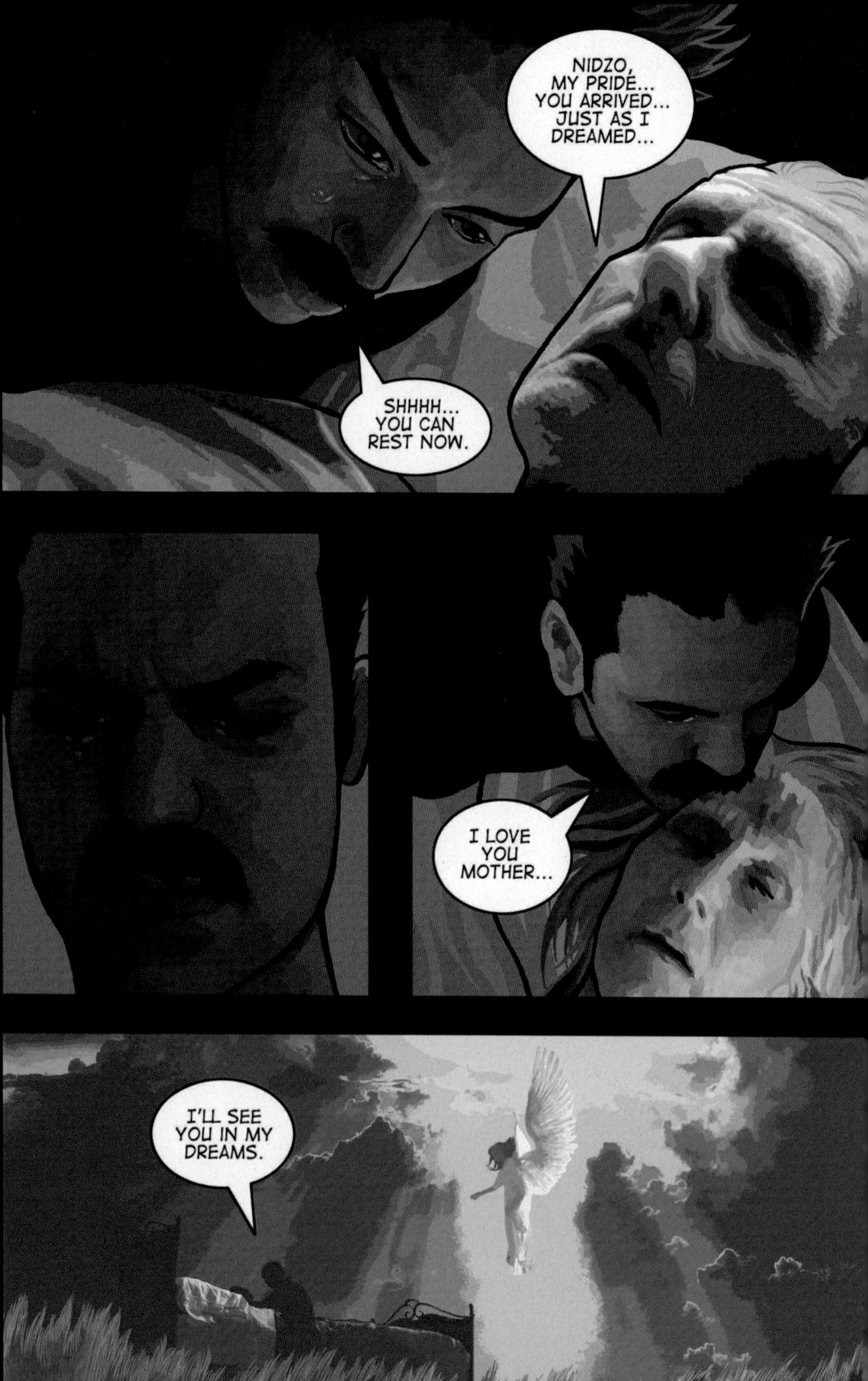
NIDZO, MY PRIDE... YOU ARRIVED... JUST AS I DREAMED...
SHHHH... YOU CAN REST NOW.
I LOVE YOU MOTHER...
I'LL SEE YOU IN MY DREAMS.

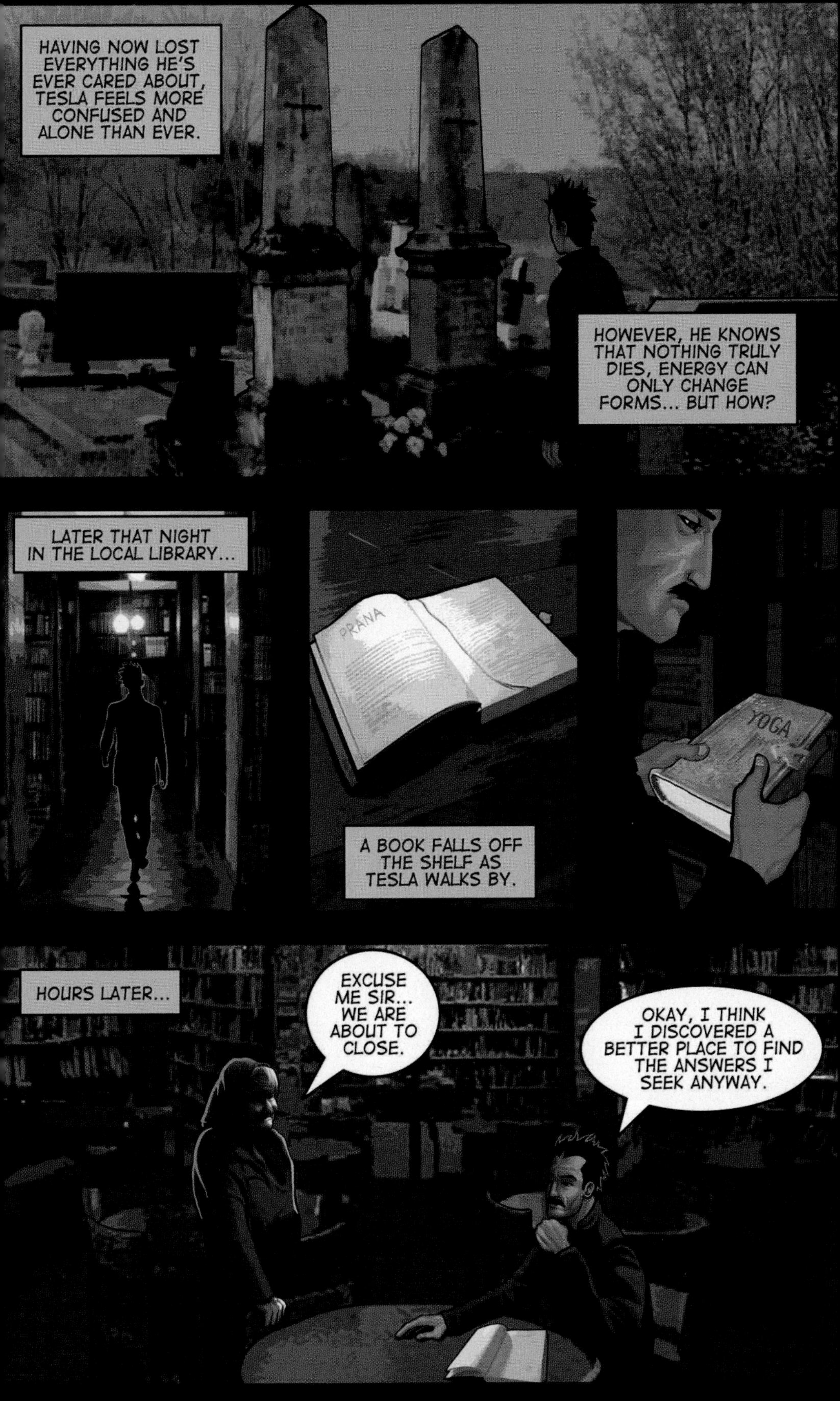
HAVING NOW LOST EVERYTHING HE'S EVER CARED ABOUT, TESLA FEELS MORE CONFUSED AND ALONE THAN EVER.
HOWEVER, HE KNOWS THAT NOTHING TRULY DIES, ENERGY CAN ONLY CHANGE FORMS... BUT HOW?
LATER THAT NIGHT IN THE LOCAL LIBRARY...
PRANA
A BOOK FALLS OFF THE SHELF AS TESLA WALKS BY.
YOGA
HOURS LATER...
EXCUSE ME SIR... WE ARE ABOUT TO CLOSE.
OKAY, I THINK I DISCOVERED A BETTER PLACE TO FIND THE ANSWERS I SEEK ANYWAY.

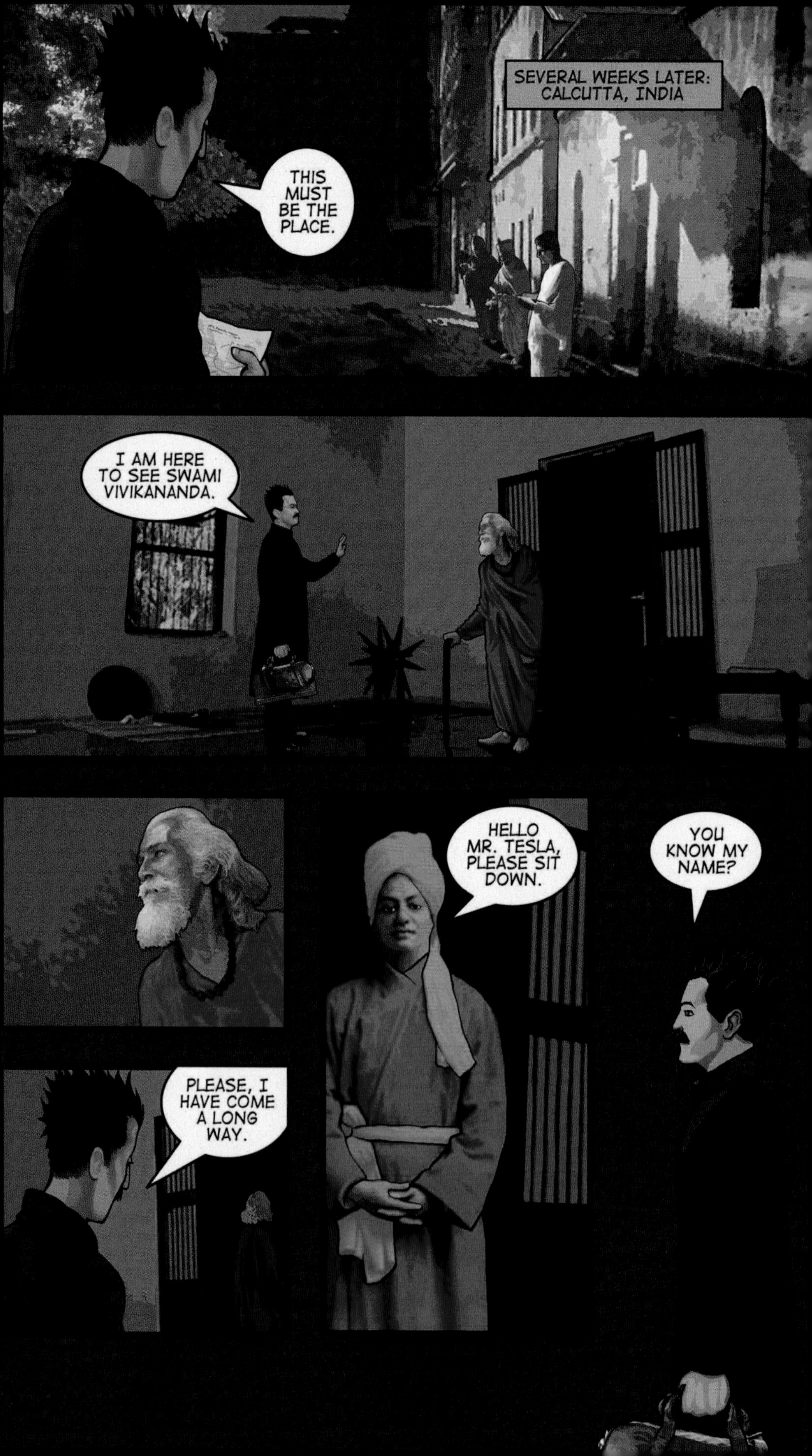
SEVERAL WEEKS LATER: CALCUTTA, INDIA
THIS MUST BE THE PLACE.
I AM HERE TO SEE SWAMI VIVIKANANDA.
HELLO MR. TESLA, PLEASE SIT DOWN.
YOU KNOW MY NAME?
PLEASE, I HAVE COME A LONG WAY.

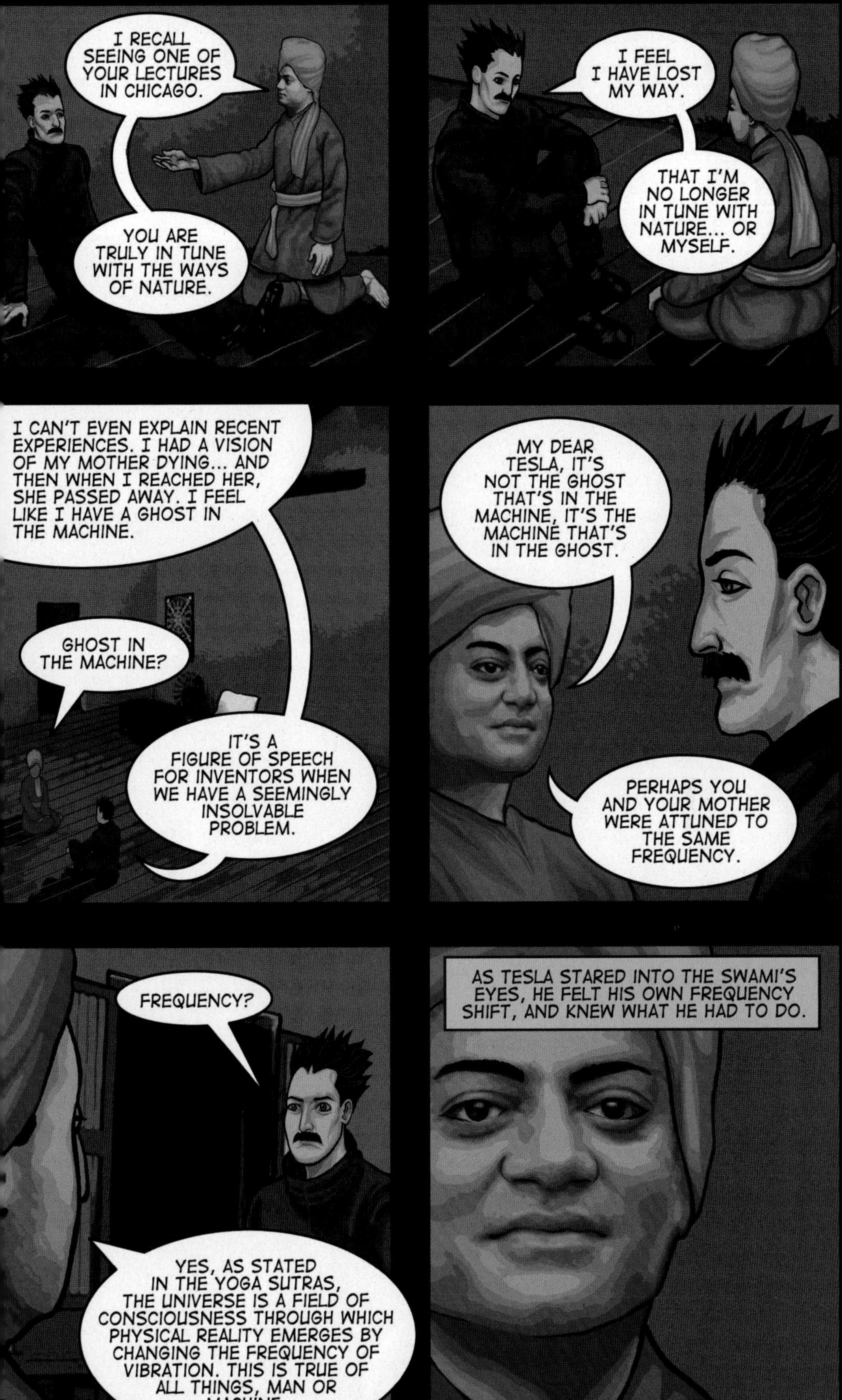
I RECALL SEEING ONE OF YOUR LECTURES IN CHICAGO.
YOU ARE TRULY IN TUNE WITH THE WAYS OF NATURE.
I FEEL I HAVE LOST MY WAY.
THAT I'M NO LONGER IN TUNE WITH NATURE... OR MYSELF.
I CAN'T EVEN EXPLAIN RECENT EXPERIENCES. I HAD A VISION OF MY MOTHER DYING... AND THEN WHEN I REACHED HER, SHE PASSED AWAY. I FEEL LIKE I HAVE A GHOST IN THE MACHINE.
GHOST IN THE MACHINE?
IT'S A FIGURE OF SPEECH FOR INVENTORS WHEN WE HAVE A SEEMINGLY INSOLVABLE PROBLEM.
MY DEAR TESLA, IT'S NOT THE GHOST THAT'S IN THE MACHINE, IT'S THE MACHINE THAT'S IN THE GHOST.
PERHAPS YOU AND YOUR MOTHER WERE ATTUNED TO THE SAME FREQUENCY.
FREQUENCY?
YES, AS STATED IN THE YOGA SUTRAS, THE UNIVERSE IS A FIELD OF CONSCIOUSNESS THROUGH WHICH PHYSICAL REALITY EMERGES BY CHANGING THE FREQUENCY OF VIBRATION. THIS IS TRUE OF ALL THINGS, MAN OR MACHINE.
AS TESLA STARED INTO THE SWAMI'S EYES, HE FELT HIS OWN FREQUENCY SHIFT, AND KNEW WHAT HE HAD TO DO.

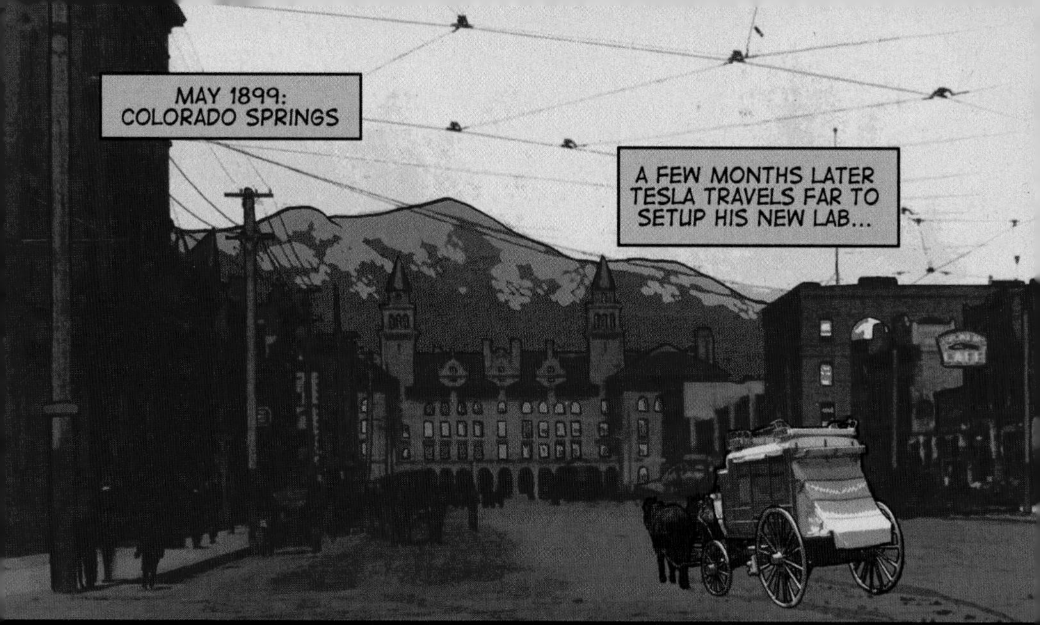
MAY 1899: COLORADO SPRINGS
A FEW MONTHS LATER TESLA TRAVELS FAR TO SETUP HIS NEW LAB...

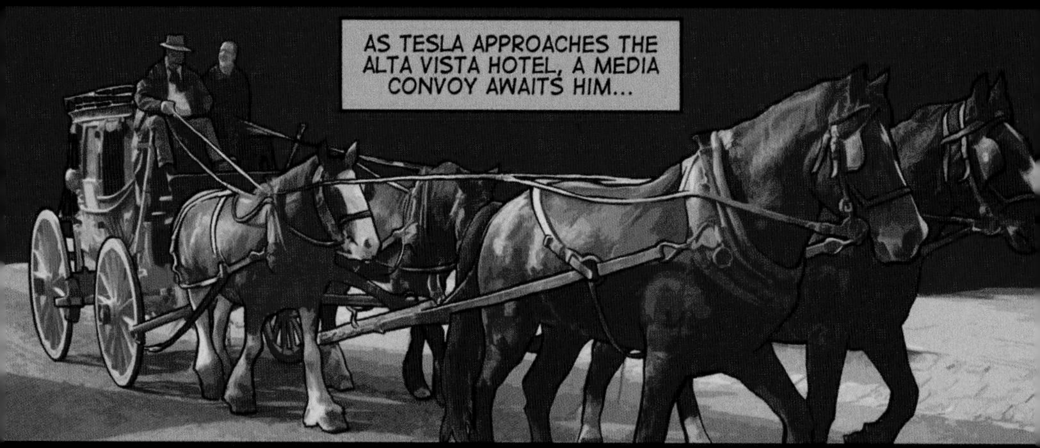
AS TESLA APPROACHES THE ALTA VISTA HOTEL, A MEDIA CONVOY AWAITS HIM...

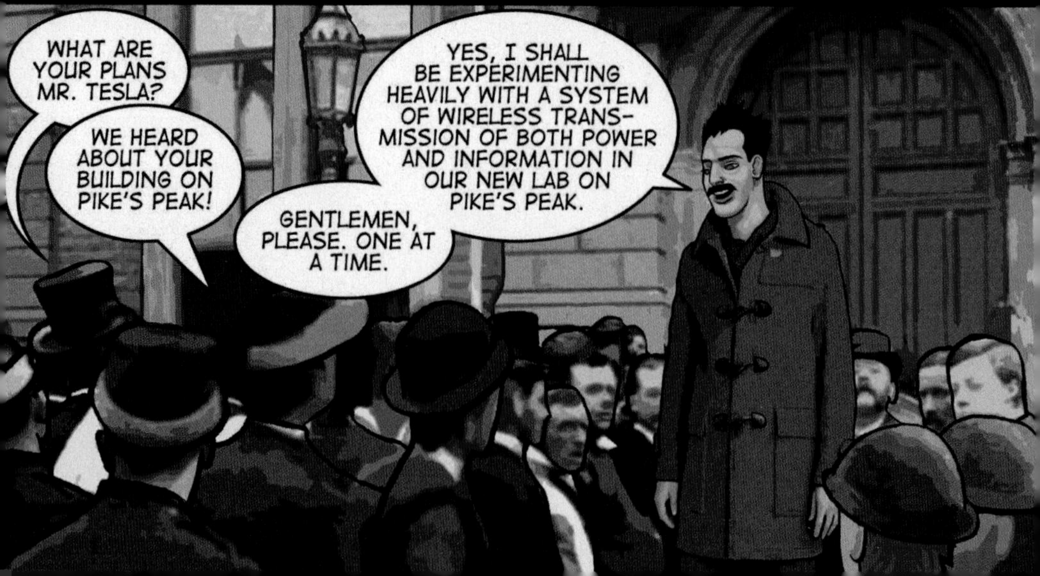
WHAT ARE YOUR PLANS MR. TESLA?
WE HEARD ABOUT YOUR BUILDING ON PIKE'S PEAK!
GENTLEMEN, PLEASE. ONE AT A TIME.
YES, I SHALL BE EXPERIMENTING HEAVILY WITH A SYSTEM OF WIRELESS TRANS-MISSION OF BOTH POWER AND INFORMATION IN OUR NEW LAB ON PIKE'S PEAK.

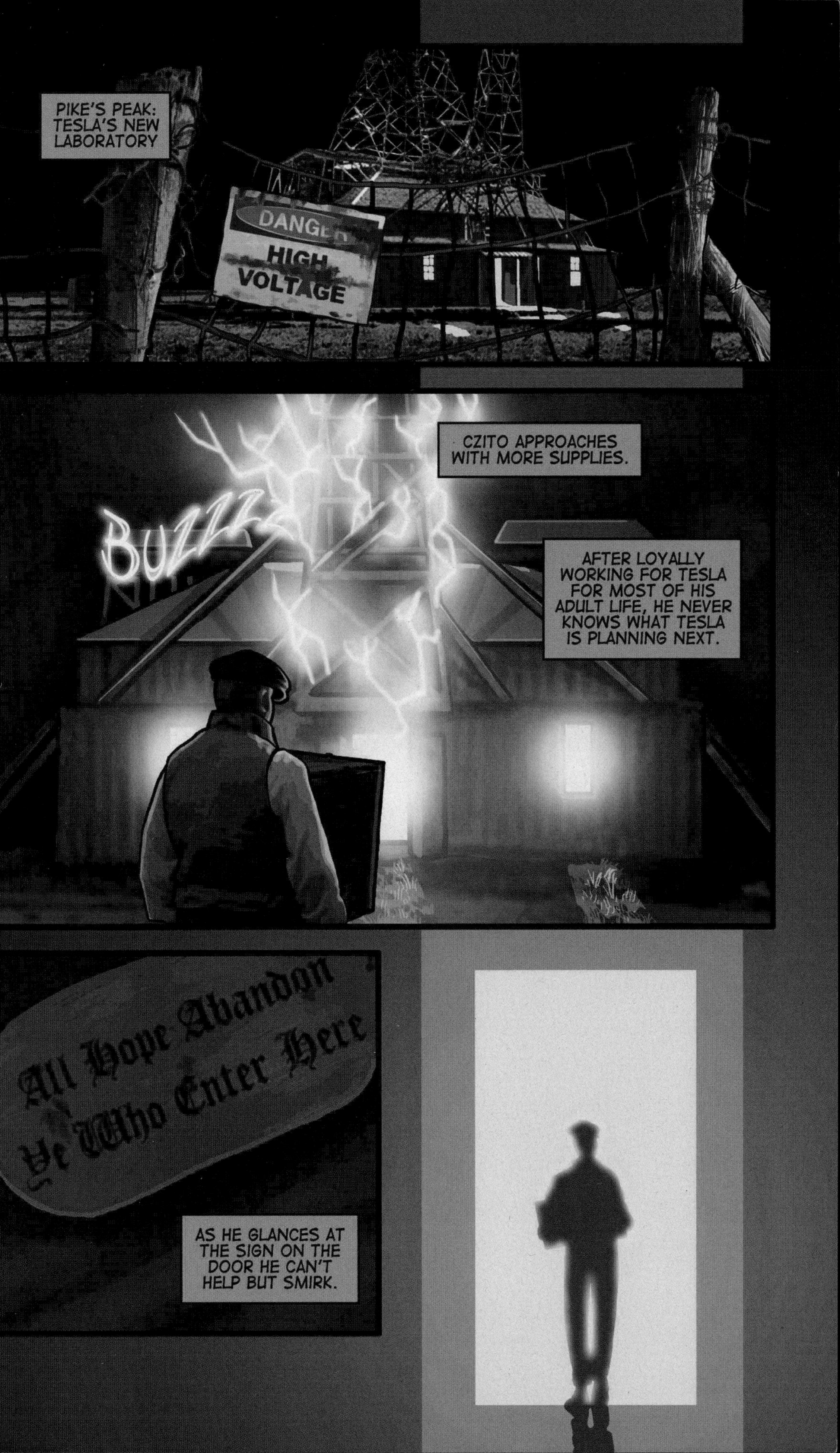
PIKE'S PEAK: TESLA'S NEW LABORATORY
HIGH VOLTAGE
CZITO APPROACHES WITH MORE SUPPLIES.
BUZZZ
AFTER LOYALLY WORKING FOR TESLA FOR MOST OF HIS ADULT LIFE, HE NEVER KNOWS WHAT TESLA IS PLANNING NEXT.
All Hope Abandon Ye Who Enter Here
AS HE GLANCES AT THE SIGN ON THE DOOR HE CAN'T HELP BUT SMIRK.

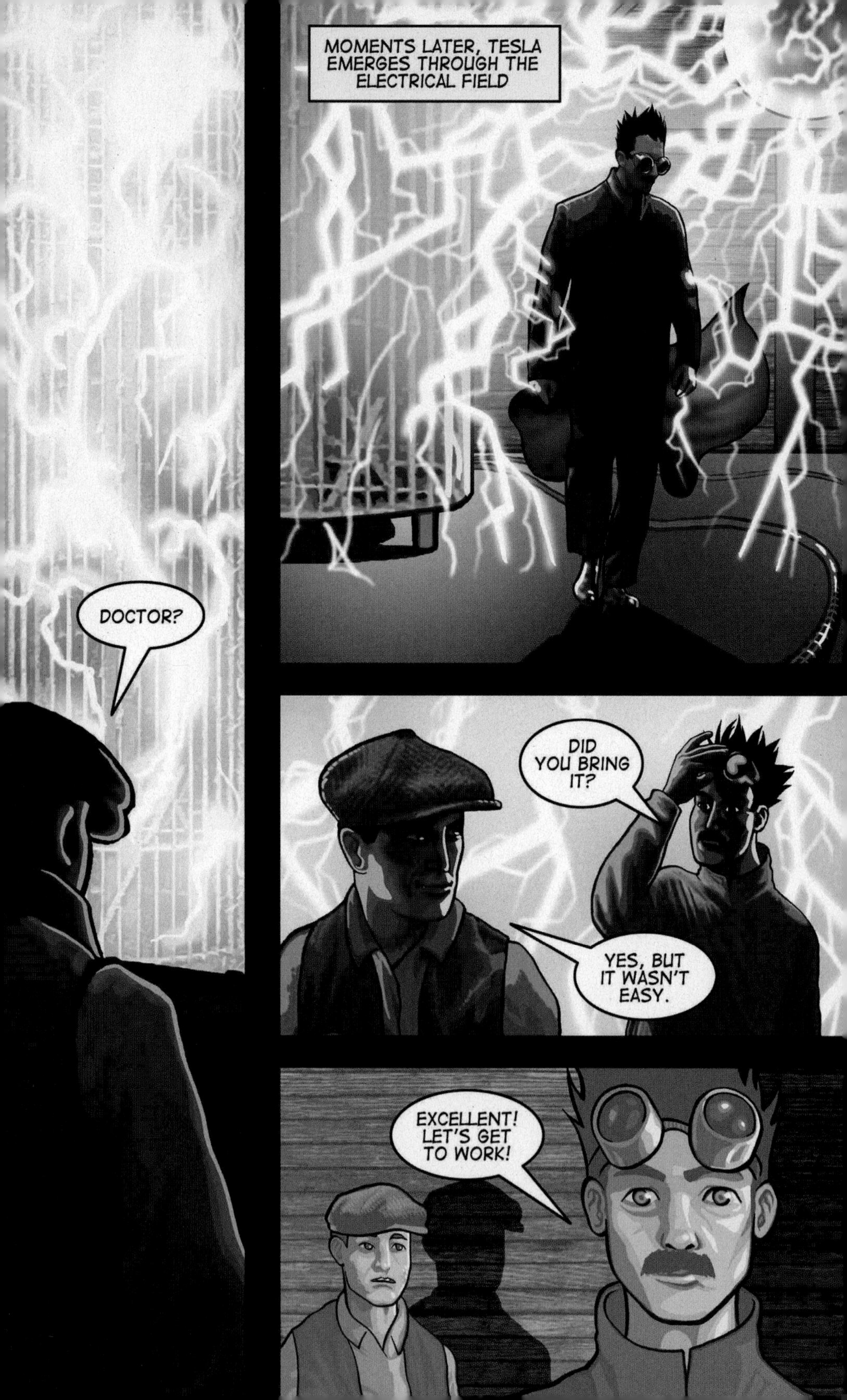
MOMENTS LATER, TESLA EMERGES THROUGH THE ELECTRICAL FIELD
DOCTOR?
DID YOU BRING IT?
YES, BUT IT WASN'T EASY.
EXCELLENT! LET'S GET TO WORK!

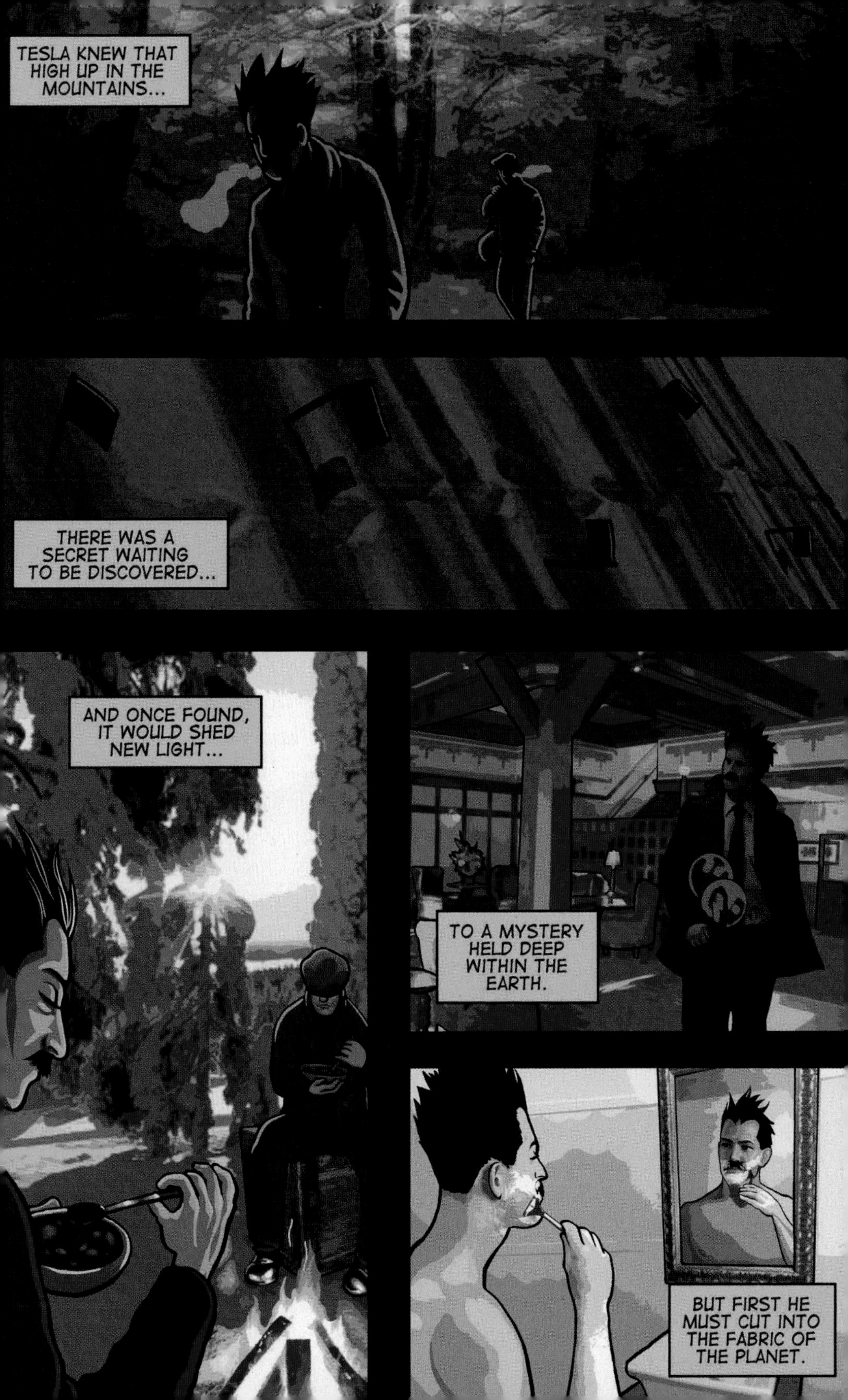
TESLA KNEW THAT HIGH UP IN THE MOUNTAINS...
THERE WAS A SECRET WAITING TO BE DISCOVERED...
AND ONCE FOUND, IT WOULD SHED NEW LIGHT...
TO A MYSTERY HELD DEEP WITHIN THE EARTH.
BUT FIRST HE MUST CUT INTO THE FABRIC OF THE PLANET.

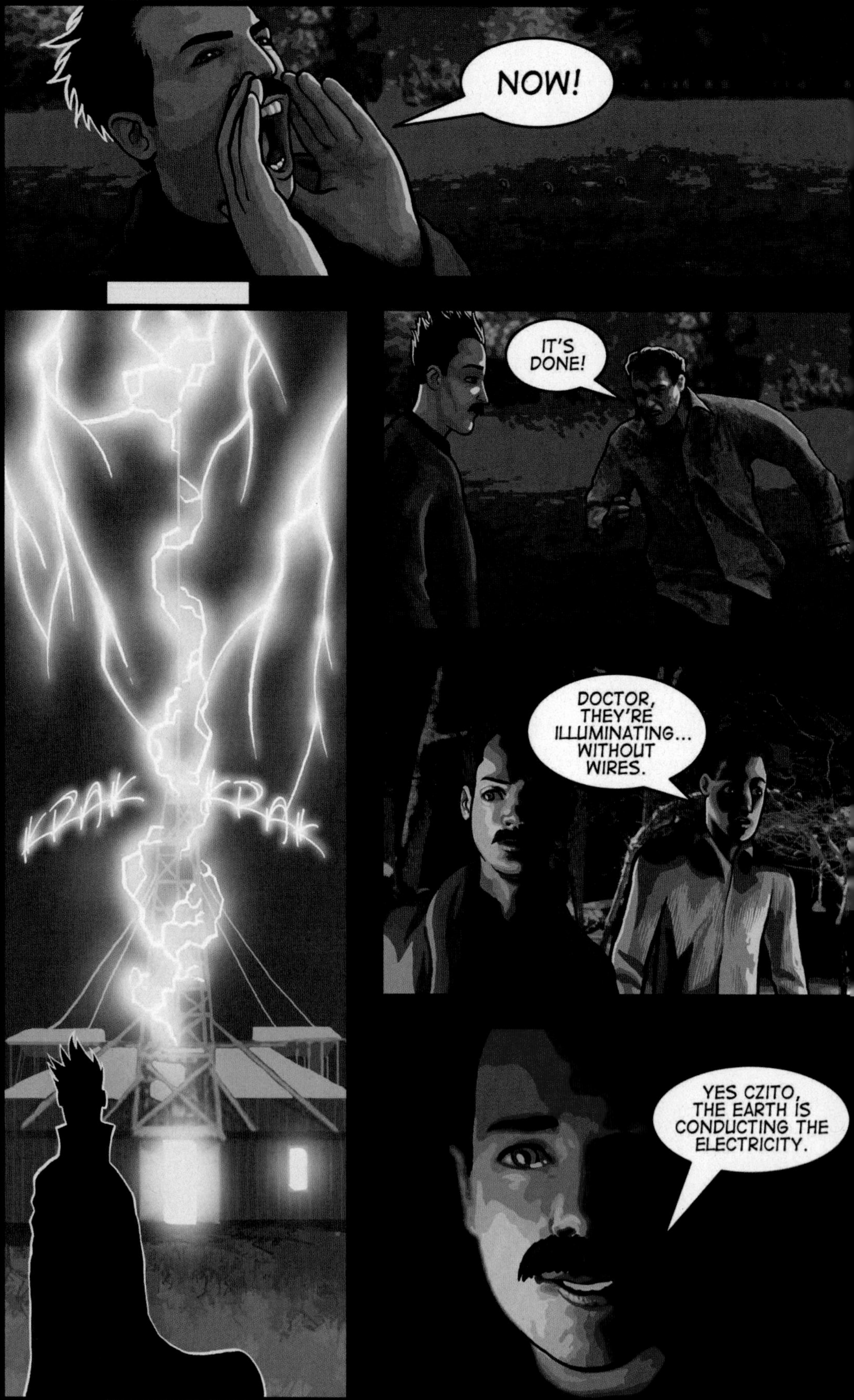
NOW!
KRAK KRAK
IT'S DONE!
DOCTOR, THEY'RE ILLUMINATING... WITHOUT WIRES.
YES CZITO, THE EARTH IS CONDUCTING THE ELECTRICITY.

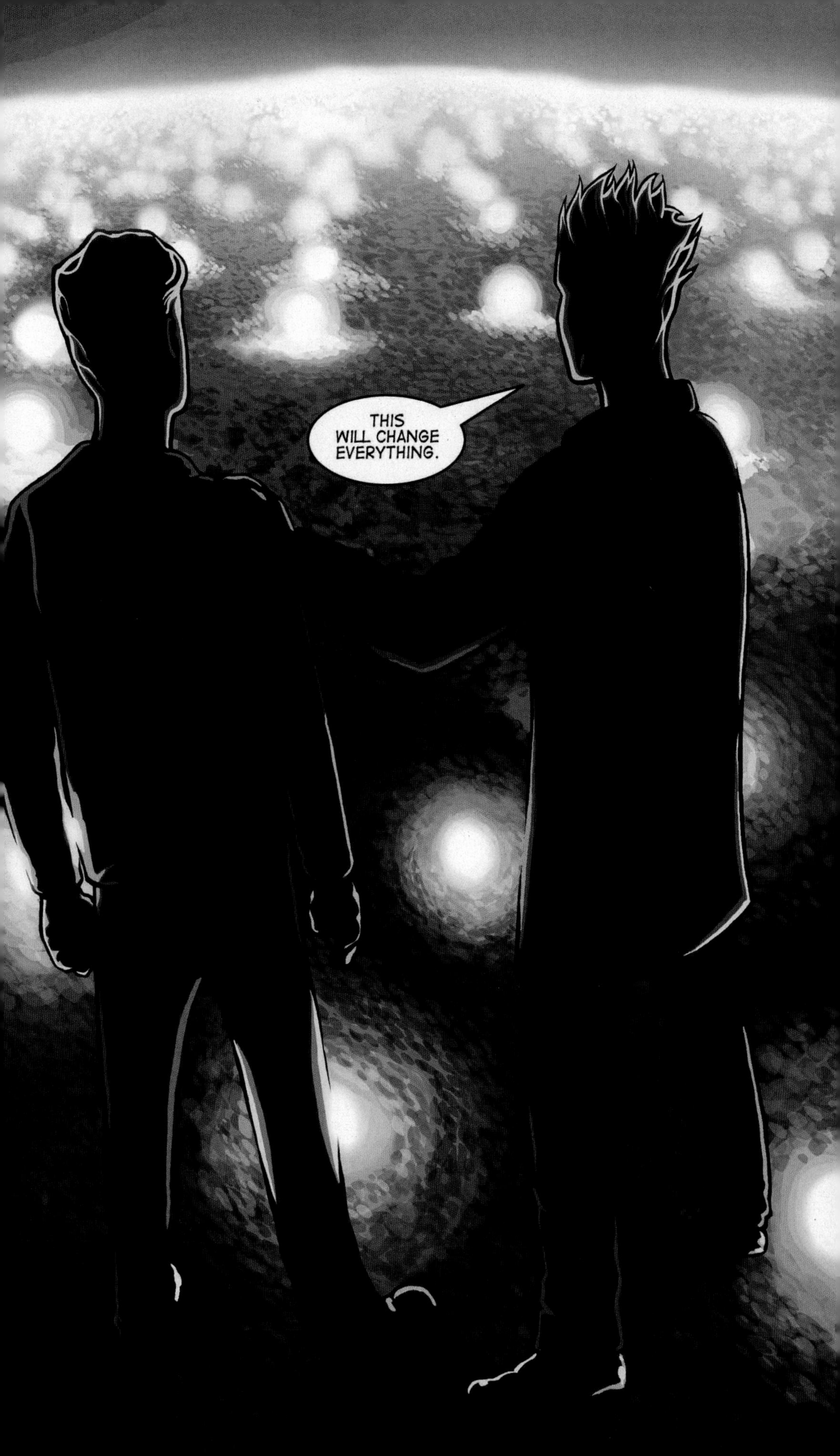
THIS WILL CHANGE EVERYTHING.

"ELECTRIC CURRENT, AFTER PASSING INTO THE EARTH TRAVELS TO THE DIAMETRICALLY OPPOSITE REGION OF THE SAME AND REBOUNDING FROM THERE, RETURNS TO ITS POINT OF DEPARTURE WITH VIRTUALLY UNDIMINISHED FORCE...SO ASTOUNDING ARE THE FACTS IN THIS CONNECTION, THAT IT WOULD SEEM AS THOUGH THE CREATOR, HIMSELF, HAD ELECTRICALLY DESIGNED THIS PLANET JUST FOR THE PURPOSE OF ENABLING US TO ACHIEVE WONDERS WHICH, BEFORE MY DISCOVERY, COULD NOT HAVE BEEN CONCEIVED BY THE WILDEST IMAGINATION."

- NIKOLA TESLA (1856-1943)

CHAPTER 6

TRANSFORMER

AFTER MUCH MORE EXPERIMENTING AND DISCOVERY IN THE MOUNTAINS, TESLA RECOGNIZES HIS TRUE PURPOSE - THE DEMOCRATIZATION OF ENERGY. ONLY UNTIL THE WORLD HAS EASY ACCESS TO ABUNDANT ENERGY, CAN THE HUMAN RACE EVOLVE BEYOND THIS AGE OF DOMINATION INTO A NEW AGE OF DOMINION. AS WARS STEM FROM THE PSYCHOLOGY OF SCARCITY AND POSSESSION, THE RELIEF OF THESE CONSTRAINTS WOULD OPEN UP A NEW RENAISSANCE LEADING TO INNOVATION IN HEALTH AND SCIENCE AS WELL AS ARTS AND SPIRITUALITY. BOUNDARIES WOULD DISSOLVE, CULTURAL EXCHANGE WOULD THRIVE AND THE WORLD WOULD COME TOGETHER AS ONE.

HOWEVER TO ACHIEVE THIS VISION, TESLA MUST SOLVE THE PRIMORDIAL PARADOX AND CONVINCE THE ULTIMATE CAPITALISTS TO HELP CREATE A WORLD IN WHICH THEIR IDEALS WOULD NO LONGER BE RELEVANT.

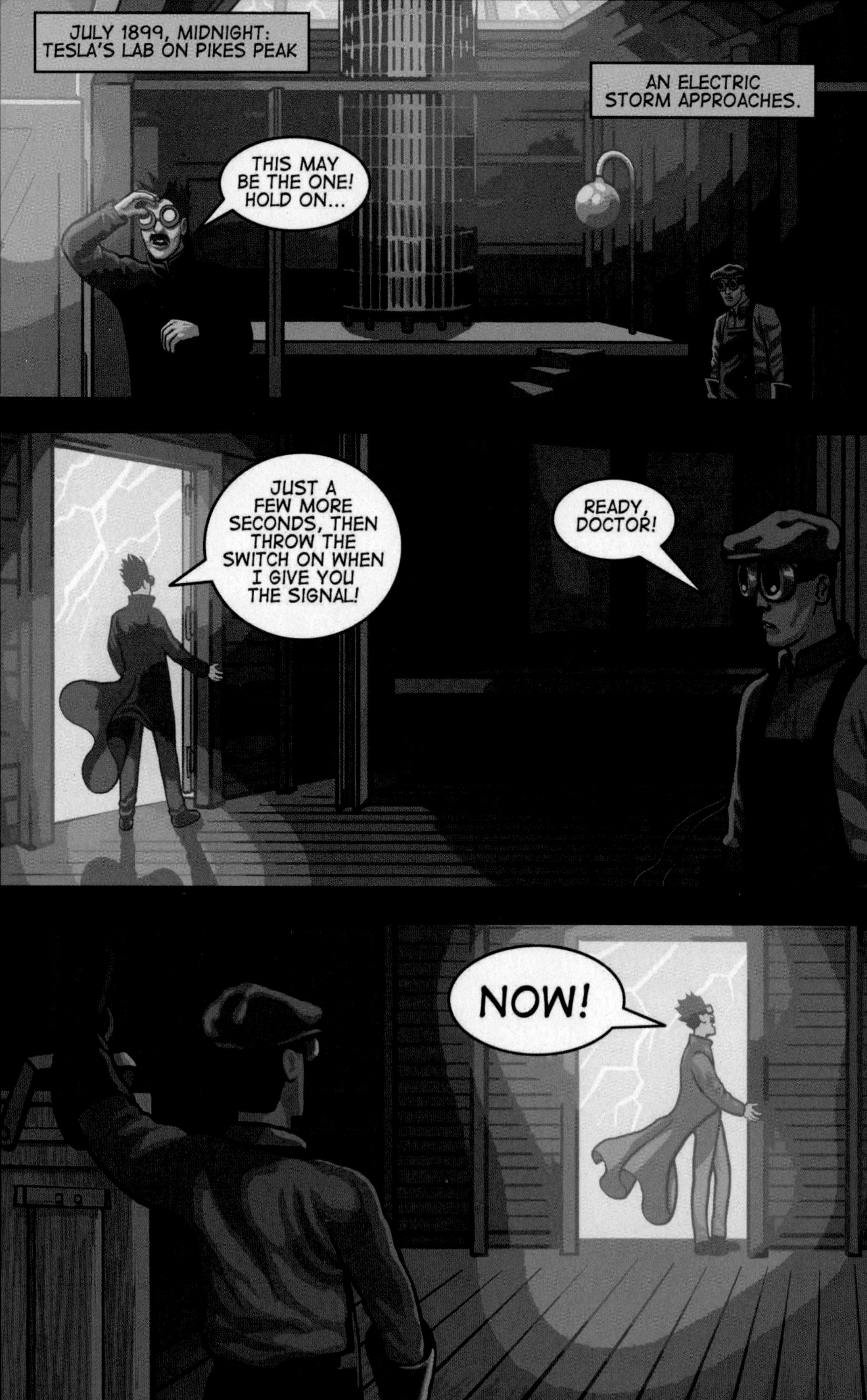
JULY 1899, MIDNIGHT: TESLA'S LAB ON PIKES PEAK
AN ELECTRIC STORM APPROACHES.
THIS MAY BE THE ONE! HOLD ON...
JUST A FEW MORE SECONDS, THEN THROW THE SWITCH ON WHEN I GIVE YOU THE SIGNAL!
READY, DOCTOR!
NOW!

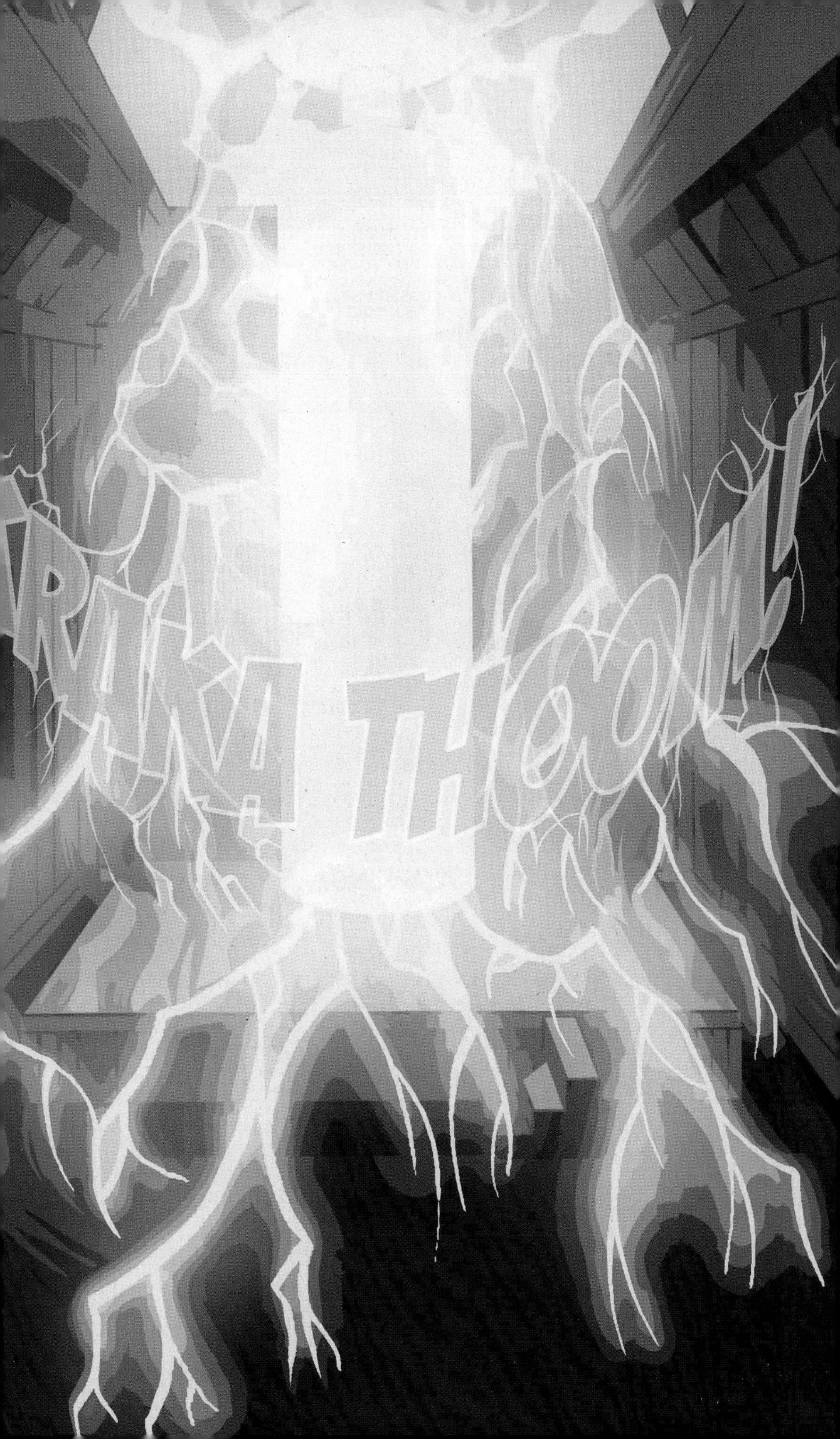
THOOM!

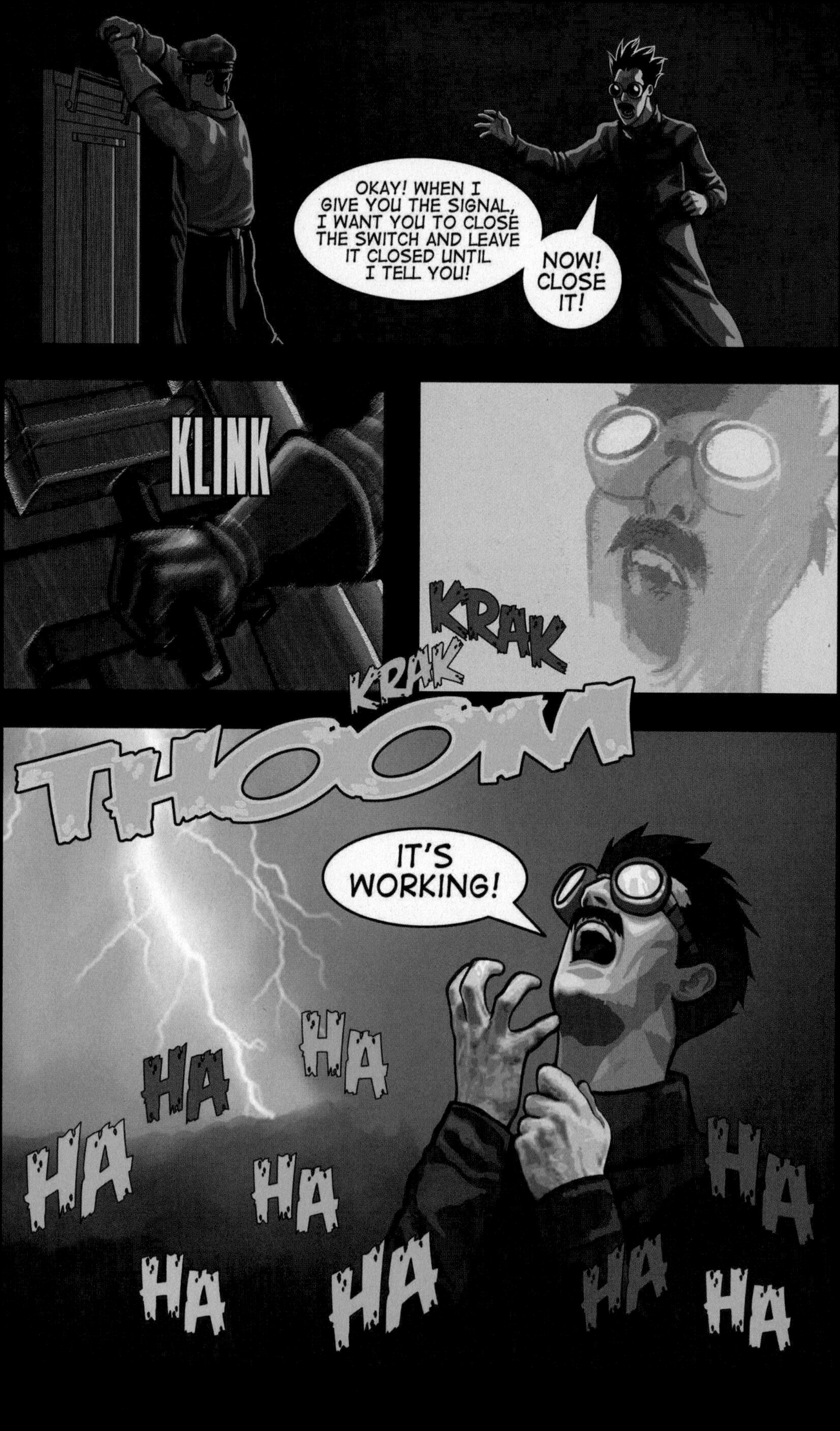
OKAY! WHEN I GIVE YOU THE SIGNAL, I WANT YOU TO CLOSE THE SWITCH AND LEAVE IT CLOSED UNTIL I TELL YOU!
NOW! CLOSE IT!
KLINK
KRAK
KRAK
THOOM
IT'S WORKING!
HA
HA
HA
HA
HA
HA
HA
HA
HA

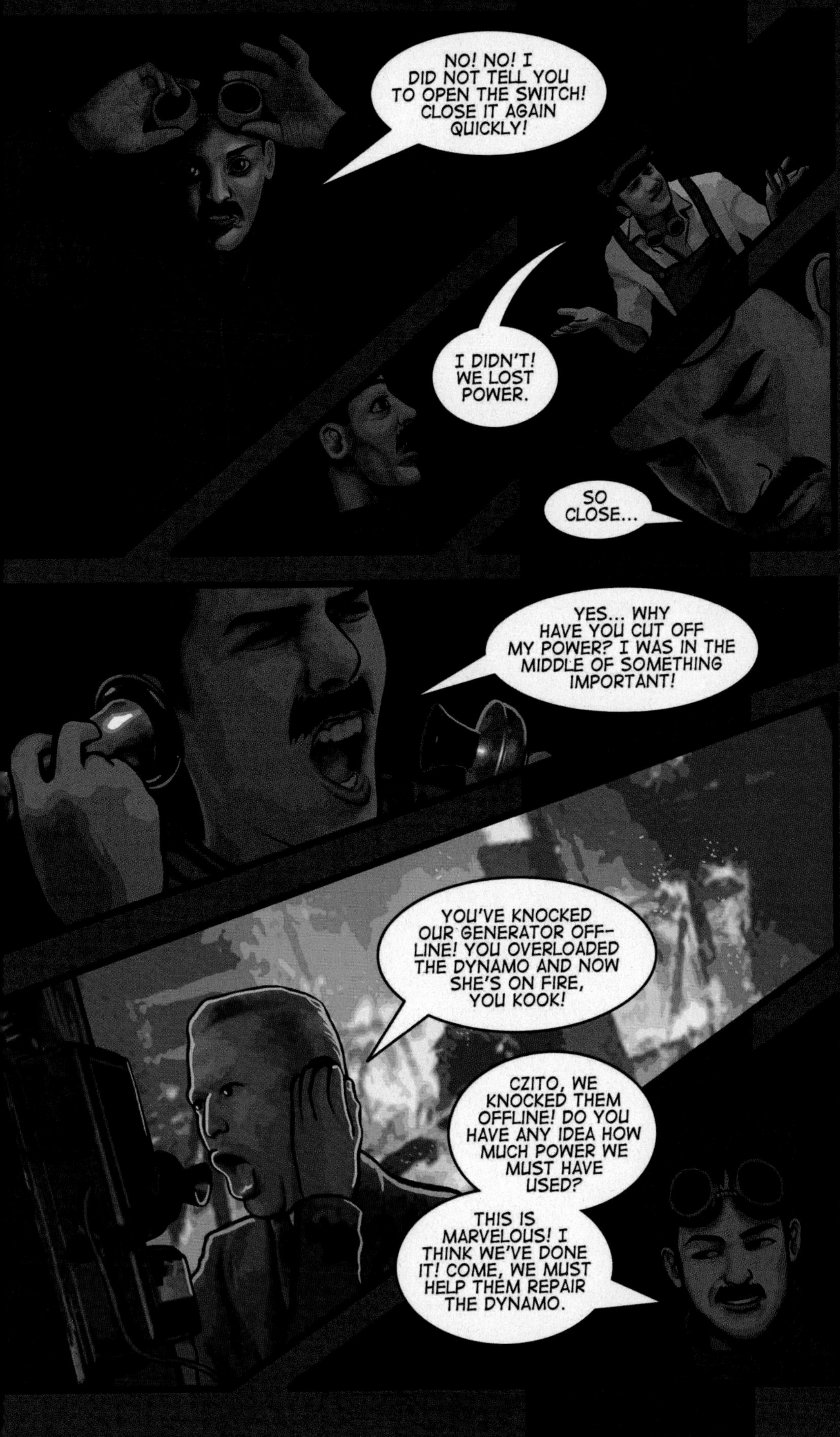
NO! NO! I DID NOT TELL YOU TO OPEN THE SWITCH! CLOSE IT AGAIN QUICKLY!
I DIDN'T! WE LOST POWER.
SO CLOSE...
YES... WHY HAVE YOU CUT OFF MY POWER? I WAS IN THE MIDDLE OF SOMETHING IMPORTANT!
YOU'VE KNOCKED OUR GENERATOR OFF-LINE! YOU OVERLOADED THE DYNAMO AND NOW SHE'S ON FIRE, YOU KOOK!
CZITO, WE KNOCKED THEM OFFLINE! DO YOU HAVE ANY IDEA HOW MUCH POWER WE MUST HAVE USED?
THIS IS MARVELOUS! I THINK WE'VE DONE IT! COME, WE MUST HELP THEM REPAIR THE DYNAMO.

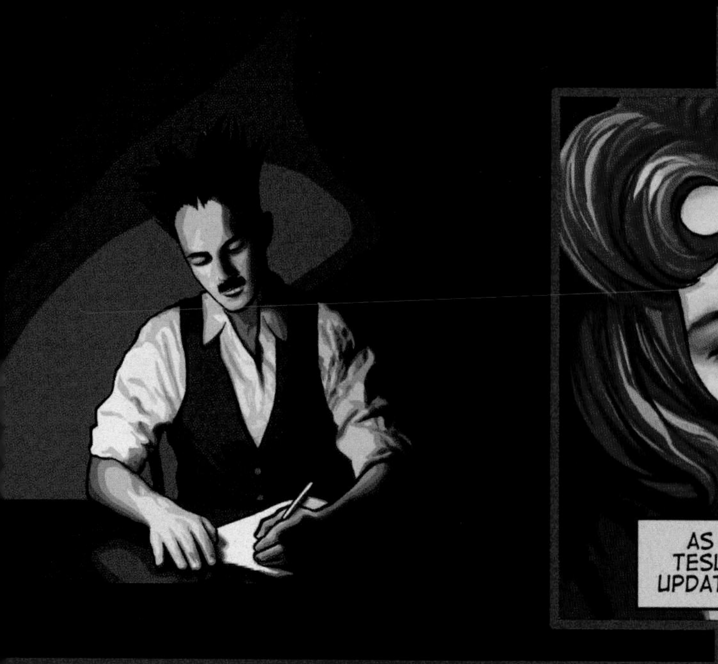

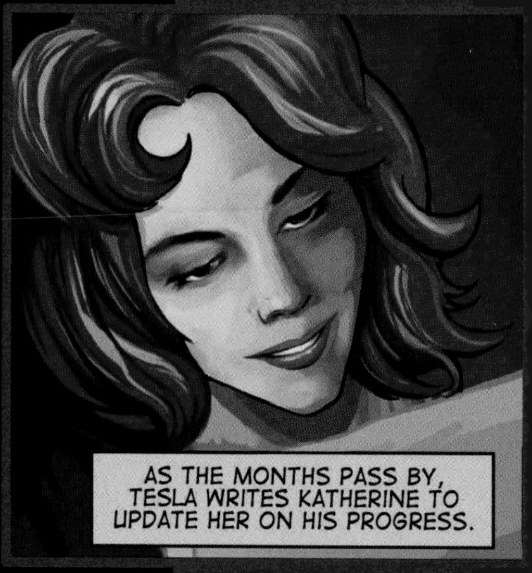
AS THE MONTHS PASS BY, TESLA WRITES KATHERINE TO UPDATE HER ON HIS PROGRESS.

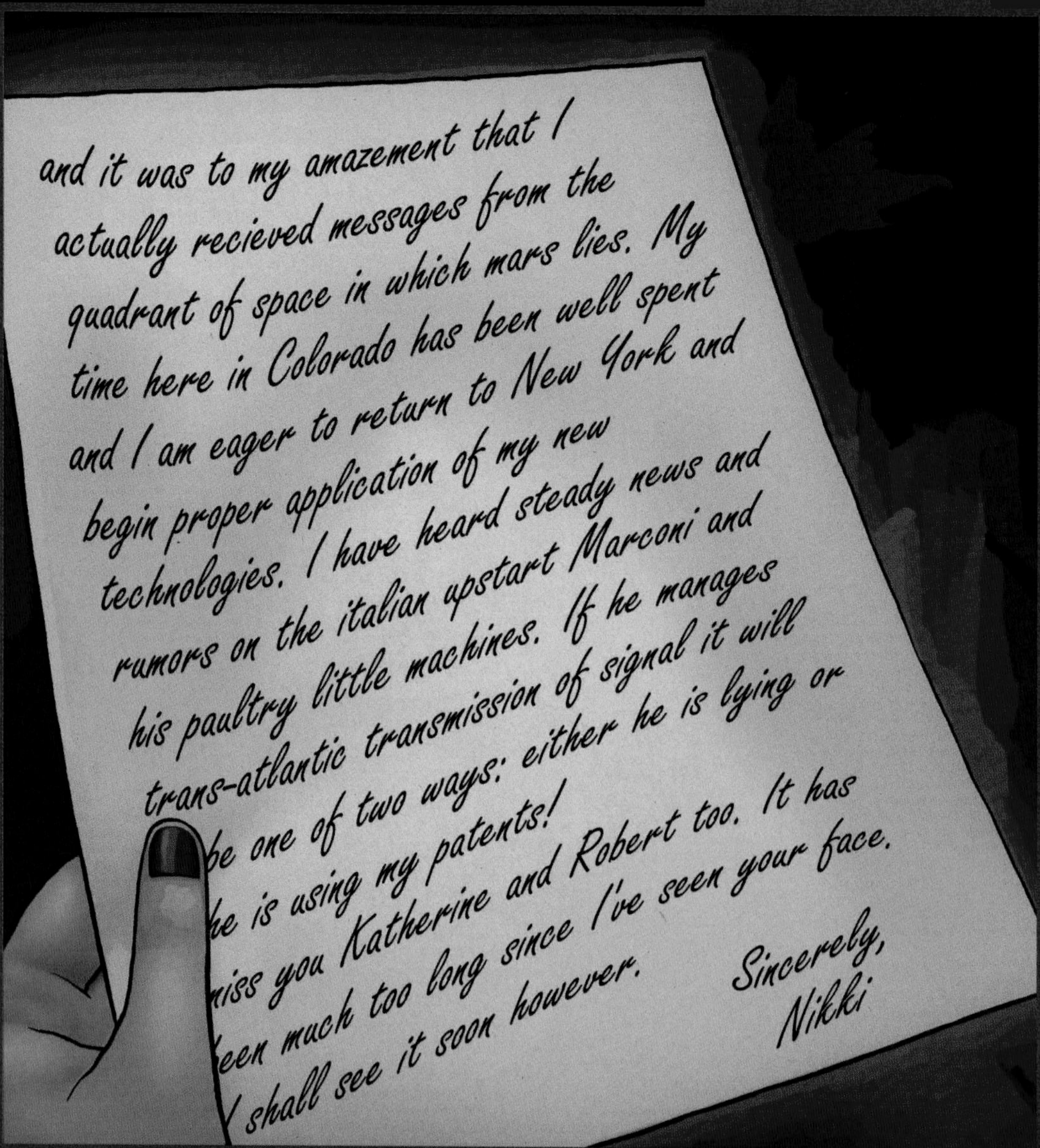
and it was to my amazement that I
actually recieved messages from the
quadrant of space in which mars lies. My
time here in Colorado has been well spent
and I am eager to return to New York and
begin proper application of my new
technologies. I have heard steady news and
rumors on the italian upstart Marconi and
his paultry little machines. If he manages
trans-atlantic transmission of signal it will
be one of two ways: either he is lying or
he is using my patents!
iss you Katherine and Robert too. It has
een much too long since I've seen your face.
shall see it soon however.
Sincerely,
Nikki

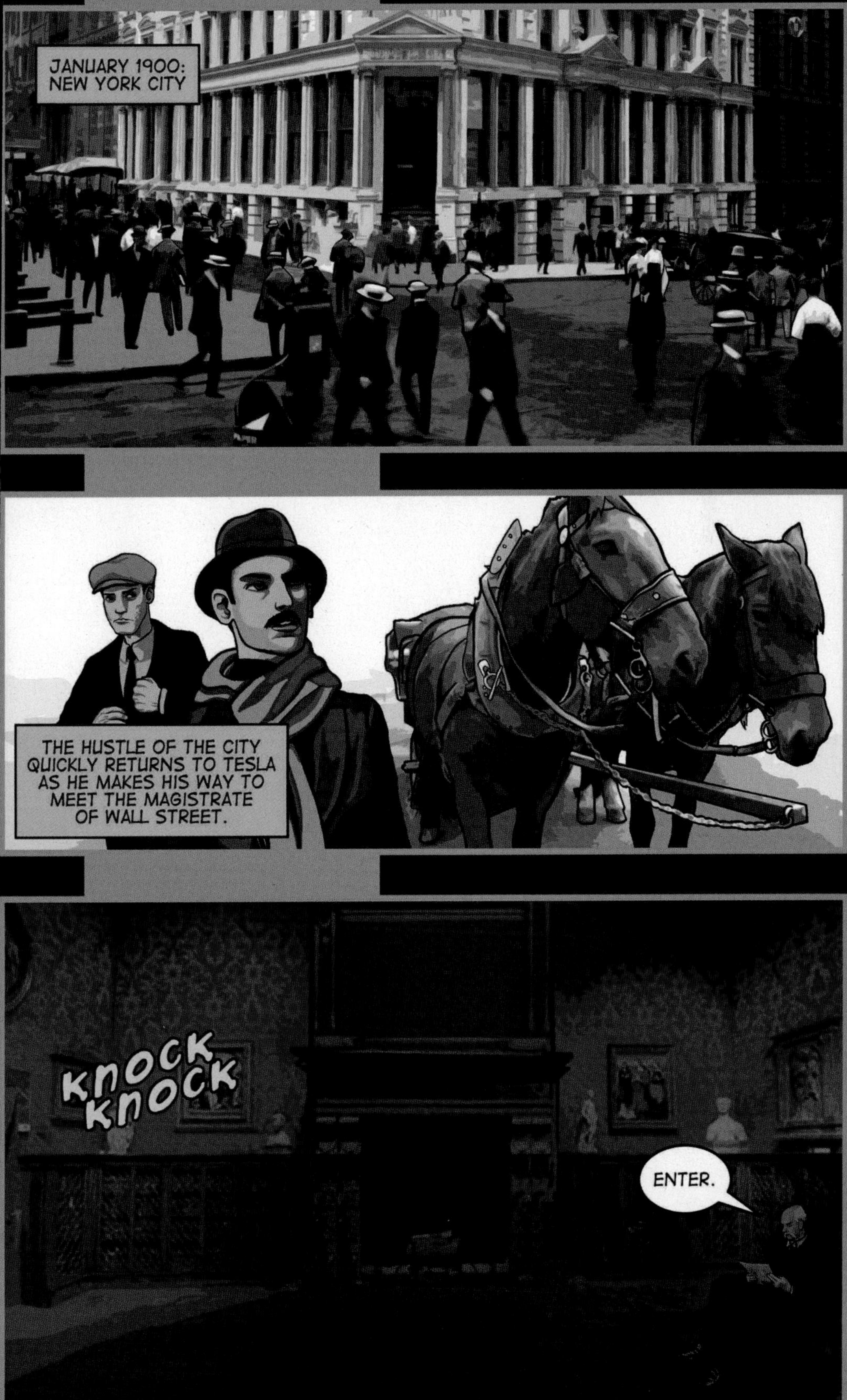
JANUARY 1900:
NEW YORK CITY
THE HUSTLE OF THE CITY QUICKLY RETURNS TO TESLA AS HE MAKES HIS WAY TO MEET THE MAGISTRATE OF WALL STREET.
KNOCK KNOCK
ENTER.

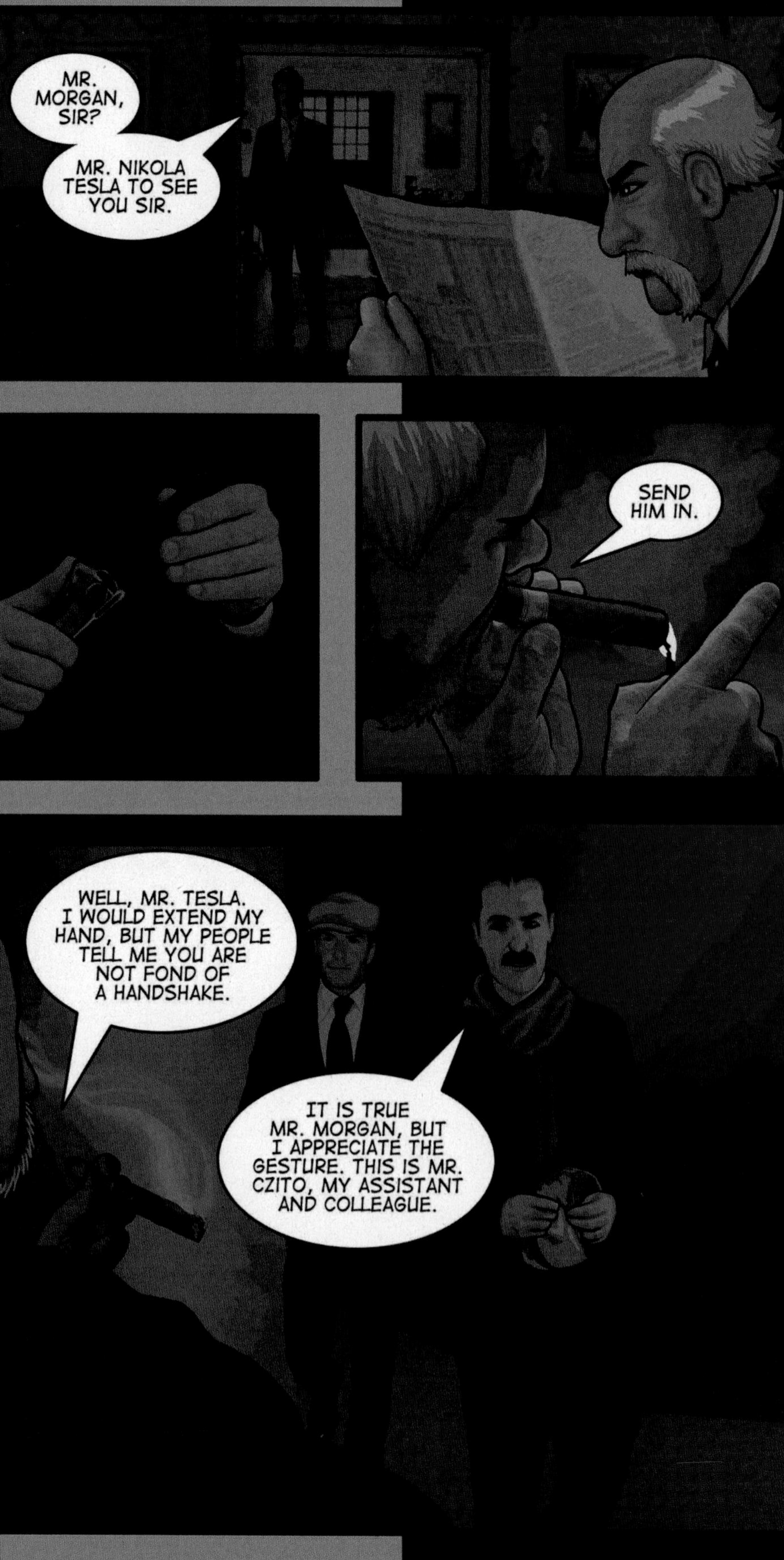

MR. MORGAN, SIR?
MR. NIKOLA TESLA TO SEE YOU SIR.
SEND HIM IN.
WELL, MR. TESLA. I WOULD EXTEND MY HAND, BUT MY PEOPLE TELL ME YOU ARE NOT FOND OF A HANDSHAKE.
IT IS TRUE MR. MORGAN, BUT I APPRECIATE THE GESTURE. THIS IS MR. CZITO, MY ASSISTANT AND COLLEAGUE.

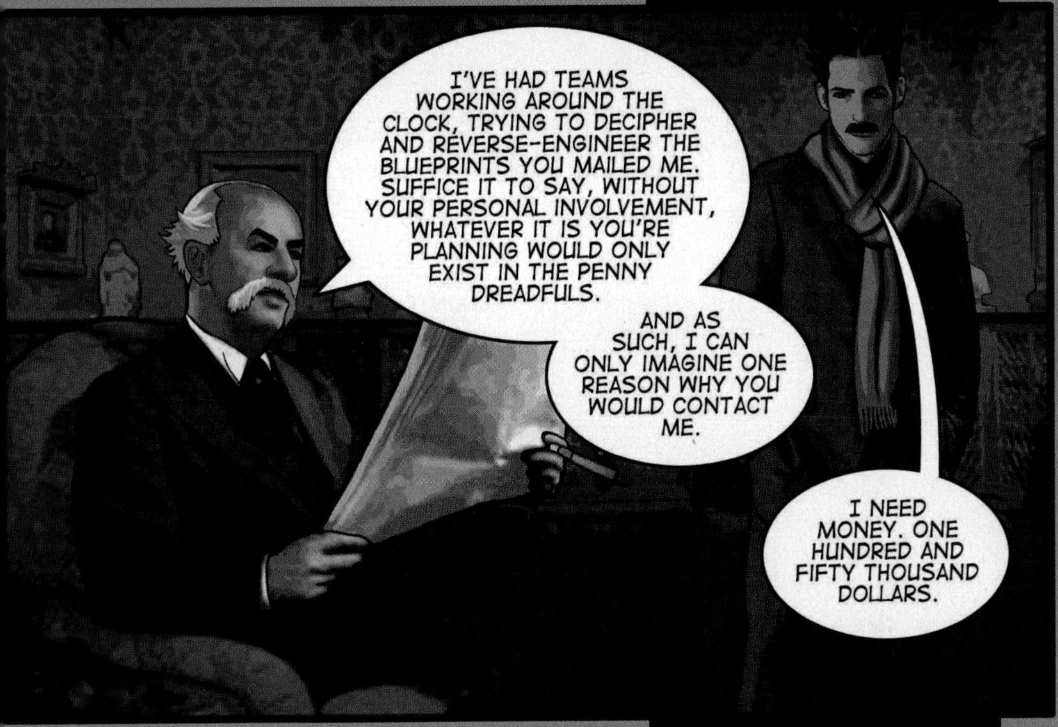
I'VE HAD TEAMS WORKING AROUND THE CLOCK, TRYING TO DECIPHER AND REVERSE-ENGINEER THE BLUEPRINTS YOU MAILED ME. SUFFICE IT TO SAY, WITHOUT YOUR PERSONAL INVOLVEMENT, WHATEVER IT IS YOU'RE PLANNING WOULD ONLY EXIST IN THE PENNY DREADFULS.
AND AS SUCH, I CAN ONLY IMAGINE ONE REASON WHY YOU WOULD CONTACT ME.
I NEED MONEY. ONE HUNDRED AND FIFTY THOUSAND DOLLARS.

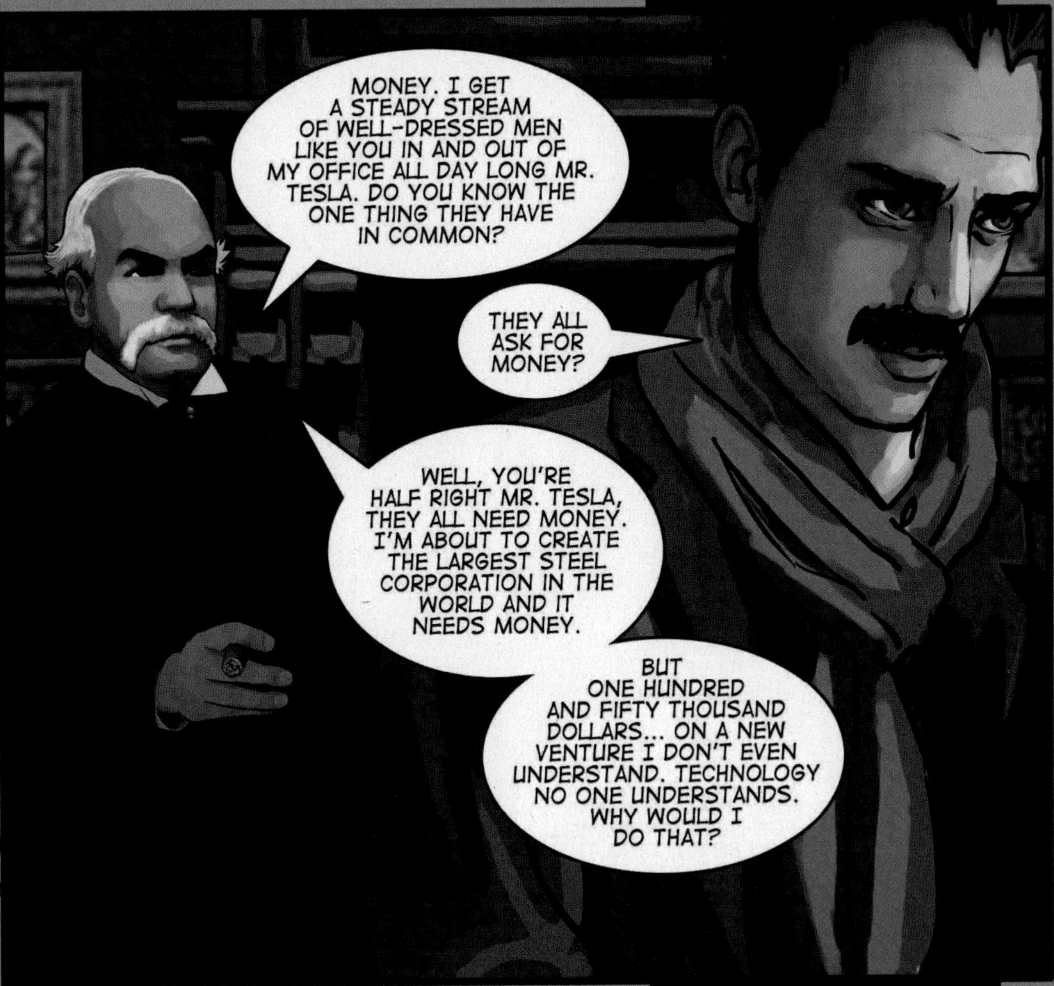
MONEY. I GET A STEADY STREAM OF WELL-DRESSED MEN LIKE YOU IN AND OUT OF MY OFFICE ALL DAY LONG MR. TESLA. DO YOU KNOW THE ONE THING THEY HAVE IN COMMON?
THEY ALL ASK FOR MONEY?
WELL, YOU'RE HALF RIGHT MR. TESLA, THEY ALL NEED MONEY. I'M ABOUT TO CREATE THE LARGEST STEEL CORPORATION IN THE WORLD AND IT NEEDS MONEY.
BUT ONE HUNDRED AND FIFTY THOUSAND DOLLARS... ON A NEW VENTURE I DON'T EVEN UNDERSTAND. TECHNOLOGY NO ONE UNDERSTANDS. WHY WOULD I DO THAT?

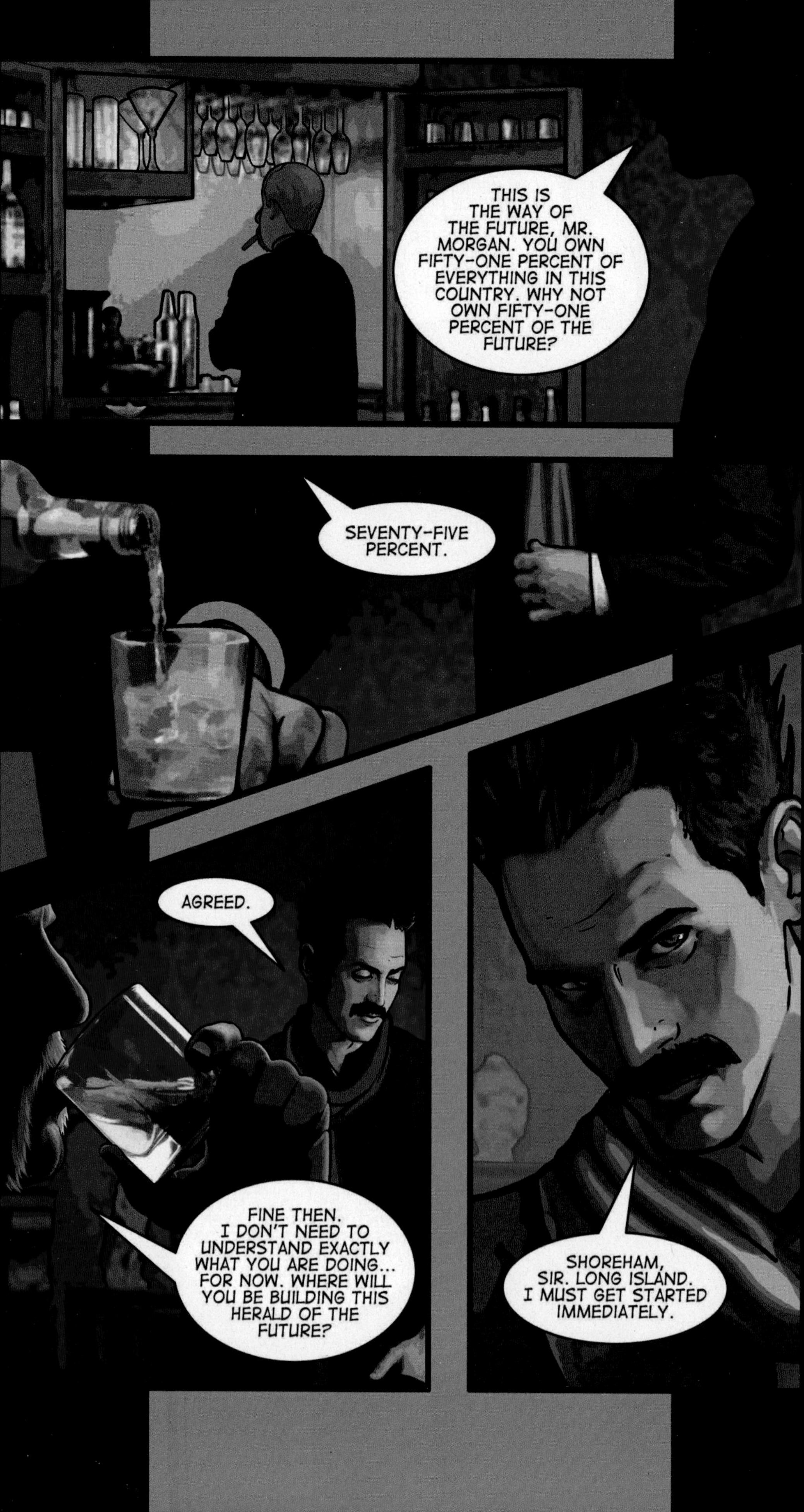
THIS IS THE WAY OF THE FUTURE, MR. MORGAN. YOU OWN FIFTY-ONE PERCENT OF EVERYTHING IN THIS COUNTRY. WHY NOT OWN FIFTY-ONE PERCENT OF THE FUTURE?
SEVENTY-FIVE PERCENT.
AGREED.
FINE THEN. I DON'T NEED TO UNDERSTAND EXACTLY WHAT YOU ARE DOING... FOR NOW. WHERE WILL YOU BE BUILDING THIS HERALD OF THE FUTURE?
SHOREHAM, SIR. LONG ISLAND. I MUST GET STARTED IMMEDIATELY.

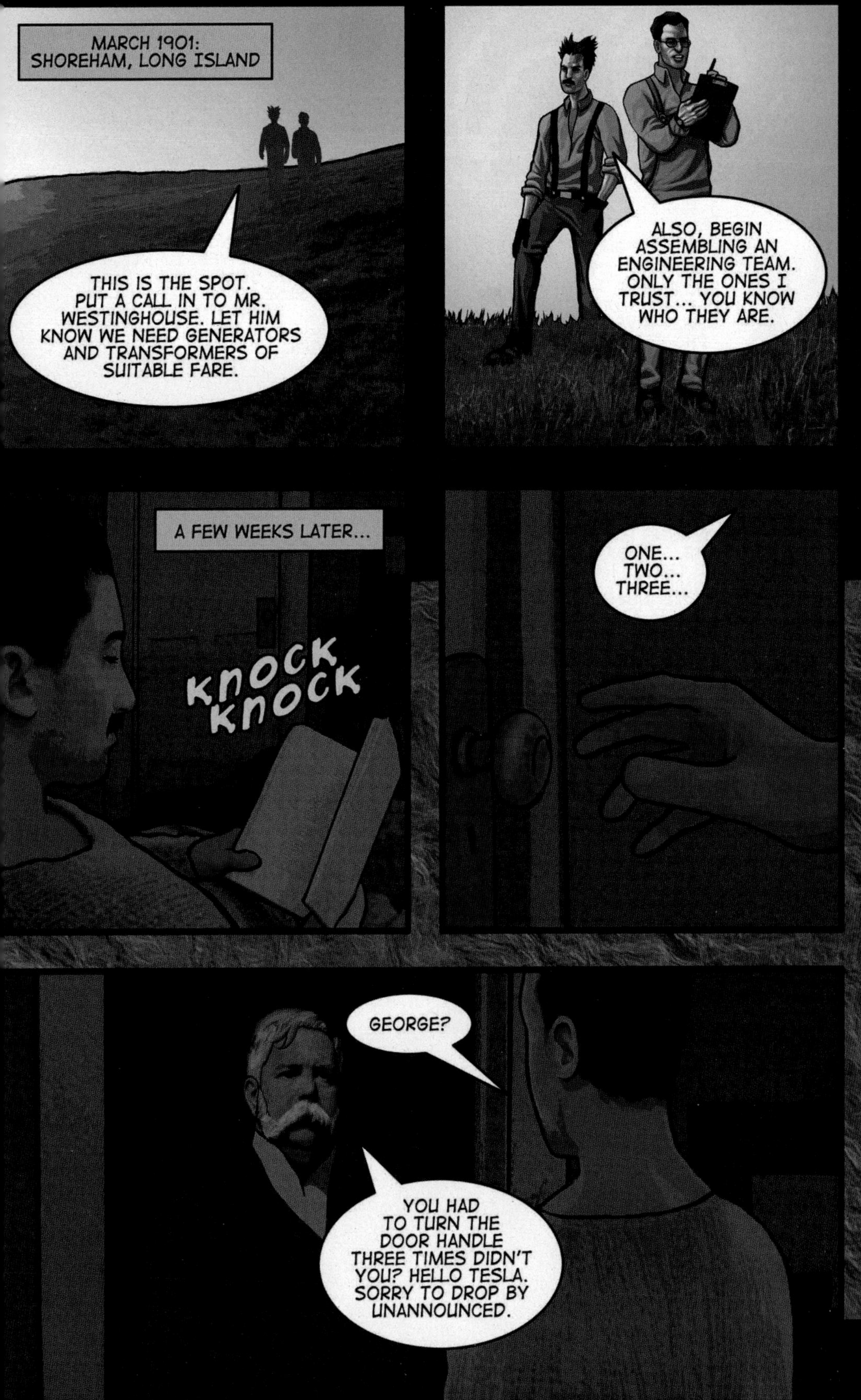
MARCH 1901: SHOREHAM, LONG ISLAND
THIS IS THE SPOT. PUT A CALL IN TO MR. WESTINGHOUSE. LET HIM KNOW WE NEED GENERATORS AND TRANSFORMERS OF SUITABLE FARE.
ALSO, BEGIN ASSEMBLING AN ENGINEERING TEAM. ONLY THE ONES I TRUST... YOU KNOW WHO THEY ARE.
A FEW WEEKS LATER...
KNOCK KNOCK
ONE... TWO... THREE...
GEORGE?
YOU HAD TO TURN THE DOOR HANDLE THREE TIMES DIDN'T YOU? HELLO TESLA. SORRY TO DROP BY UNANNOUNCED.

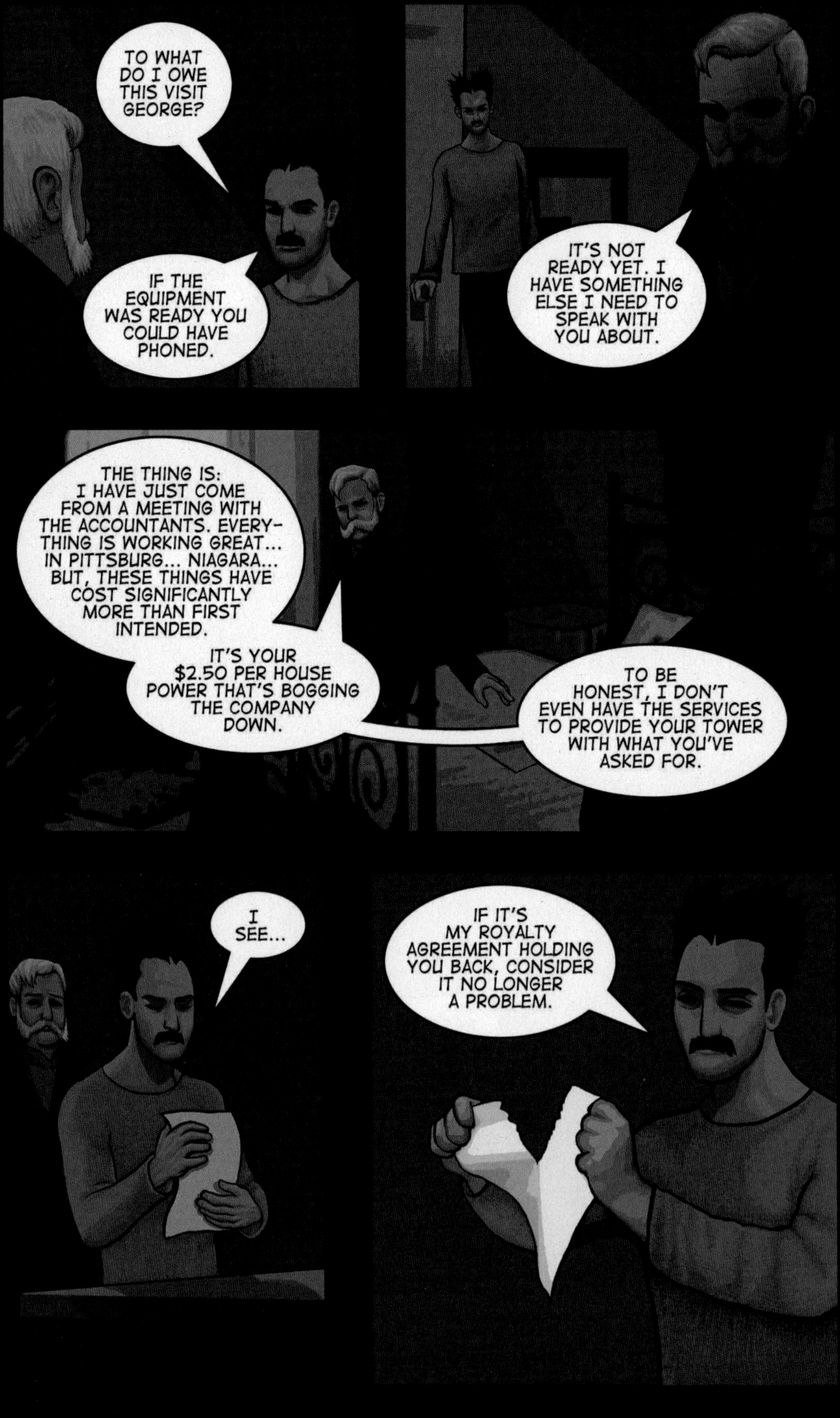
TO WHAT DO I OWE THIS VISIT GEORGE?
IF THE EQUIPMENT WAS READY YOU COULD HAVE PHONED.
IT'S NOT READY YET. I HAVE SOMETHING ELSE I NEED TO SPEAK WITH YOU ABOUT.
THE THING IS: I HAVE JUST COME FROM A MEETING WITH THE ACCOUNTANTS. EVERY-THING IS WORKING GREAT... IN PITTSBURG... NIAGARA... BUT, THESE THINGS HAVE COST SIGNIFICANTLY MORE THAN FIRST INTENDED.
IT'S YOUR $2.50 PER HOUSE POWER THAT'S BOGGING THE COMPANY DOWN.
TO BE HONEST, I DON'T EVEN HAVE THE SERVICES TO PROVIDE YOUR TOWER WITH WHAT YOU'VE ASKED FOR.
I SEE...
IF IT'S MY ROYALTY AGREEMENT HOLDING YOU BACK, CONSIDER IT NO LONGER A PROBLEM.

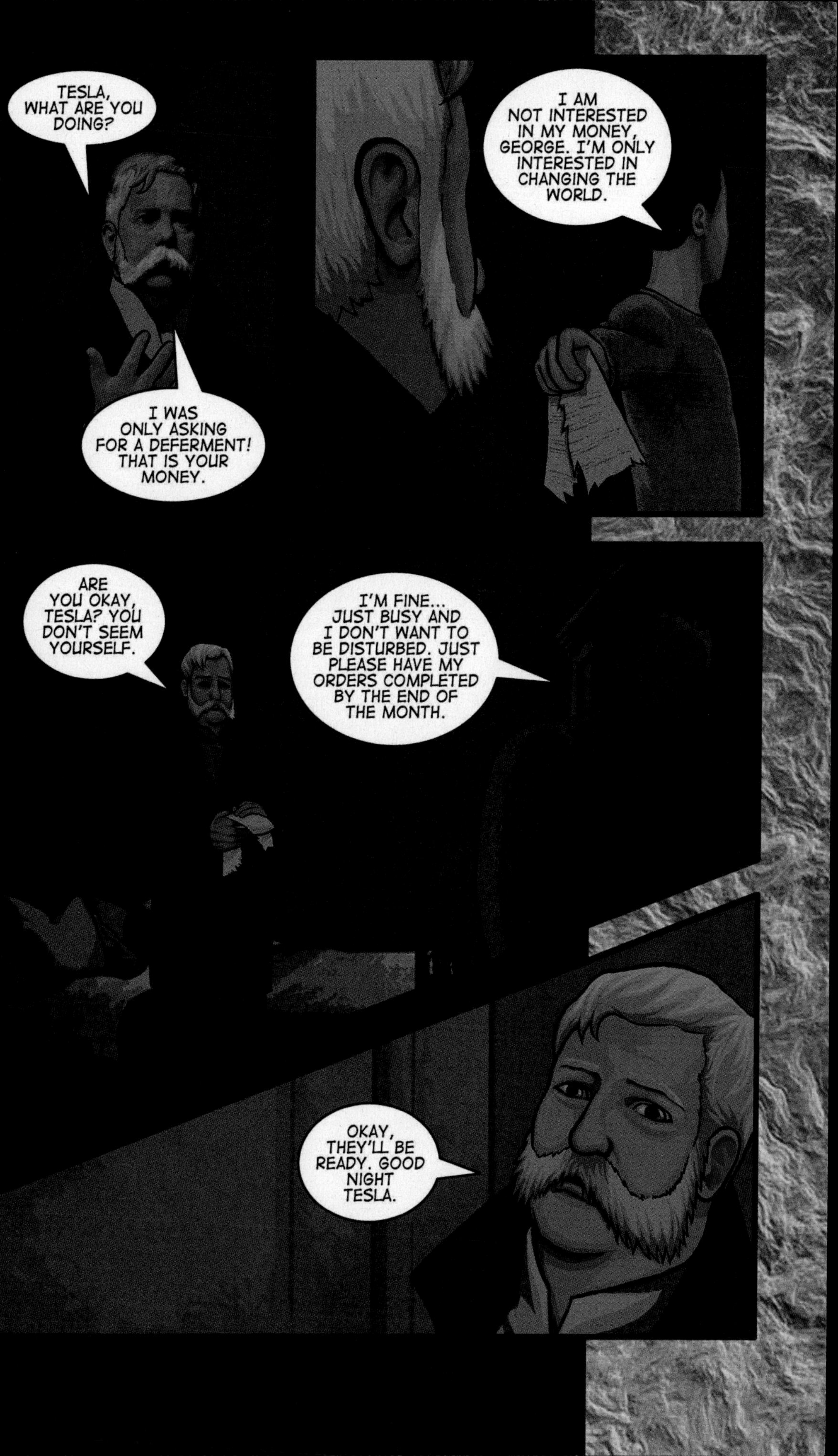
TESLA, WHAT ARE YOU DOING?
I WAS ONLY ASKING FOR A DEFERMENT! THAT IS YOUR MONEY.
I AM NOT INTERESTED IN MY MONEY, GEORGE. I'M ONLY INTERESTED IN CHANGING THE WORLD.
ARE YOU OKAY, TESLA? YOU DON'T SEEM YOURSELF.
I'M FINE... JUST BUSY AND I DON'T WANT TO BE DISTURBED. JUST PLEASE HAVE MY ORDERS COMPLETED BY THE END OF THE MONTH.
OKAY, THEY'LL BE READY. GOOD NIGHT TESLA.

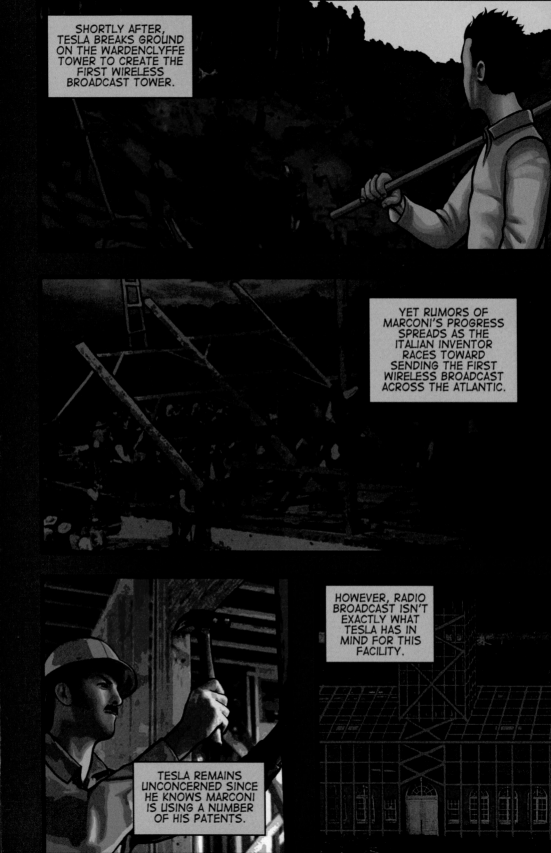

SHORTLY AFTER, TESLA BREAKS GROUND ON THE WARDENCLYFFE TOWER TO CREATE THE FIRST WIRELESS BROADCAST TOWER.

YET RUMORS OF MARCONI'S PROGRESS SPREADS AS THE ITALIAN INVENTOR RACES TOWARD SENDING THE FIRST WIRELESS BROADCAST ACROSS THE ATLANTIC.

HOWEVER, RADIO BROADCAST ISN'T EXACTLY WHAT TESLA HAS IN MIND FOR THIS FACILITY.

TESLA REMAINS UNCONCERNED SINCE HE KNOWS MARCONI IS USING A NUMBER OF HIS PATENTS.

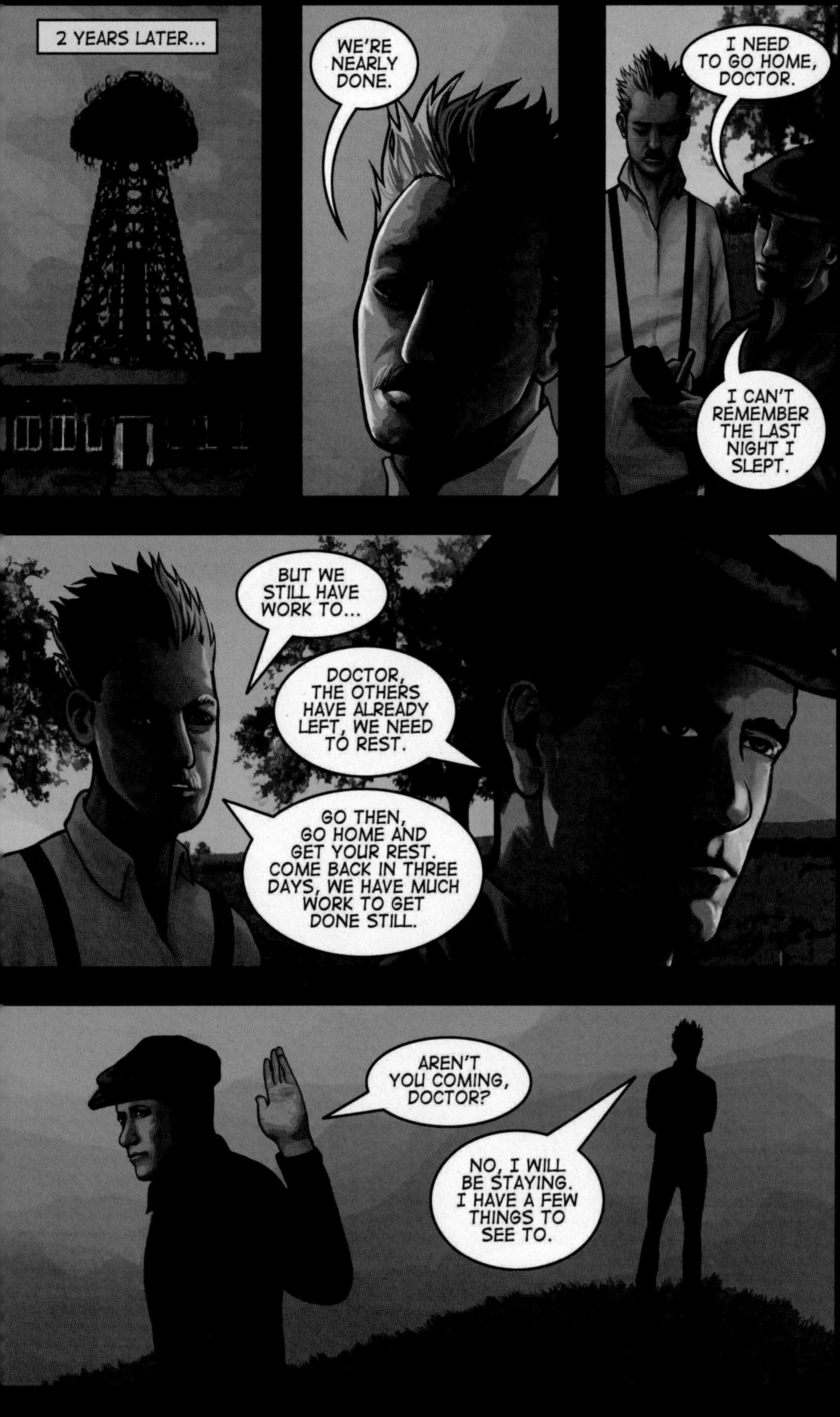
2 YEARS LATER...
WE'RE NEARLY DONE.
I NEED TO GO HOME, DOCTOR.
I CAN'T REMEMBER THE LAST NIGHT I SLEPT.
BUT WE STILL HAVE WORK TO...
DOCTOR, THE OTHERS HAVE ALREADY LEFT, WE NEED TO REST.
GO THEN, GO HOME AND GET YOUR REST. COME BACK IN THREE DAYS, WE HAVE MUCH WORK TO GET DONE STILL.
AREN'T YOU COMING, DOCTOR?
NO, I WILL BE STAYING. I HAVE A FEW THINGS TO SEE TO.

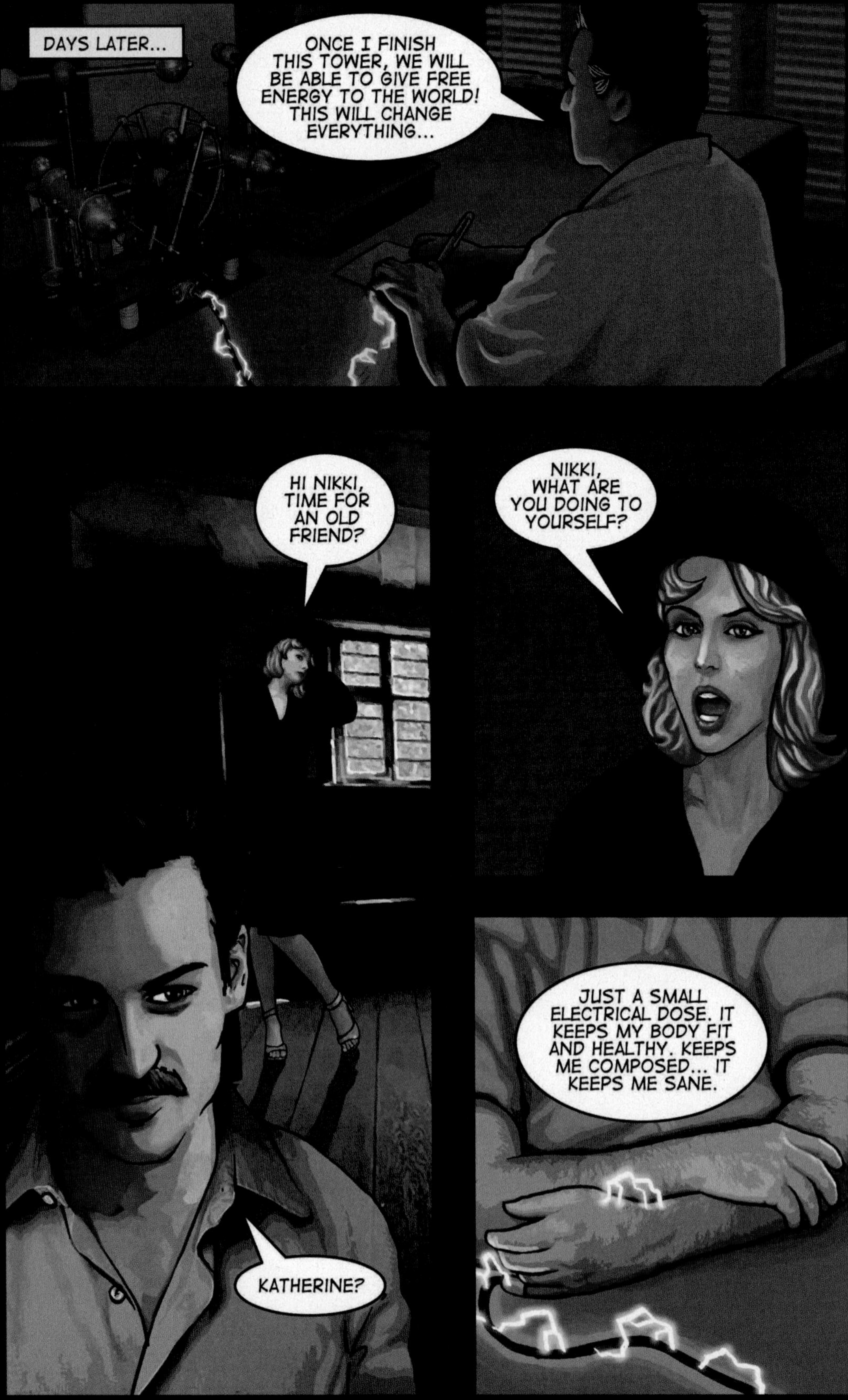
DAYS LATER...
ONCE I FINISH THIS TOWER, WE WILL BE ABLE TO GIVE FREE ENERGY TO THE WORLD! THIS WILL CHANGE EVERYTHING...
HI NIKKI, TIME FOR AN OLD FRIEND?
NIKKI, WHAT ARE YOU DOING TO YOURSELF?
KATHERINE?
JUST A SMALL ELECTRICAL DOSE. IT KEEPS MY BODY FIT AND HEALTHY. KEEPS ME COMPOSED... IT KEEPS ME SANE.

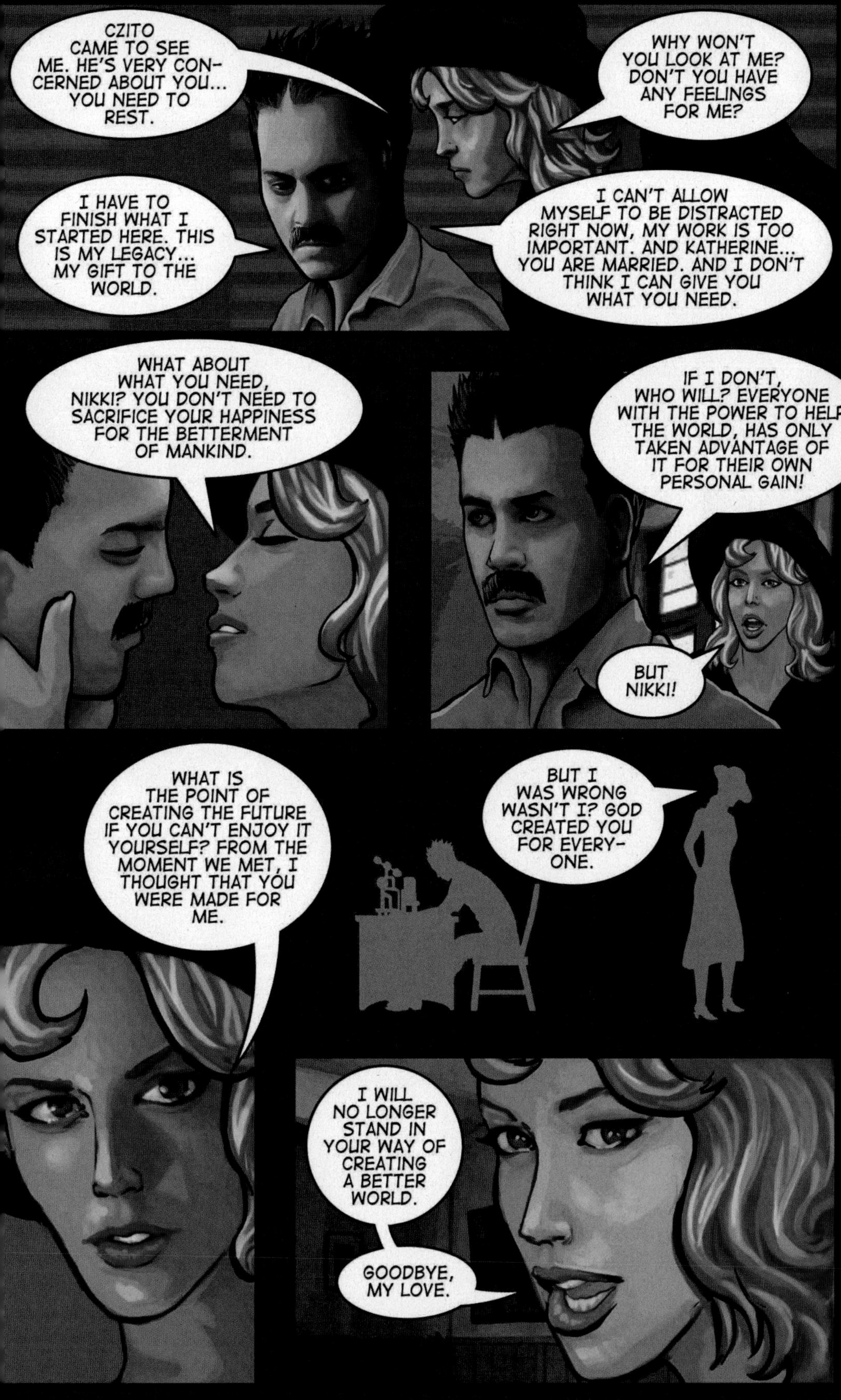
CZITO CAME TO SEE ME. HE'S VERY CON-CERNED ABOUT YOU... YOU NEED TO REST.
WHY WON'T YOU LOOK AT ME? DON'T YOU HAVE ANY FEELINGS FOR ME?
I HAVE TO FINISH WHAT I STARTED HERE. THIS IS MY LEGACY... MY GIFT TO THE WORLD.
I CAN'T ALLOW MYSELF TO BE DISTRACTED RIGHT NOW, MY WORK IS TOO IMPORTANT. AND KATHERINE... YOU ARE MARRIED. AND I DON'T THINK I CAN GIVE YOU WHAT YOU NEED.
WHAT ABOUT WHAT YOU NEED, NIKKI? YOU DON'T NEED TO SACRIFICE YOUR HAPPINESS FOR THE BETTERMENT OF MANKIND.
IF I DON'T, WHO WILL? EVERYONE WITH THE POWER TO HELP THE WORLD, HAS ONLY TAKEN ADVANTAGE OF IT FOR THEIR OWN PERSONAL GAIN!
BUT NIKKI!
WHAT IS THE POINT OF CREATING THE FUTURE IF YOU CAN'T ENJOY IT YOURSELF? FROM THE MOMENT WE MET, I THOUGHT THAT YOU WERE MADE FOR ME.
BUT I WAS WRONG WASN'T I? GOD CREATED YOU FOR EVERY-ONE.
I WILL NO LONGER STAND IN YOUR WAY OF CREATING A BETTER WORLD.
GOODBYE, MY LOVE.

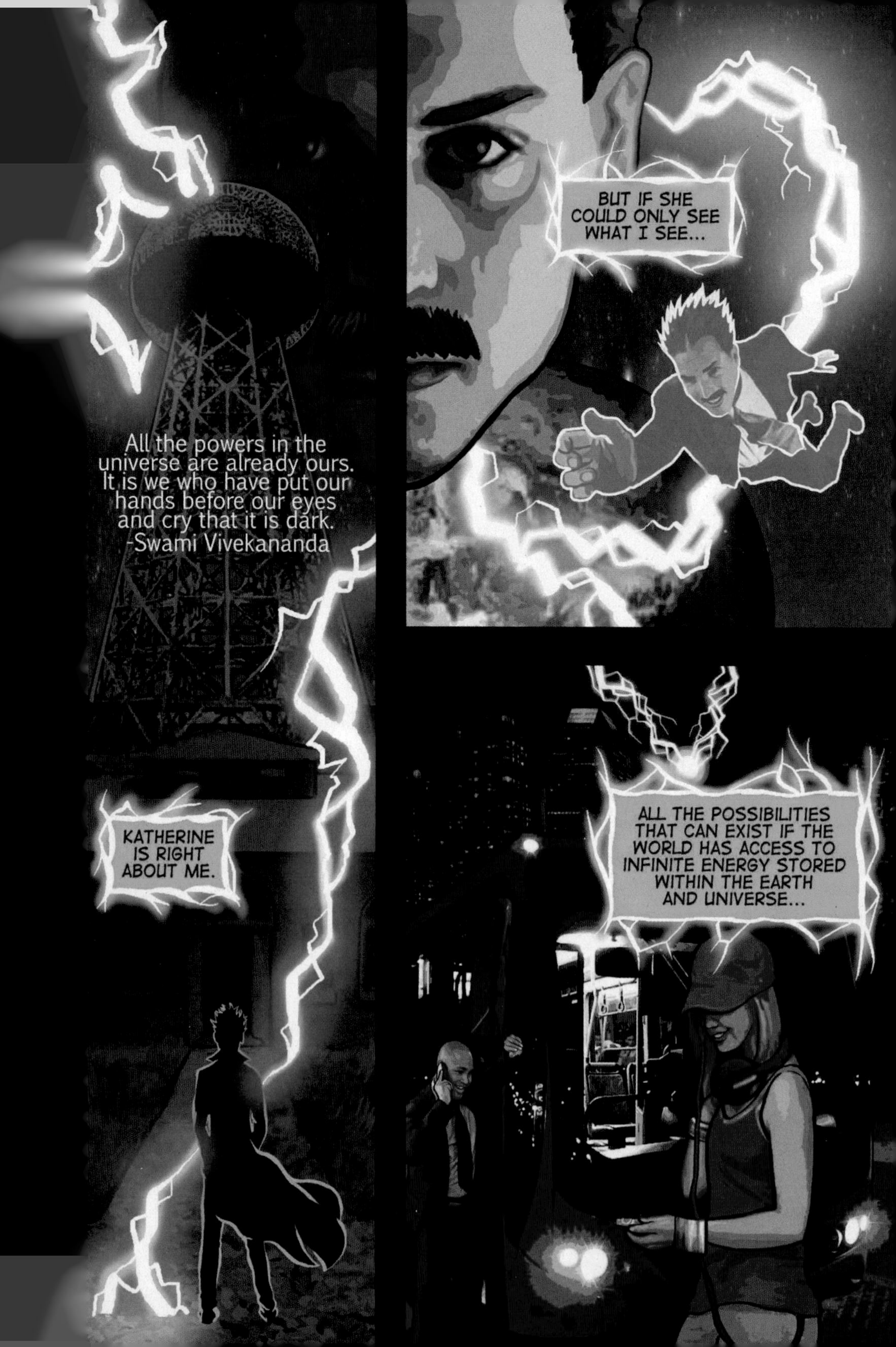
All the powers in the universe are already ours. It is we who have put our hands before our eyes and cry that it is dark.
-Swami Vivekananda
BUT IF SHE COULD ONLY SEE WHAT I SEE...
KATHERINE IS RIGHT ABOUT ME.
ALL THE POSSIBILITIES THAT CAN EXIST IF THE WORLD HAS ACCESS TO INFINITE ENERGY STORED WITHIN THE EARTH AND UNIVERSE...

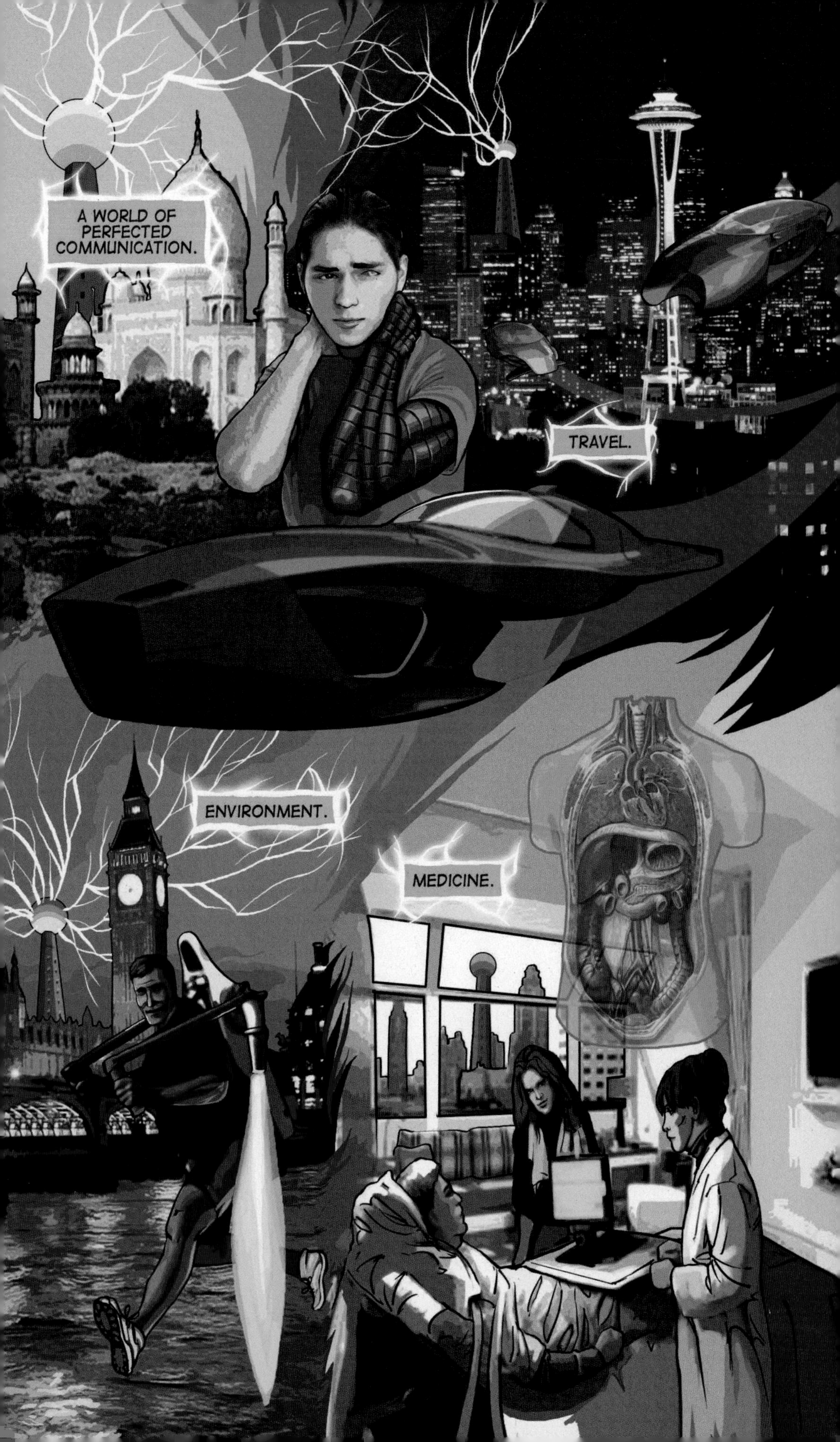
A WORLD OF PERFECTED COMMUNICATION.
TRAVEL.
ENVIRONMENT.
MEDICINE.

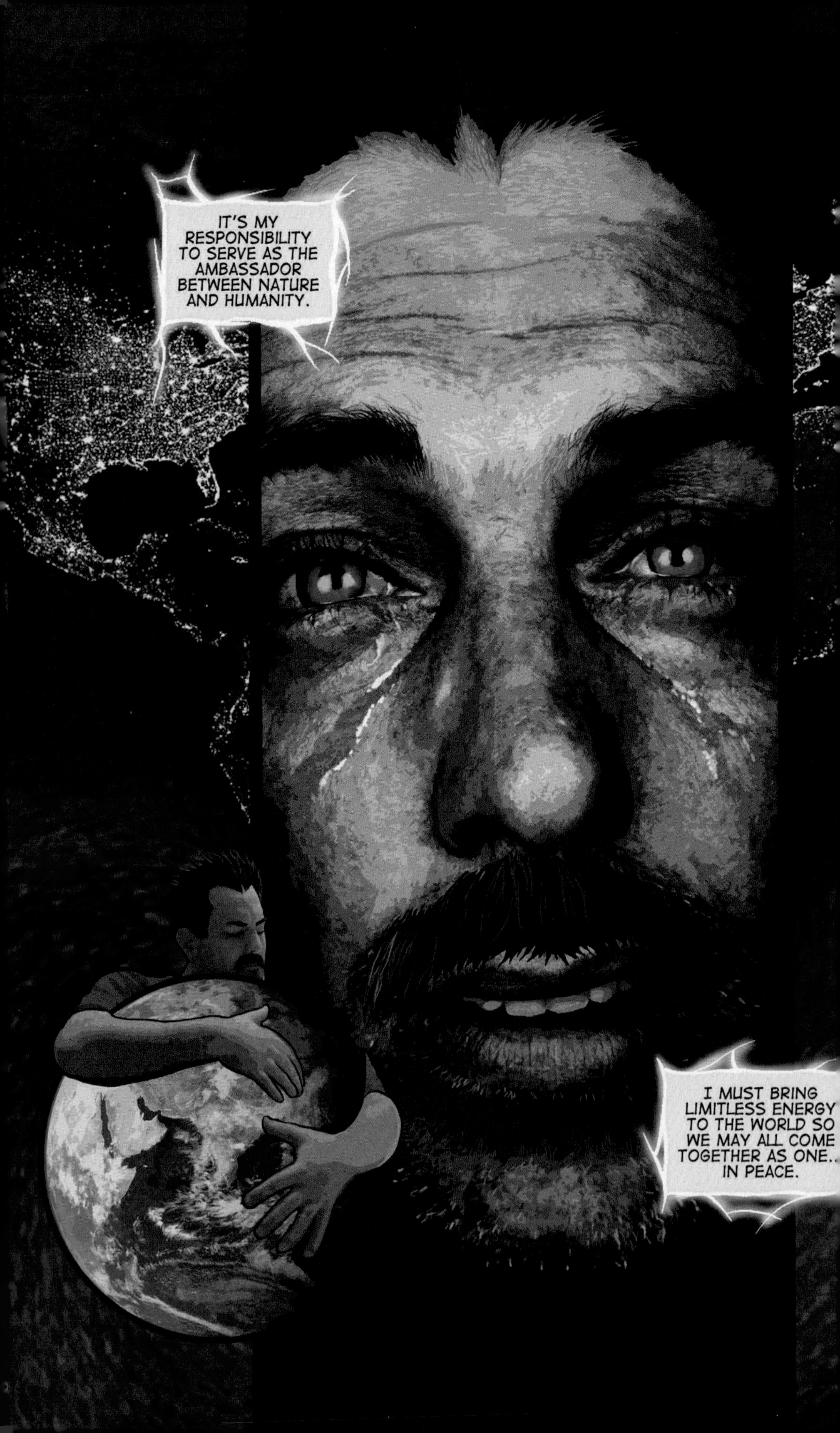
IT'S MY RESPONSIBILITY TO SERVE AS THE AMBASSADOR BETWEEN NATURE AND HUMANITY.
I MUST BRING LIMITLESS ENERGY TO THE WORLD SO WE MAY ALL COME TOGETHER AS ONE... IN PEACE.

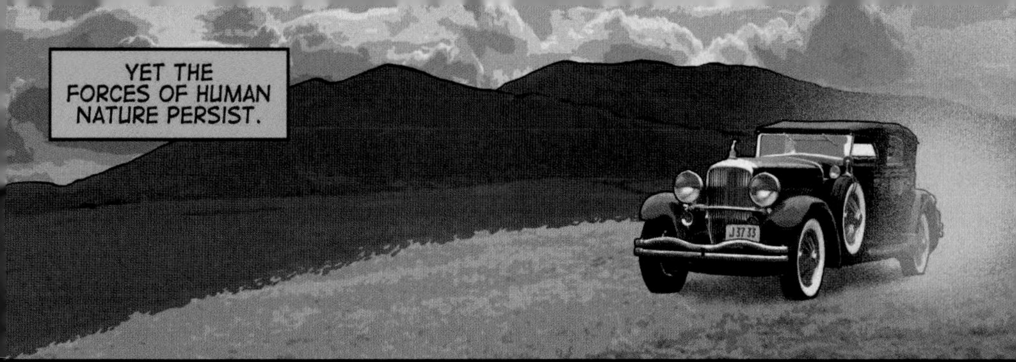
YET THE FORCES OF HUMAN NATURE PERSIST.
J37 33

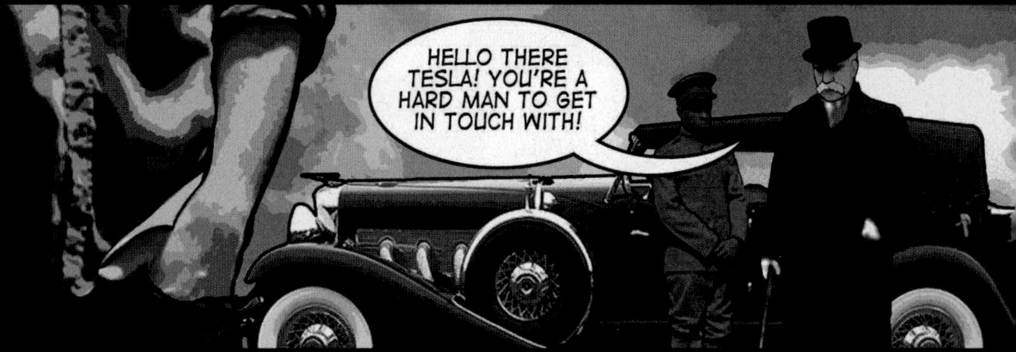
HELLO THERE TESLA! YOU'RE A HARD MAN TO GET IN TOUCH WITH!

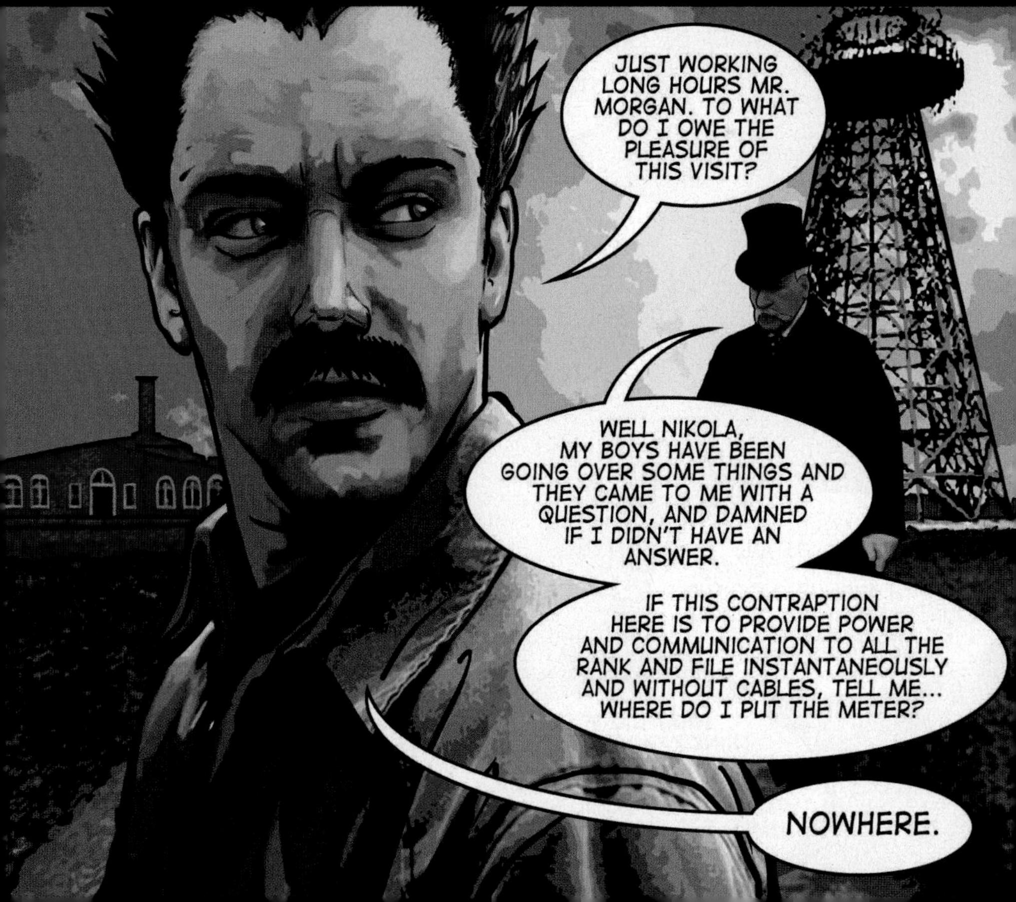
JUST WORKING LONG HOURS MR. MORGAN. TO WHAT DO I OWE THE PLEASURE OF THIS VISIT?
WELL NIKOLA, MY BOYS HAVE BEEN GOING OVER SOME THINGS AND THEY CAME TO ME WITH A QUESTION, AND DAMNED IF I DIDN'T HAVE AN ANSWER.
IF THIS CONTRAPTION HERE IS TO PROVIDE POWER AND COMMUNICATION TO ALL THE RANK AND FILE INSTANTANEOUSLY AND WITHOUT CABLES, TELL ME... WHERE DO I PUT THE METER?
NOWHERE.

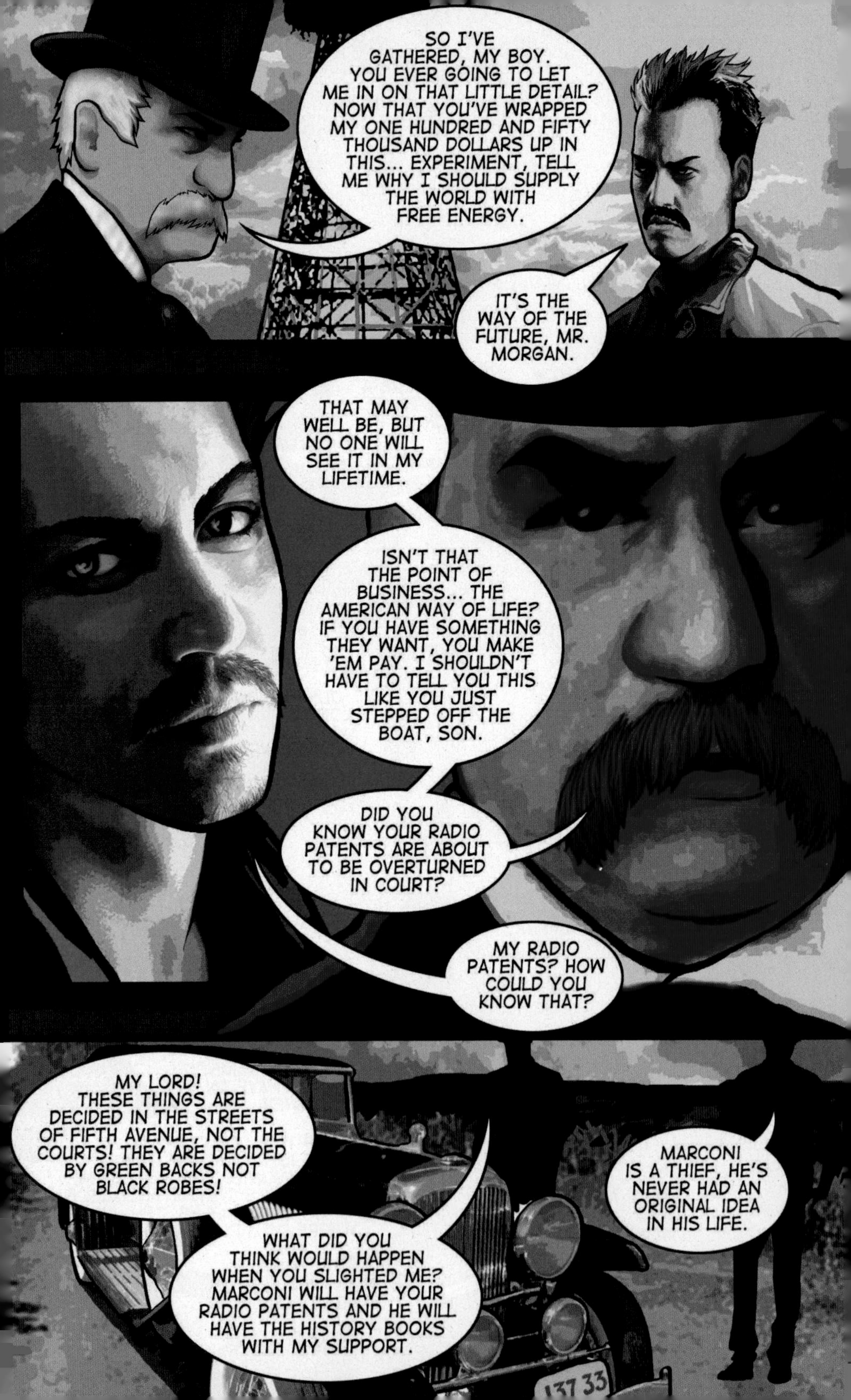
SO I'VE GATHERED, MY BOY. YOU EVER GOING TO LET ME IN ON THAT LITTLE DETAIL? NOW THAT YOU'VE WRAPPED MY ONE HUNDRED AND FIFTY THOUSAND DOLLARS UP IN THIS... EXPERIMENT, TELL ME WHY I SHOULD SUPPLY THE WORLD WITH FREE ENERGY.
IT'S THE WAY OF THE FUTURE, MR. MORGAN.
THAT MAY WELL BE, BUT NO ONE WILL SEE IT IN MY LIFETIME.
ISN'T THAT THE POINT OF BUSINESS... THE AMERICAN WAY OF LIFE? IF YOU HAVE SOMETHING THEY WANT, YOU MAKE 'EM PAY. I SHOULDN'T HAVE TO TELL YOU THIS LIKE YOU JUST STEPPED OFF THE BOAT, SON.
DID YOU KNOW YOUR RADIO PATENTS ARE ABOUT TO BE OVERTURNED IN COURT?
MY RADIO PATENTS? HOW COULD YOU KNOW THAT?
MY LORD! THESE THINGS ARE DECIDED IN THE STREETS OF FIFTH AVENUE, NOT THE COURTS! THEY ARE DECIDED BY GREEN BACKS NOT BLACK ROBES!
MARCONI IS A THIEF, HE'S NEVER HAD AN ORIGINAL IDEA IN HIS LIFE.
WHAT DID YOU THINK WOULD HAPPEN WHEN YOU SLIGHTED ME? MARCONI WILL HAVE YOUR RADIO PATENTS AND HE WILL HAVE THE HISTORY BOOKS WITH MY SUPPORT.

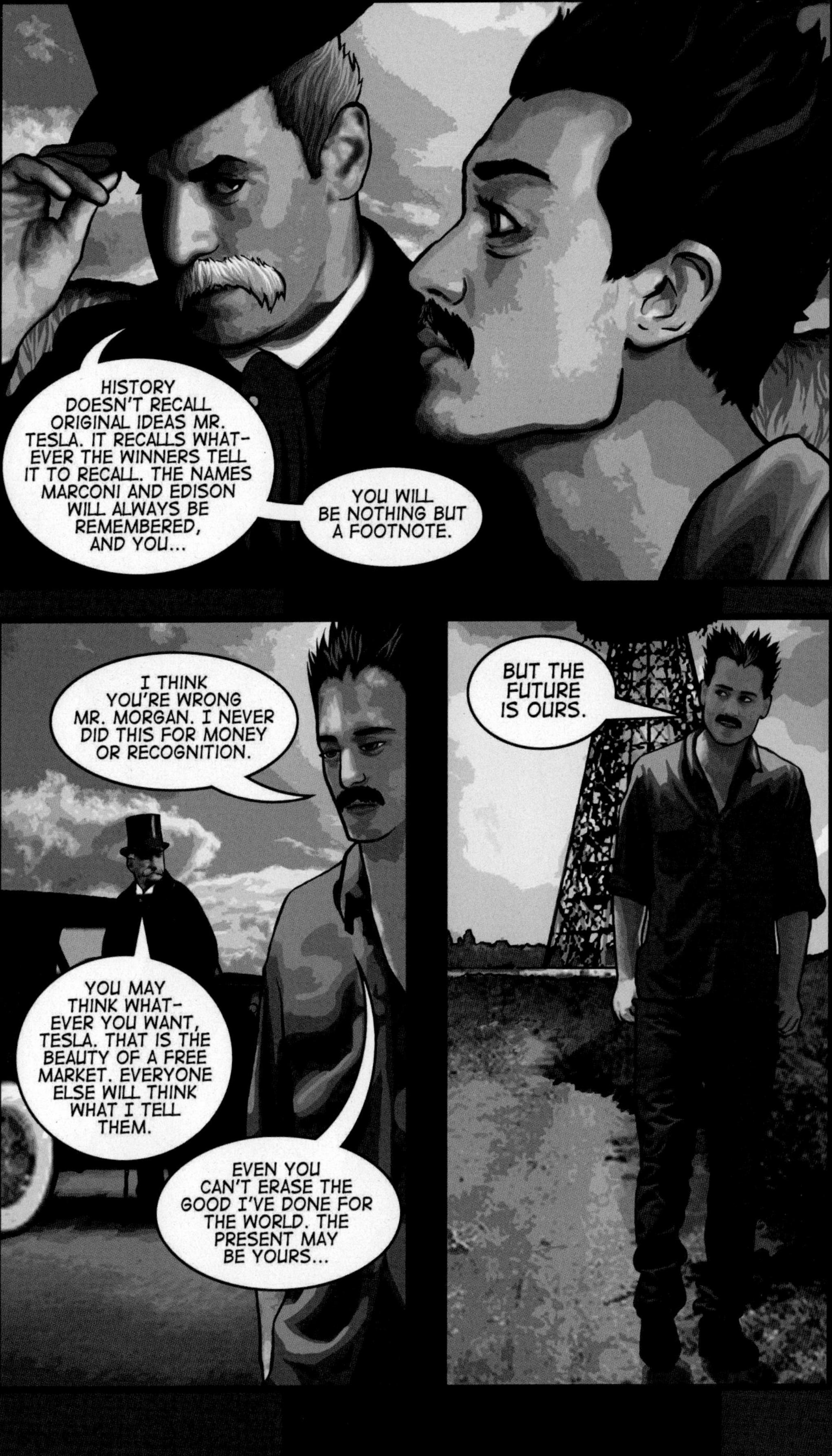
HISTORY DOESN'T RECALL ORIGINAL IDEAS MR. TESLA. IT RECALLS WHAT-EVER THE WINNERS TELL IT TO RECALL. THE NAMES MARCONI AND EDISON WILL ALWAYS BE REMEMBERED, AND YOU...
YOU WILL BE NOTHING BUT A FOOTNOTE.
I THINK YOU'RE WRONG MR. MORGAN. I NEVER DID THIS FOR MONEY OR RECOGNITION.
YOU MAY THINK WHAT-EVER YOU WANT, TESLA. THAT IS THE BEAUTY OF A FREE MARKET. EVERYONE ELSE WILL THINK WHAT I TELL THEM.
EVEN YOU CAN'T ERASE THE GOOD I'VE DONE FOR THE WORLD. THE PRESENT MAY BE YOURS...
BUT THE FUTURE IS OURS.

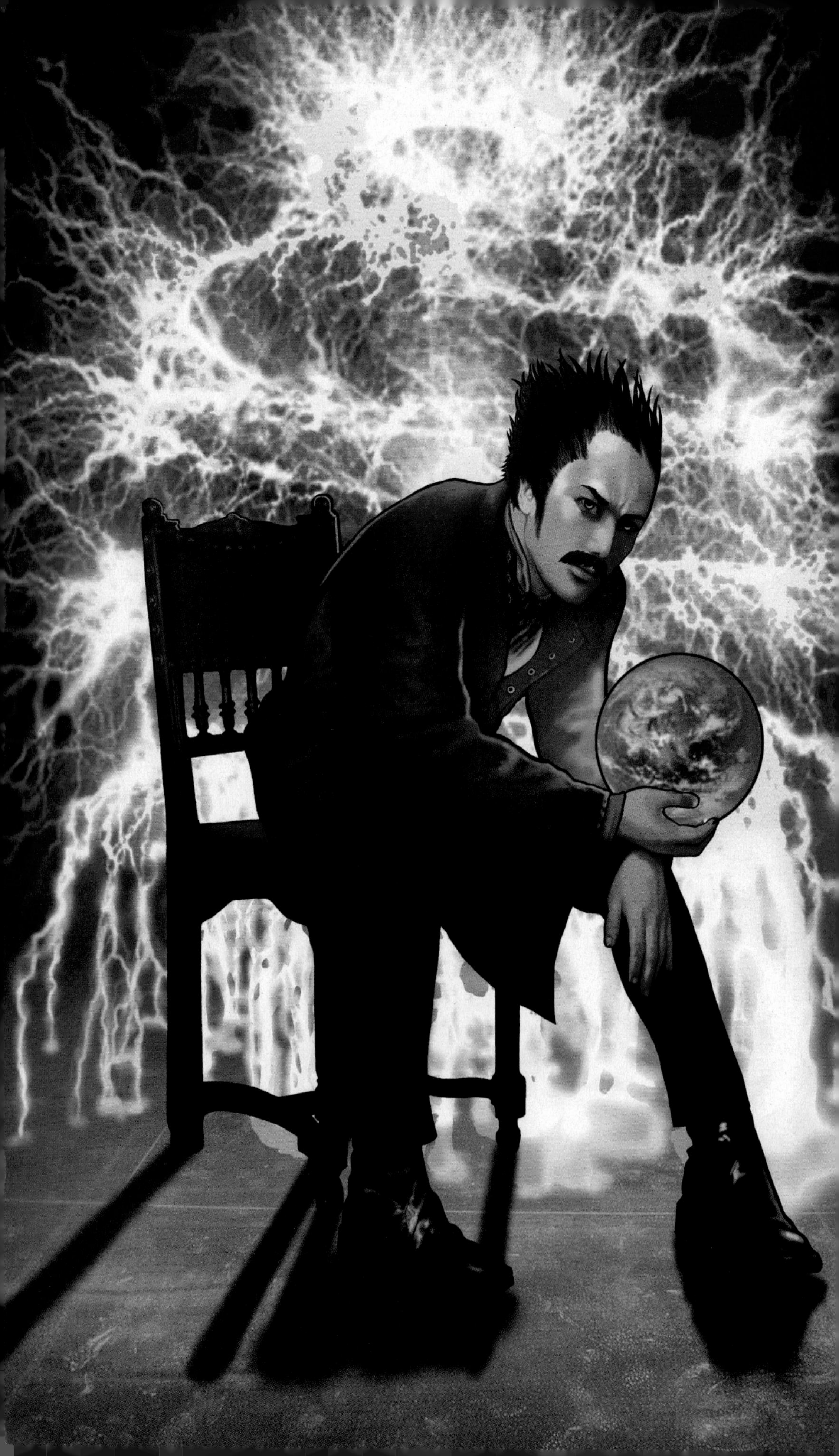

FAST FORWARD...

AS YOU MAY HAVE GUESSED, THE STORY DOES NOT END HERE. MARCONI WENT ON TO RECEIVE TESLA'S RADIO PATENTS AND WON THE NOBLE PRIZE IN PHYSICS, WHILE EARNING J.P. MORGAN A HEAVY RETURN ON HIS INVESTMENT. J.P. MORGAN GREW INTO ONE OF THE LARGEST GLOBAL BANKS KNOWN TODAY AS J.P. MORGAN CHASE. EDISON WAS RECOGNIZED AS ONE OF THE GREATEST INVENTORS OF OUR TIME AS HIS EDISON GENERAL ELECTRIC CO., NOW KNOWN AS G.E., STILL REMAINS IN THE FORTUNE TOP 10 COMPANIES. G.E.'S RIVAL WESTINGHOUSE CORPORATION CONTINUES TO THRIVE AS ONE OF THE LARGEST POWER AND ELECTRICAL COMPANIES AND AT ONE POINT OWNED INFINITI BROADCASTING AND CBS. SWAMI VIVEKANANDA BECAME ONE OF THE MOST INFLUENTIAL INDIAN MYSTICS INTRODUCING YOGA TO THE WESTERN WORLD, AND MARK TWAIN IS RECOGNIZED AS ONE OF THE MOST PROLIFIC WRITERS AND SATIRISTS OF OUR TIME.

SO WHAT HAPPENED TO TESLA? AFTER HIS ATTEMPT TO DISTRIBUTE FREE WIRELESS ENERGY WAS STIFLED, TESLA CONTINUED TO PURSUE OTHER INVENTIONS SUCH AS THE REMOTE CONTROL, ROBOTICS, WIRELESS POWER TRANSMISSION, OSCILLATOR DEVICES, RADAR, DREAM RECORDER, PARTICLE BEAMS AND OTHER CREATIONS THAT INFLUENCED THE DIRECTION OF HISTORY AND FICTION. DESPITE HIS ON-GOING INNOVATION, HIS COMMERCIAL TIMING NEVER SEEMED RIGHT AND SOON WENT BANKRUPT AND SPENT THE REMAINING YEARS OF HIS LIFE ALONE IN A ROOM AT THE NEW YORKER HOTEL WITH HIS PIGEONS AND JOURNALS. SOON AFTER HIS DEATH, THE U.S. GOVERNMENT CONFISCATED AND IMPOUNDED ALL HIS NOTES AND JOURNALS WHICH WERE LATER DECLARED BY THE U.S. GOVERNRMENT AS TOP SECRET IN THE NAME OF NATIONAL SECURITY. WHAT WERE IN THOSE SECRET JOURNALS? WELL, THAT'S A WHOLE OTHER STORY...

THANK YOU

I WOULD LIKE TO START BY THANKING MY FATHER, VIPIN MEHTA, WHO HAS ALWAYS BEEN THERE FOR ME THROUGH THICK AND THIN AND WHOSE 'CHANGE THE MINDSET, CHANGE THE WORLD' THEME FROM HIS 'GLOBAL HEALING' BOOK SERIES WAS PART OF MY INSPIRATION FOR CREATING THIS BOOK. MY MOTHER, HANSA MEHTA, WHOSE INEXHAUSTIBLE LOVE AND SUPPORT HAS ALWAYS ALLOWED ME TO REACH BEYOND MYSELF. MY SISTER, RADHA MEHTA, WHO SUPPORTED ME IN THIS AND ALL MY ENDEAVORS, AND WHOSE AMAZING VOCAL TALENT PUTS ME TO TEARS EVEN TO THIS DAY.

I WOULD LIKE TO ESPECIALLY THANK MY AMAZING ARTIST, ERIK WILLIAMS, WHOSE UTMOST PASSION FOR TESLA AND THIS PROJECT HELPED FUEL THE FIRE TO GET THIS DONE. IT WAS FATE THAT I DISCOVERED ERIK WHEN I DID, BECAUSE IT WAS ONLY AFTER OUR FIRST CONVERSATION THAT I INSTANTLY KNEW I HAD THE PERFECT ARTIST FOR THIS BOOK. I AM HIS BIGGEST FAN!

I WOULD LIKE TO THANK ALAN BOYKO, ERIC COMPTON, ED MASESSA AND THE SCHOLASTIC TEAM FOR BEING SUCH AN AMAZING PUBLISHING PARTNER AND HELPING US GET TESLA'S STORY OUT THERE.

I WOULD LIKE TO THANK DAN LAUER, ALEC ANDERSON, JACK WARREN, DAVID LONNER, DEEPAK CHOPRA, LEVAR BURTON, JASON REED, SEAN O'REILY, VERONICA RUELAS, CURT MARVIS, ALEX BARKLOFF, JOEL SERFACE, MONIKA OKAPIEC, CHRIS OLMSTEAD, ELLE SENINA AND THE MANY OTHERS WHO'VE HELPED ME ALONG THIS JOURNEY. THIS WAS TRULY A TEAM EFFORT AND WITHOUT EACH PERSON'S CONTRIBUTION, SMALL OR LARGE, I COULD NOT HAVE FINISHED THIS.

I WOULD LIKE TO THANK ALL THE TESLA FANS FOR KEEPING HIS NAME ALIVE THROUGH THE YEARS AND CONTINUING TO CHEER HIM ON.

FINALLY, I WOULD LIKE TO THANK NIKOLA TESLA FOR HIS CONTRIBUTION TO OUR WORLD AND VISION FOR A BETTER HUMANITY. AS HE ONCE SAID...

"LET THE FUTURE TELL THE TRUTH AND EVALUATE EACH ONE ACCORDING TO HIS WORK AND ACCOMPLISHMENTS. THE PRESENT IS THEIRS; THE FUTURE, FOR WHICH I REALLY WORKED, IS MINE."

THE FUTURE IS NOW!

- RAVÉ MEHTA